GET WOMEN TO WANT YOU

MICHAEL ANTHONY

THE INSTITUTE OF HUMAN UNDERSTANDING

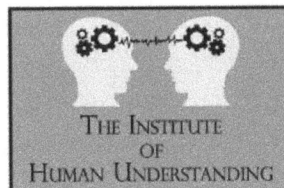

THE INSTITUTE
OF
HUMAN UNDERSTANDING

ONLINE DATING STATISTICS

- In the United States, 40 million people use online dating services, equating to 40% of the single adult population.

- The US Census Bureau estimates that 44% of the adult population is single.

- The Institute of Human Understanding estimates 74% of the adult population has either tried or knows someone who has tried online dating or a dating app.

- According to MBAPrograms.org, the online dating industry has gone from a $900 million industry in 2007 to a $1.9 billion industry in 2012, and in 2017 IBISWorld, the market research company, reported total revenue was up to 2.7 billion.

- Mobile dating sites have grown 576% in the past year.

- One in five relationships start online, according to Match.com.

- It's a bigger industry than porn.

CONTENTS

FOREWORD

When Michael came to me with the news he *finally* wrote this book, I was ecstatic. I had been telling him he needed to put together a book, a manual, a guide, or something since his understanding of women is off the charts. His knowledge and strategies helped our group of friends a lot with meeting and connecting with women, and I experienced women treating me differently from before. If I needed to know what sites to use, what to say, how to say it; whether I should text, email, or just call and when, Michael had the answers. Those answers led me to *a lot* of success.

I'm at best an average-looking guy and nervous around women. When I do say something, it always seems to come out wrong, despite the number of times I've rehearsed it in my head.

One of the most exciting things for me was to understand how a woman thinks and makes decisions. As a result, I knew how to talk to them and connect with them. I used some of Michael's knowledge but never actually understood the details. To be honest, I took them for granted since I could always call on him because he's one of my best friends.

After I read this book, I gained a thorough understanding of how to act with women and the ability to analyze any situation to see whether it made sense for me to invest the time and energy. Time is the most valuable thing we all have, so I place a high priority on mine.

What I found the most valuable was learning how to position myself to get women to want me. I had women reaching out to me, which is new and different. I also had women I never thought I had a chance with before returning text messages. My confidence increased, and I was no longer nervous with women because I had the skills to effectively communicate with them.

If you're looking for an easy-to-read, step-by-step manual, you've found it here. Make sure to pay attention to the details as the details *do* make the difference. It may seem too easy after reading this, and honestly, it can be. We complicate things by over-thinking.

In the past, I've been guilty of over-thinking things, as well. Now, I have a distinct advantage with women. My group of friends know of my successes, and others often envy me when they regularly see me with different women. Chances are, I'm the guy you looked at and wondered, "How did that guy get that girl?"

Austin Cole

INTRODUCTION

A single mother raised me, and other women always surrounded us. Her friends were around the house, and the girl talk never left me with a dull moment. I heard all their stories about dating, guys attempting to pick them up, etc. To be honest, I probably heard too much! My mother is a beautiful woman, and there was never a shortage of guys shamelessly trying to pick her up. As pathetic as it may sound, they would often do it in front of me, giving me a front row seat to what *not* to do. I quickly saw the power an attractive woman has over men. I also noticed the number of options a woman has. These experiences have proven invaluable to me over the years.

As I entered high school, my attention was on sports and girls. Obviously, one of the reasons for this was that my teenage hormones were going crazy, but it was also because each girl posed a different challenge. I easily understood the dynamics, or lack thereof, in a relationship or interaction. Through observation and focus, I could identify what was and was not attractive to the girl based on other guys' failures. When I combined my knowledge and observations with the ability to successfully find and push the hot buttons of each girl, I realized this was a game changer.

As the new millennium arrived, the Internet became the driving force in everyday life. The Internet has been great for improving efficiency in all aspects of life, including making it easier to meet women. The probability of connecting with a woman online is much greater than meeting them offline. While meeting women at random places isn't unheard of, the odds are against it. Most people are too busy, tired, or shy to even attempt meeting someone while out. Thinking about the fear of rejection and how intimidating it is to approach a woman in person makes online dating even more attractive.

Having recognized that, I decided to research dating sites, mobile apps, and social networking sites. I used many of my friends, asking them to join these sites and test my theories. The overwhelming response was obvious. Once they experienced success with one site, they simply implemented the same strategy with the other sites, as well.

My approach is universal. It's identical to that of a well-run business: There's a research-based system in place for maximum efficiency. If the person follows the steps, the results (success) will follow. As I told a good friend of mine, "I'll do everything for you but show up; you have to bring something to the table."

Many people have already tested and proven the methods in this book. The 27 case studies throughout this book are real-life, detailed examples. This is the only book compiled of actual case studies that have experienced success in getting women to want to date them.

As the founder of IHU: The Institute of Human Understanding, I would like to commend you for making the commitment to change your life. You'll no longer have to wonder why women choose one man over the other; you'll understand it. You'll no longer have to wonder what to say to a woman; you'll know what to say and when to say it. You'll no longer have to wonder if a woman likes you; she'll like you naturally.

Once you become the man a woman desires, you'll automatically become more desirable to other women. Think about it: So many people want what they can't have, particularly women. They continually want what they perceive to be the best. Sure, a leather purse may be a leather purse to you, but the brands Coach and Louis Vuitton have a much higher value to some women. The same is true for jewelry, shoes, cars, sunglasses, and clothes. These women want what they perceive to be the most desirable—not only to themselves, but also to others.

Taking this into consideration, the most valuable accessory many women can have is the man at her side. The more desirable she sees you, the more valuable you are to her.

Have you ever been in the situation where a woman has turned you down, and you couldn't help but want her more? Well, you're not alone, many men have. In this book, you'll learn how to turn the tables and play hard-to-get. As a result, she may want you more. This increases the woman's interest in you because she perceives your value to be greater. This also presents a challenge, and many women love a challenge. This is the type of case study displayed in this book.

You can connect with more women and have control over your choices and future.

Take a moment to reread that last statement. How exciting would it be to control *your* own future and live life on *your* terms based on what *you* want, when *you* want it?

Now think of something you consider yourself good at and how easy it comes to you. Now imagine you're good at connecting initially with women. Think of the life you could have and the options. It's exciting, isn't it? Now think of the women you could pursue, the confidence you'd have, the experiences and the stories you could tell. Are you excited yet? You should be. This book will change your life. The information in this book may focus on getting women, but it can easily apply to other areas in life so you communicate better or can be a better friend or a better you.

New apps and online dating sites are being created daily. Many will come, and most will go. The strategies, insights and analysis provided within this book are universal. They have stood the test of time and are currently working today.

I have incorporated what guys who have had success with dating women online and on apps say, what they talk about, where they meet, and how they stand out. Online you don't have to compete with someone who may have more to offer in the bar scene or in public by flashing wealth or appearance. After finishing this book, you'll possess the dialogue and knowledge to be at a distinct advantage online. That advantage begins now.

Michael Anthony

SECTION I:

WHY ONLINE DATING AND WHAT YOU SHOULD EXPECT

CHAPTER 1:
THE CHANGE YOU'LL EXPERIENCE

"There is nothing noble in being superior to your fellow man. True nobility lies in being superior to your former self."

—Ernest Hemingway

Chances are you've heard friends and coworkers talk about experiences using an online dating site or a dating app. You may have even checked one out to see what all the talk was about. What you soon discover is how easy it is to sign up and start searching for women; however, many fail to realize how many pitfalls exist. Online, everyone starts out on a level playing field.

These sites and apps can be a bit overwhelming since the details can create information overload. This book simplifies all the details and help you digest the information overload by breaking it down step-by-step. For your understanding, I've condensed the information into a comprehensive, detailed analysis. These details, as are what can prevent you from blending in an overcrowded dating scene. You'll learn how to become her most desirable option through proven universal concepts and strategies.

There are many additional details outlined for you to get women to want you. These details, include determining which site and apps are the best fit for you, how to design your profile, choosing the right type of pictures, avoiding common pitfalls, identifying the different types of women and how to connect once you've identified her type.

From there, you'll also understand how to communicate effectively, use the various means of communication to your advantage, make progress each time you talk to a woman, and how to create enough comfort for her to want to meet you. Simply put, you'll take away all the extensive research The Institute of Human Understanding and I have compiled in more than 10 years of research and development as this book concludes with a specific plan for you to implement for success.

The change you'll experience is ultimately the change you choose. Not everyone can experience the change; it takes a strong mind, a desire, and the ability to concentrate. You determine your future, and the decisions you make now will have a direct impact on your future with women, your confidence, and your overall quality of life. As the American entertainer Pearl Bailey said, "The first and worst of all frauds is to cheat one's self."

Your commitment to reading this book cover to cover will enhance your understanding of women more than you could ever imagine. With the straightforward delivery and detailed analysis, you'll dramatically and immediately improve your knowledge. This book is only meant for those with a strong desire to learn how to communicate and understand women. It all starts with a commitment for a better life.

CHAPTER 2:
WHY ONLINE DATING?

"People aren't naturally well-behaved."

- Clay Shirky, Harvard Business Review

THE ONLINE PROCESS

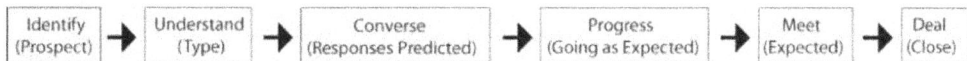

Identify (Prospect) → Understand (Type) → Converse (Responses Predicted) → Progress (Going as Expected) → Meet (Expected) → Deal (Close)

The Online Process summarized above details the steps you'll master in this book to succeed in meeting women and getting them to feel comfortable with you and wanting to know more about you online.

Let's be honest: Our jobs take up a good portion of our lives, and we don't want to go out each night attempting to meet someone new. We're done with that rodeo.

- No more nights coming home feeling rejected
- No more wasting money on drinks for women, hoping to get a number and maybe more
- No more brainless conversations
- No more nights regretting you didn't approach a woman
- No more waiting for the "right time" to approach a woman
- No more over-thinking a conversation
- No more cold feet and being afraid to say something
- No more last-minute searches around the bar to find a woman before it closes
- No more frustrations

No more of it all!

You'll learn step-by-step how to have exponential success meeting women online. You'll see first-hand not only how it works, but you'll also understand the steps to take to duplicate the process. There are instructions on how to dissect how to locate women and what to say to them. Then, you can review the responses and how to implement what you've learned.

When most people first consider online dating, they're skeptical and hesitant to take the initial jump into one of the dating sites or apps. However, once you sign up, you immediately see the potential. Wow! There are so many other benefits, including:

Convenience: You don't have to plan around your schedule. This is huge since some people are busy, work a lot, or just like a little time for themselves. You don't have to dress up, fix your hair, iron your clothes, throw cologne on, drive somewhere, or waste money. You can interact on *your* terms. You can even sign up online in your underwear while eating a bowl of ice cream, and no one will ever know.

Endless Possibilities: You can look at literally hundreds, if not thousands, of women—they're all at your fingertips at any time. It's like looking at a menu at a restaurant; first, you eliminate whatever you aren't interested in, then you decide what you *are* interested in. You can review their interests, careers, location, hobbies, and more after you establish you have an interest.

Now think back to a time when you met someone and were interested in her, only to find out much later something about her that turned you off. When many of my friends were younger, they didn't want to date a woman with kids. One friend met a woman who intrigued him, only to find out she was divorced twice and had six kids. Now imagine the time, energy, and effort he could have saved if he'd seen her profile online and had known this information beforehand. This is just one of the ways that online dating and apps make sense and is much more time-effective.

The following is an example of how you can narrow down the women using an age range, location, and other criteria:

I'm A	Male ▼	Seeking	Female ▼	25 ▼	To	40 ▼	All Profiles ▼	For	Anything ▼
All Ethnicities ▼	United States ▼	Hawaii ▼	City	Honolulu ▼	Zip Code		▼	Search	

The following is an example of the search results you will see when searching for women online:

The following is another example of how results appear when searching for women online:

I think we can agree that more choices are better, especially when you're the decision maker. The less specific you are when you search, the more prospects will appear. You can narrow down prospects based on age, ZIP code, distance from ZIP code, race, religion, etc. The more specific you are, the fewer results you'll have. At first be vague and get the maximum number of women to choose from.

<u>Cost</u>: Now think of a time when you went out, dressed up, fixed your hair, shaved, put on cologne, cleaned your car, drove to a bar, paid for parking, paid to enter a bar, purchased numerous drinks throughout the night, only to pay for a taxi to take you home. This is a typical night for most men. This typical night can quickly cost more than $100. In more expensive locations, this typical night can easily cost $250 or more. Hell, some of the drinks in Miami, New York, and LA cost more than $20 each.

Part of the attraction with online dating and apps is that it can be inexpensive, but perhaps the best part is the flexibility it offers. Not only can you check out the women in your area, but you can search areas that may be 15, 30, or 45 miles or more away. The possibilities are endless. The only limits you have are the ones you put on yourself. You can even change your personal location on the site based on where you may travel for work or go on vacation. This has proven to be great for meeting women when out of town.

Time is the one thing we don't have an excess of, so we must leverage it to do as many things as possible, efficiently as possible.

Since you can maximize your time and exposure to women, you can also be more selective based on what you're looking for. Say goodbye to the days of going out to the bar to hopelessly try to meet a random woman because you need a date for an upcoming event or boring lunch dates or blind dates in a feeble attempt to find the "one."

You know what you like and don't like better than anyone else. Shouldn't you be in charge of eliminating matches for you? You should decide if you feel an attraction based on their photos, or after reviewing a little background information on them, including their likes and dislikes, etc. if you want to pursue them. This eliminates the awkwardness and wasted time if the woman isn't a good match.

This is the exact reason most people search for someone who interests them on Google, Facebook, and Instagram before agreeing to meet them. They want to have an idea of who they're meeting, and they want some background information. This is what the online dating sites and apps take care of for you. They practically give you an online resume for you to review to help you decide. Talk about a gift from above; this seems to be as close as it gets for us men.

In *Trading Up: Why Consumers Want New Luxury Goods—and How Companies Create Them* by Michael J. Silverstein and Neil Fiske, the authors say

> The rules and practices of dating have changed dramatically in the past twenty years; today, for many singles, dating is a marketing exercise that must be undertaken with great seriousness. Would-be connectors seek every possible advantage through the savvy use of goods. There are new dating rules. While it is mostly women who make up the rules and enforce them, females can get just as frustrated and confused by the process as men. This is primarily because they're generally more interested in marriage than men are; although both women and men are delaying marriage, men delay longer. These facts take on particular significance when viewed in the light of long-term changes in sexual behavior.

> The most sexually active women are eighteen to twenty-nine years old, and the great majorities have had their first sexual intercourse while in high school. So, because most women (as well

as men) come into their dating years with early sexual experience and because they are delaying marriage, the median time between first sexual encounter and marriage has dramatically increased, from 1.3 to 8.1 years. That means the period of active dating is very much longer than it used to be.

Even the window for "hookups" is longer, the pace of the dating game has not slowed, and the business of finding a lover who might become a suitable mate seems as fraught as ever. This is partially because of the greater sophistication of the dating "consumer,"— people are seeking the best possible companion available and thanks to the popular media, they have a much larger pool to evaluate, at least virtually. It's also because everybody is so pressed for time—working harder, doing more, and trying to cram more into everything into life. Accordingly, the dating process has been streamlined and facilitated via a number of new methods, including dating services and web dating. [1]

This passage directly highlights how retailers cater and position themselves for maximum profitability. These retailers use years of studies and statistics on human behavior to understand how humans make their decisions. In doing so, these large retailers, including Victoria's Secret, BMW, and Panera (among others) can cater directly to what the customers want before the customers know they want it. This book is very insightful for life and dating. The excerpt above details through their studies that most people today go through a longer dating stage, that hooking up is more common, and that people need and use online dating more than ever.

SECTION II:

IDENTIFYING AND UNDERSTANDING

CHAPTER 3:
THE SIGNIFICANCE OF TIMING

"You're giving me too much time to think. When I have time to think, that's not good for you."

—Actress speaking to Johnny Drama on the show *Entourage*

Timing is everything. Timing can be the difference between someone being interested in you, giving you the time of day, ignoring you, laughing at your joke, deciding to hang out with you, and anything that may result. Timing in life can vary from wanting to focus on work, casually dating, not wanting a relationship, or wanting to commit and start a family.

The following examples are of late-night interactions with various modes of communication:

THE LATE-NIGHT TEXT

The general premise that she's reaching out to you at this level indicates her interest. The reality is that if the person is texting you late at night and asking what you're up to, it's obvious they're bored and thinking about you. When someone feels bored late at night, they're typically looking for ways to occupy their time.

- CASE STUDY -

The following is an excerpt from a text conversation from Tyler:

Girl: hey!
Tyler: whats up
Girl: Not much, just bored

> *Feedback—She's letting it be known from the start she's bored and looking for something to do.*

Tyler: that's no good
Girl: What are you doing?
Tyler: I was thinking about watching the new Will Ferrell movie that just came on Netflix!

Feedback—Showing her you have something to do, though not giving her a direct invitation to come over. You're waiting to see if she invites herself or comments on it.

Girl: That sounds like fun!

Feedback—And she does comment!

Tyler: Yea, im excited, its such a great movie...

Feedback—Create a sense of her missing out.

Girl: I haven't seen it
Tyler: Really? Wow, youre missing out! Without a doubt a top one of the best!

Feedback—Reiterating she's missing out, you two may not have the same tastes, though the goal is to make it seem better than it is.

Tyler: I would say you could come by and watch it..though im afraid you may steal all the popcorn;)

Feedback—Fun and innocent poke.

Girl: I don't even like popcorn..
Tyler: Fine, then as long as you promise to behave, youre more than welcome to come by...

Feedback—Showing her your sense of humor and formally inviting her since she hasn't invited herself, though has expressed an interest.

Girl: Where do you live?

Feedback—She's considering it as she figures out in her mind how far she is.

Tyler: I am about 5 minutes from the Target off of Broad Street, where are you?

Feedback—Gave her a landmark she's most certain to know because it will make her more comfortable with location and increases the odds of her coming over.

Girl: I am off of Main and Third

Feedback—No matter what she says, spin it into a positive in terms of not being too far away to meet up.

Tyler: Wow! You're close! You're 10 min from me!

Feedback—Downplaying the 10-minute distance as being very close and using exclamation points instead of periods to convey you're excited. This is helping her confirm in her mind she should come over.

Tyler: the movie starts at 11:00pm, better get on it....133 High Street ps im hoping youre not a stalker seeing as you will know where I live now...

Feedback—Telling her to hurry up, giving her your address and poking fun at her a little makes the details you just gave her to come over less intense.

*__Note__: A late-night text is recommended over a late-night phone call; it's less personal and easier to do.

LATE-NIGHT EMAIL

The late-night email has the same general premise as the late-night text or phone call but without the urgency. They're similar since the contact is at a time when the person is obviously on their mind. However, with an email there's no certainty of a reply from the other person that night. The reason for this is that many people have their phones with them all the time, so when they receive a text or a phone call, they receive it as soon as they check their phone. Responses from an email can take much longer, sometimes the following day or even days later, depending on how often the person checks their email. Text messages, phone calls, and app messages are by far the quickest ways to get an immediate response.

The most important things to take from a late-night email are that the woman is thinking about you while she's alone at night. Also, she's taking her time to write you. You can conclude that she isn't doing anything or is already in for the evening, if the time of the email is later than 11:30 p.m. It's important to check the time the email was sent because that can provide valuable information to you.

There are three classifications of the late-night email regarding times sent and the rationale for each:

1. If she sends an email before 10:30 p.m., don't look too far into it. The rationale is she still had time to go out, meet friends, or go on a date.
2. If she sends an email between 10:30 and 11:30 p.m., she has most likely been in for the night or had an early night after dinner. Most people are already out between 10:30 and 11:30 p.m., so chances are she did nothing or went out with friends, family, or even had an early date. She's reaching out to you at this hour because she wants to be doing something other than being home. If she did go out with someone else earlier, her interest in them isn't enough to prevent her from reaching out to you. She's showing she's interested in hanging out with you.
3. If she sends the email at 11:30 p.m. or later, you can bet she went out, maybe had a drink or two, and is either lonely or looking for fun. If she's reaching out to you at this hour, she's interested in hanging out. This could also lead to a fun night in together. The biggest issue is she sent it via email. If this was real-time messaging, i.e., a text message, a phone call, or an instant message, you could respond immediately to hang out that night. It's highly doubtful you'll be on your email at the exact same time, and if you were to respond immediately via email, it makes you look boring for being online or checking your phone at that hour. You never want to be the one emailing at this hour. As in sales, response time is important for you to jump on the opportunity to hang out when she's interested.

LATE-NIGHT APP MESSAGING

An app messaging conversation can establish mutual interest, create excitement, and can be very effective in meeting women. A late-night conversation can escalate the latter more quickly than a conversation during the day or early evening.

Once you start messaging, you expose yourself to a whole new world of communication. It's almost as if you become a kid again since the excitement is such a rush. Many describe this feeling as sitting on the edge of their seat anticipating the next message.

This can also lead to discussions about sex. Sex talks come about when someone talks about how long it may have been since they last had sex, how long it's been since they last dated someone, and why they're online rather than being out. Sometimes women will even volunteer that information based on their frustration with life, guys, players, or a personal issue. You should never be the one that pushes this conversation.

One of the most effective ways to gauge a woman's comfort and willingness to talk about sex is by copying a very effective management technique, "the sandwich approach." If the opportunity presents itself and is not totally off base, use this proven approach that management in nearly all the Fortune 500 companies use. The "sandwich approach" is when a manager has an issue they need to address, and they decide to sandwich the issue between a couple of compliments or jokes. For example, "You did a great job on the presentation today. Be sure to spell check next time; you misspelled many words. Overall, I see you have such great presence on stage."

An example of the sandwich approach, which you can use in the online dating scene is commenting about how long it has been since you had sex. For example, "There are so many weirdos on here just looking for sex. Don't get me wrong, it has been a while for me too, though messaging people with the exact number of days it has been since their last time is a bit overboard!"

This is the most effective way to get them to open up because they're sure to have a response or comment regarding that statement. Their response could range from mentioning an experience she had with one of the weirdos on the site, how creepy it is, how it has been a while for her too, and commenting on your not having had sex for some time.

If the opening is there, continue with the conversation since it will eventually progress, and she will open up further and feel more comfortable with you.

These are delicate conversations to have. You must be careful if you're the one transitioning from an innocent subject to one with some type of sexual undertone. These transitions can easily turn off a woman if the timing isn't right or it's inappropriate.

Never be too direct in your questioning; you don't want to appear as though you're interrogating them. If they feel this way, it will make them uncomfortable. There should never be any sort of self-pitying, either; no woman cares or wants to hear it.

Your likelihood of interacting with and getting the "good girl" to want you increases when communicating through messages. The reason for this is that no one will judge them because no one will know other than the two of you, unless one of you says something. Think about it: You and a woman message back and forth, meet, hang out, and part ways afterwards. You two are the only ones involved. The major attraction for the "good girl" is that she knows it's discreet, and there's a thrill to it.

In comparison, if she were to meet and leave with a guy from the bar, almost all her friends and his friends know. There's little doubt that more friends and people will eventually find out through gossip. All women hate to be "judged," and the more people who know, the more judgment.

You can also be certain that others in the crowd will see them leave together, and you can bet the woman is cautious; she wants to avoid any possibility of someone she knows seeing her leave with him. As you can tell from this viewpoint, the likelihood of a "good girl" doing this is not very high. This situation is very uncomfortable for most women. Most women do not want people to view her as a girl who leaves with random guys from a bar and will go to drastic measures to protect their reputations. This is one of the major reasons getting women online is such a successful avenue; a woman can act on her inhibitions without everyone knowing, judging her, or physically watching her.

The quote below is important. Women like the idea of a man they can trust who will stay quiet and doesn't kiss and tell.

> *"I am a man despised by many women in public, though behind closed doors they like me. In fact, many have reached out to me without their friends ever knowing, and they never will, which is why they contact me in the first place."*

> —Derik Sinveg

THE THREE BEST THINGS ABOUT APP MESSAGING:

1. You can have multiple conversations at a time, which means you can be talking to multiple women simultaneously. I've witnessed some of our case studies having conversations with as many as five women at one time. Talk about efficiency and covering your bases to ensure success!

2. The second and one of the hidden gems about some messaging services is the ability to go "offline" while still actually being online. This is great for avoiding people you don't wish to talk to and for limiting distractions so that you can focus solely on one conversation. The capabilities to message are still in place; the only difference is that others won't know you're online unless you message them.

3. The third and most important thing is that some app messengers allow you to organize the various women you're talking to. You can do this by creating labels for each one or creating groups. As covered later in the book, you must keep the different women you're talking to organized. For instance, an example of a name label would be "Sarah 21 NYC Student." If you follow that example, you can organize each woman's name, age, location, and occupation. This is vital because whenever you get a message from them, or whenever you message them, the title helps you remember who they are. If they see that you don't remember them and are just playing games, they won't bother talking to you. Unfortunately, many of their names on sites and apps don't provide any information on who they are to help you remember them. So, these labels are very important, and you should use them when entering cell numbers in your phone as well. One misstep can ruin an opportunity.

EXAMPLES:

<u>FRIENDS LIST</u>

Sarah 21 Nyc Student—Citygurl223

Abbey 27 Nurse Upstate—Abbsusc

Trinity 31 Bronx Florist—Flowapowa

Jackie 24 Nyc Waitress—Js1986

The primary point with any of these late-night messages is that if a woman reaches out to you, you can conclude she's interested in you. Combine her interest in you with any times she may be "bored," and you're in a very good position to interact further to connect and possibly hang out. When you hear people say that someone has "too much time on their hands," this typically indicates they did something strictly out of boredom. This is great news for you because if she's bored, she has too much time on her hands. Your job is to give her something to do.

THE REBOUND

The rebound occurs once someone becomes single after being in a relationship. Most people desire what they don't have. For instance, when someone is single they want to be in a relationship, or when someone is in a relationship, they think of the opportunities if they were single. The rebound happens once a relationship ends or once someone gets out of an exclusive dating setup. Once that happens, they tend to act on past desires to make up for "lost time."

A woman who is on the rebound looks at this as her opportunity to live it up. She was previously in an exclusive relationship and was envious of her single friends. Now, she can live the life she envied. Fresh in her mind are the crazy experiences her friends bragged about and the times she witnessed her friends go through guy after guy. All of this happened while she felt tied down in a relationship. Now is her time to shine. This is an opportunity, a great opportunity.

This woman typically is looking to relive her single days. She's looking for something new and exciting. Most relationships lose the excitement and can become stale over time. It's safe to assume that before she was on the rebound, this was her experience, as well.

To connect with a woman when she's in her rebound state, you want to appeal to her by not only being different, **but better**. The goal is to get her to want to hang out with you by using the various conversation methods you'll learn to ultimately get her to want you, too.

The guy may have dumped her or she's still upset and is searching for someone to fill that empty feeling. If the woman doesn't feel comfortable enough or doesn't want to come over for one reason or another, you must pick a location to meet where it's comfortable for both of you. Considering she's looking for something new and exciting, do something atypical; she's more than likely had her fair share of dinners and movies. Go dancing, go to the zoo, play bumper cars, go to a fair, or something else that's different. This will fulfill her desired change of pace.

If you're to meet her and she decides to drink, prepare for an eventful night. She's sure to be somewhat upset over her breakup and how things played out. It's common for this woman to drink herself to drunkenness. She goes overboard and thinks she can handle her liquor. She doesn't realize she doesn't have the same tolerance she had when she was drinking on a regular basis. She gets too caught up in being "free" and making up for lost time.

A woman on the rebound is a very delicate person to interact with. You must not pry into her life but be respectful. She's looking for a distraction from that time of her life. If she starts to discuss that part of her life, be respectful, though change the subject quickly. It's crucial to have her focus on the moment and allow her to enjoy the time she's with you and away from the past. This also means not supporting her drinking too much; you want her to remember the time she had with you as positive.

Remember, when you're in the moment, you define it, or it defines you.

CHAPTER 4:
CLARIFYING WHO YOU'LL BECOME

"If you could do whatever you wanted with no chance of failure,
what would you do? That is what you should be doing then."

—Tony Robbins

Imagine you can start over and be whoever you want to be. You can pick your personality, how you look, how others look at you, and you can have control of your life.

Is there someone you know who gets women who are out of his league, often dating more than one at a time? Do you wonder, "How does he do it?" Usually, this guy is what society calls a player.

This player could very well have some of the same characteristics you may have found in yourself after determining who you are in Chapter 5 based on your characteristics,

He's the guy who knows what it takes to get women, what he has to offer, and it has become irritatingly easy for him. This guy has had success in the past, and his confidence can be intimidating, though admirable. Chances are you and he may have many similar features. The difference is he highlights his attractive and most successful characteristics to women. He does this by design, and that design is for success. You're about to learn to do the same.

What's stopping you from being like him or even better? Nothing, now. You have everything you need in this book.

A decisive moment of realization is now: You have something to offer to women. You know deep down inside you're unique, and you have desirable characteristics. Chances are the characteristics you possess could give you a natural advantage over the guy who is currently having success with women. The only difference is in the way he highlights what he has to offer. His confidence continually grows, and he has the track record that affirms this.

We all have lost to someone who wasn't as good as we are. You may be smarter, funnier, stronger, more driven, happier, more adventurous, better looking, have more characteristics in common with a woman, and have an all-around better personality. Despite having all of this to offer, if you don't present it effectively, it's all wasted. Can you recall a time when you felt you were the right match for a woman, and for one reason or another, you couldn't get her?

Wouldn't it be great to combine what you've learned from the men who experience a great deal of success with the attributes you already possess? Be ready; you're about to do that and more. You're going to be "that" guy. You'll learn how to incorporate the actions, movements, and charm they possess that bring them great results. This is your cheat sheet so that you can duplicate their results consistently.

There's a reason the world's most famous golfer Tiger Woods still uses a golf coach; the

CEOs of Fortune 500 companies must report regularly to the board of directors; Arnold Schwarzenegger had a lifting partner despite having won a record seven Mr. Olympias in bodybuilding; and some colleges require their business students to intern at a company.

The reason? These people need an outside perspective, accountability, and insight. The top professions in every field have their own "coach" guide them along the way. I'm your coach on this journey to a better life.

This book, which some would refer to as a cheat sheet, is the partner you need. It will help condition you for continual progress, which will then create momentum. Momentum will then lead you to unimaginable success, yielding what you may have once considered unattainable.

During the Chicago Bulls' NBA record-setting season for wins, I recall Michael Jordan stating he thought they were never going to lose since the game became so easy to him. The same will happen for you once you start to get women. Your confidence will increase, your game will sharpen, and everything will become easier for you.

THE 10 GOLDEN COMMANDMENTS:

A FRAMEWORK FOR ACTION

1. In every relationship, always ask, "What's in it for me?"
2. Help yourself, and let others help themselves.
3. Know what you want.
4. Be energetic and persistent in pursuit.
5. Know when to break the rules.
6. Don't be nice, be charming and sexy.
7. Be flexible and aware of shifting opportunities.
8. Don't be angry; get what you want.
9. Don't be negative.
10. Understand that what others do is not about you. [2]

This comes directly from a book *for women* regarding high net worth dating. Take it to the bank, my friend, and get on it. If you're questioning how some women may perceive you, the following quote illustrates the reality of life. *"While most women would not admit to certain things or act a certain way in public, we all know people act differently behind closed doors. Oftentimes, women find solace knowing they can act on their inhibitions in private and keep it private."* The woman who told me this made me promise not to put her name with the quote, though you can be certain she isn't the only woman who feels this way.

"Identification through classification and understanding is not only the true way for one to learn, it is also the best way to implement what one has learned."

—Unknown

I want you to reflect on a person you admire, a person who has the life you want and desire. Make a list of what they have that you want.

Using the following list, place in order the most important items in life with a ranking of 1 for the most important to the least important item numbered 12. Give this itemization great thought because this will be your guideline for what you'd like to see in yourself. Remember, be honest with yourself. You cannot pretend for too long because you'll eventually be found out. [3] If you're not true to yourself you can't get as much as possible from this book.

____ Power

____ Respect

____ Reputation

____ Time

____ Quality of Life

____ Experiences

____ Fun

____ Sense of Humor

____ Appearance

____ Options

____ Style

____ Presence

The numerical order you just completed displays the value you place on the characteristics you admire most.

Using the different profile assessment characteristics above, review each of these and relate them to yourself by identifying your strengths and weaknesses for each. Brutal honesty is your only path to success. If you're not honest with where you stand, you're only hurting yourself and your potential growth in those areas. However, if you're honest in your assessment, you should expect growth and be on the path to possessing the characteristics you admire.

The next step in the process is self-awareness. Becoming self-aware is the first and most important step toward change. Now, you have to become conscious about these characteristics, and if you monitor your actions and vocabulary, you should expect consistent improvement. This improvement takes time, though there can be a quick change with discipline. You can strengthen the features you currently possess by combining the new disciplines you'll gain through self-awareness. This will result in an increase in focus and confidence.

If you're doing this online, it's very easy to create the persona you want. It's also important to remember that women will eventually find out if you're legit or not. If you're going to play the part, be the part. This is the chance to be who you've always wanted to be.

For the following questions, write down your answers in detail. This is very important. Once you can determine the answers and have written them down so that you can visualize them, it will increase your success rate drastically. In fact, in 1964, all members of the Harvard Business School graduating class stated at graduation the clear goals they wanted to accomplish. Among them, 5 percent took the time to write down their goals on paper. In 1984, Harvard did a follow-up study, and it discovered that 95 percent of those who wrote down their goals achieved them within 20 years. Among the "lazy" majority, only 5 percent of them reached their expected goals. An earlier study at Yale University also had similar results. This time, only 3 percent of the 1953 graduating class made written goals. Twenty years later, in 1973, 3 percent of Yale graduates accomplished more goals than the rest of the other 97 other combined. [4]

If you're serious about success, you must write down your goals. Answer each question by summarizing, i.e., confidence, style, The specifics will come later in this book.

Why do you want to change?

_____

_____

What do you hope to gain from this book?

_____

_____

How soon will you implement what you learn?

_____

_____

How will this affect your confidence?

_____

_____

How will this change your life if you experience the success you desire?

_____

_____

CHAPTER 5:

IDENTIFYING WHO YOU ARE

"If you cannot tell me who you are, how can you change to who you want to become?"

—Matthew Romano

As you read the different types of men, you must be honest with yourself. If you see characteristics you may not have noticed about yourself, this is a good thing. If you're honest with yourself regarding who you are, you'll grow rapidly. It's called self-actualization. You cannot grow if you aren't honest with yourself, you can't improve.

THE EIGHT DIFFERENT TYPES OF MEN

1. Awkward Guy: This guy is socially awkward. He's clueless about what to say and when. His habits range from being tough on himself and questioning what's wrong with him to blaming others for his lack of success. Rather than improving on any past successes, he psyches himself out before, during, and after any communication. It's common for him to say inappropriate things and appear nervous. This makes any communication he has even more awkward. He does this regularly by continually thinking of any past failures and shortcomings. To change, he must redirect his thoughts to those of success to prevent creating an awkward situation before a situation presents itself.

2. Clingy Guy: Characteristics include being too emotionally open with the woman from the start. This guy may have wondered why things ended too early with a woman in the past. He's quick to be emotionally invested. After a breakup, this guy is clueless about what went wrong. He dissects every conversation and moment they were together. Unfortunately, he isn't honest enough with himself to realize the obvious: He came across as clingy. Women don't want to know that you're just a normal guy looking to settle down with someone. They want to feel as though they got "a good one" and feel lucky. They do not want you to constantly text them or call them, and you don't need to know where they are at all the times. You don't want to come across as wanting to see them all the time.

   The Clingy Guy scares many women away because he compliments them too often and even says, "I love you" quickly. He also makes the mistake of offering commitment too quickly by saying, "I'm not seeing anyone else" and "I feel like we're meant to be," which can scare a woman not looking for commitment just yet. He asks specific questions regarding the number of kids she wants, the age she wants to get married, etc. There's no set timetable to have discussions about these topics. It's always better to wait until she brings up any of them. If you bring them up, it can creep them out and turn them off.

3. <u>Touchy/Feely Guy</u>: The best two words for this guy is back off! Being too touchy can instantly turn off a woman. There's no reason to go overboard immediately. Believe it or not, a hug, a kiss, or even holding hands has a very emotional and psychological effect on most women. You must restrain yourself until the moment is right. Later in this book, you'll learn to identify when the moment is, in fact, right. You want to avoid—at all costs—the potential for her to feel turned off or disrespected. If you're too touchy right off the bat, her guard will immediately go up and create awkwardness. Her thought process will go straight to, "I wonder how many other girls he has done this to?" This makes you look like a playboy because you're going too fast. This also can make a woman uncomfortable, which is exactly what you never want. Most smart women will see through this guy.

4. <u>Too Intense Guy</u>: The best example of this is a head coach of a football team; most are too intense, rarely calm, and their strong nature can come across as very confrontational. Each person must possess different speeds. Sometimes women want to experience a rush such as skydiving or zip-lining, or they want to be spontaneous enough to go out on an adventure such as traveling somewhere exotic. Other times women want to relax and be lazy. The Too Intense Guy doesn't recognize the different emotional states the woman is in because his foot is always on the gas pedal. If you're intense too often, you'll come across as overbearing and will create distance between you and her or anyone for that matter. Identifying what state a woman is in and her type is pivotal in communicating effectively with her.

5. <u>Life of the Party Guy</u>: This guy sees himself as hilarious. He often takes jokes too far, thinks everyone is waiting for him to entertain them, and sometimes talks just to hear himself talk. He's too loud and can make offensive comments, which embarrasses himself and others around him. This person can feel awkward if he sits back and tries to fit in with the crowd. This character must learn to scale it back.

    Remember, women often try to find a reason not to like you, and acting this way will give them that reason. Instead, be calm, cool, and collected. The key is not to be offensive and to come across as likeable. Simple enough, isn't it? Once you develop a sense of comfort between the two of you and have identified that you both have a similar sense of humor, the time is right to test the waters. You can ease into jokes that may be a little more risqué and make more outlandish comments that are sure to get a reaction. If only one person is enjoying the jokes and conversation, you're making no headway. However, if both people are on the same page, it can elevate the connection and enjoyment for both of you.

6. <u>Moneybags Guy</u>: This guy likes to overcompensate for his insecurities by flashing money. He may try to impress her by taking her to an expensive restaurant, buying drinks, spending cash in excess, and trying to dress and live up to an image he created for himself. The reality is this guy is paying for her attention. In contrast, living this moneybags lifestyle can cause you to spend tons of money

and, more importantly, tons of time in the courting stage. If you're okay with this and have the cash and time to live this lifestyle, be prepared; expectations are that it's forever. The truly successful men are those who don't need to spend a dime.

7. <u>The Natural Guy</u>: This is the guy who has it down. He's a "natural" in a social setting and is rarely uncomfortable, can easily strike up a conversation, and is genuinely enjoyable to be around. Both men and women enjoy his company. He's very smooth with women, without needing to flash money or by not being genuine as he understands how to communicate and interact in a respectful, yet attractive manner.

8. <u>Nice Guy</u>: This guy is the perfect gentlemen. He's the image of what most parents teach their sons to be from a young age. He's very polite and compliments the woman often. These compliments include, "You're pretty," "You're beautiful," "You're amazing," and "I like you so much." He opens the door for the woman, treats her like a princess, and women classify him as a friend or maybe he's even like a brother. **Note**: A woman wants a guy with an edge. How many times have you been interested in a woman, only to watch her go to some guy who doesn't treat her nearly as well as you would? Not only is she attracted to this guy, she literally treats him like a king.

   The old saying, "Nice guys finish last" applies here. **Women want a guy with an edge, someone who intrigues them and poses some sort of challenge**. We see this repeatedly; women feel more attracted to assholes. **Note**: An asshole is not always the mean image you may have in mind. He's more unpredictable than any guy described thus far. The definition of insanity is doing the same thing again and again while expecting a different result. When you're the nice guy, you relinquish all control you could have; you're always attempting to appease her. Many women want someone to take charge, so take the lead. Most nice guys will never realize they're even doing anything wrong.

Chances are you compared yourself to each of these descriptions while you read them. You may have even seen bits of yourself in the characteristics described in each of these eight types. Each of us is very diverse and has varying characteristics. Once you've identified the characteristics you possess, you can then understand how a woman may view you. From there, you can adjust your characteristics to be a more well-rounded person.

Remember, if you want a fake woman, be a fake man. If you'd like to compliment a woman, do so because she deserves it not because she wants or expects it. Brutal honesty is important to your success and to experience any growth. Self-actualization is essential for growth. To get where you're going, you must have a clear vision of where you want to go, but also a clear picture of where you are currently.

CHAPTER 6:
THROUGH A WOMAN'S EYES

"One of the biggest challenges we'll encounter in life is to unlearn many of the things we were taught was right."

—Michael Anthony

To gain a better understanding of what a woman experiences when she's on dating sites and apps, I created three different fake profiles on both Plenty of Fish and Match.com over a two-month period. Each profile had five photos, and the "About Me" section had four sentences. I used each of the three profiles for a period of three days in a certain ZIP code; after the three days were up, I used the same profile but changed the ZIP code to a location in another state; and after those three days were up, I used the same profile again and changed the ZIP code to yet another state. In total, I created 18 profiles: nine for Plenty of Fish and nine for Match.com: the six originals duplicated two additional times.

I followed the same outline regarding age, number of pictures, types of pictures, and wrote four sentences for each profile. To get the pictures, I joined Shutterstock and downloaded stock images. I uploaded these photos to each site/app and then typed four sentences in the "about me" section that described each fictional woman as being new to the area with a couple of generic sentences regarding liking the beach and vacationing. Because Plenty of Fish is free, I was not under much of a time crunch, but I was with Match so I used the free trial period.

In total there were three profiles, each displayed in a total of three states for three days apiece. The activity on these profiles was unimaginable as were the messages. Look at just how much competition there is online for a woman's attention and why differentiating yourself is so important.

Within just three days, people viewed the profile 126 times, and it received 78 emails and 92 winks. The following is an example of the behind-the-scenes profile settings for the profile we created. As you can imagine, there was a lot to sort through from the number of emails, winks, and profile views received in just three days. Some of this information was entertaining to say the least.

Following the behind-the-scenes profile settings, you can see some of the various messages received. All phone numbers and personal information are hidden for privacy purposes.

In comparison, the male profile had no profile views, no emails, and no winks in three days. Though the profile was bland and filled with "no-no's," the competition for females is far more active.

- CASE STUDY -

BELOW ARE ACTUAL EMAIL EXCERPTS WITH INFORMATION REMOVED FOR PRIVACY

To: MissyE@gmail.com

From: alwaysTim@gmail.com

Subject: We should hang out...

Text me (123) 456-7890

To: bosslady@gmail.com

From: joey25@gmail.com

Subject: Did you move here for work? Where do you work at? Do you like it?

To: hollabackmama@gmail.com

From: ashtonKusher@gmail.com

Subject: Are you a model??

Because you could be if you wanted to. You look just like a model from the Victoria Secret catalog.

To: mandy34@gmail.com

From: bigJIMguy@yahoo.com

Subject: You are HOTT

Im sure you already knew this :P

To: amanda_uf@gmail.com
From: mafiamaan@yahoo.com
Subject: New to this too!

I am new to this too!

To: chrisBoy@aol.com
From: JeniLily@yahoo.com
Subject: Summer is my favorite season too

Though summer can get too hot. I am not a big fan of humidity and sweating, lol

To: shawnda4@aol.com
From: stanleyswiz@yahoo.com
Subject: Best time of your life ;)

That I will be for you. You have never experienced what I can give you babe!

To: stewguy@aol.com
From: christy65@yahoo.com
Subject: Please write me back!

Stuart

I really like you :)

To: victoriaSec@gmail.com

From: jonnyV@yahoo.com

Subject: You and I are a lot alike!

You and I both like to stay in shape, like the outdoors (from the looks for your pictures) and are new to this site. Sounds like a match made in heaven! Possibly even our destiny!

Prince Charming

To: jennbabe@gmail.com

From: sebastian@yahoo.com

Subject: Hey Beautiful :D

How do you like living downtown? The weather has not been the greatest, though it does get better ☺ So do you model for a living? The reason I ask is because you are very attractive. I do not say this often, though you are beautiful. How long have you been on here? Have you met anyone yet? Write me back! Sebastian

---

To: MatJson@gmail.com

From: Megan36@gmail.com

Subject: I love California!

It is probably my favorite state in the United States, though I prefer to travel Europe as it makes the United States look pathetic. Europe is amazing. Have you been to Paris? You would love it there ;)

To: fieldhockyGurl@gmail.com

From: SAMY33@gmail.com

Subject: Drinks?

You look like a girl who likes martinis! We should go out tonight for drinks at the Martini Bar downtown.

To: ILoveDisneyMovies@aol.com
From: SmithM33@msn.com
Subject: Can't wait to talk to you again :D

You seem like the total package and you are so pretty.

To: MsJones@aol.com
From: SmittyM@msn.com
Subject: Can't wait to talk to you again :D

Have a great day! I am really looking forward to talking to you again, I woke up this morning thinking about you and you seem like a great girl. I will be on my email throughout the day, if you're bored and want to email back :) I will get online tonight around 9 to chat some more!
-Max

To: M_RN_317@aol.com
From: RoofDoctor@yahoo.com
Subject: Interested?

So what did you think of the chat last night? Did you have fun? I sure did, you were really easy to talk to. Not only do you look beautiful, you seem to be smart too. I like that ;) I have a pretty busy day today, driving from where I live by (location removed for privacy) to the jobs I have today should make for a tiring day. I guess it could be worst, right? Luckily, our work phone is (123) 456-ROOF, as it keeps us busy. So do you enjoy your job as a nurse? Which hospital do you work at? I could only imagine how sexy you look in your little nurse outfit. text me at (123) 456-7890 and we can message back and forth throughout the day.

Talk to you soon sweetie,
Justin

- CASE STUDY -

INSTANT MESSAGES

There's an option on Plenty of Fish and many other dating sites to have your settings show whether you're online at that moment. You can enable or disable that feature. The instant messenger service allows any person who sees you online to instantly message you. Within just 10 minutes, you'll have to turn this feature off because the number of messages coming in exceeds 20. The instant messages included compliments about her looks, simple small talk, pictures of half-naked bodies, and promises to take her on the best date ever. The following are some condensed excerpts of instant messages sent to "her." Below the excerpts is my feedback for you to correct your thinking. Remember, this is the overwhelming response a fake profile received; just imagine what a normal woman deals with...

- **Hey hot stuff**

  Feedback—Turn-off since it appears you're playing games already and have intentions on her based solely on looks. Not a good start.

- **What are you doing tonight gorgeous?**

  Feedback—Insinuating she's considering hanging out with you tonight, when she doesn't know you and hasn't even talked to you yet.

- **HEY!**

  Feedback—All capital letters is the equivalency of yelling online. Simmer down!

- **I think I fell in love once I saw your pictures!**

  Feedback—This is creepy. This is sure to make her feel uncomfortable.

- **When are you free to hang out?**

  Feedback—Odd, assuming she wants to hang out even though she hasn't talked to you.

- **Have you been to the new piano bar?**

  Feedback—Not such a bad question, though not a good icebreaker.

- **I can show you around since you're new to town**

  Feedback—This screams desperation. She's on an online dating site, not there to find a tour guide.

- CASE STUDY -

TEXT MESSAGES

As if creating a fake profile wasn't enough, I then purchased a prepaid phone for each profile. The voicemail was set up with the generic computer automated voice, which reads back the phone number as the voicemail greeting, so no voice was present on the voicemail greeting. During the chat and emails, texting was suggested as the best way to contact "her." Though this was pushing my comfort zone, I knew it was necessary for this book to have detailed and accurate case studies.

I specifically asked for a different area code when I purchased the phone and prepaid card. This would align with the story if anyone questioned where "she" was from since the area code was in line with her story of recently moving in her profile description. As you can imagine, she had quite the array of text messages sent to her. Some were rude, others sounded very desperate, and all were very easy to see through.

The following are examples of text messages sent to "her" with my feedback beneath each.

- **What are you doing?**

  Feedback—Seems very possessive as if you need to know what she's doing.

- **Are you busy? You still haven't messaged me back??**

  Feedback—Can we say desperation?

- **If you don't like me, just tell me...**

  Feedback—Women want confidence, not insecurity. This makes you come across weak and inferior.

- **Where do you live?**

  Feedback—Creepy, and no woman would reveal this information to a stranger.

- **Are you dating anyone?**

  Feedback—Obviously if on a dating site, she's not. Asking this question scares the woman as it insinuates you're thinking about a relationship, when she doesn't know you.

- **I would satisfy you more than you ever have been before.**

  Feedback—Inappropriate and a surefire way for her to block you and not respond.

- **Can't wait to meet you!**

  Feedback—Seems too anxious and creates doubt about why you must be so excited. Is it because you're a creep, and everyone else turns you down?

- **I promise you'll like me...**

  Feedback—This reeks desperation again. Stating something such as this raises concern about why this you sent this.

- **How long have you been single?**

  Feedback—In the beginning stages of talking to someone, the last thing you need to discuss is her last relationship.

- **Are you there?**

Feedback—Terrible ice breaker, if she responds she's there, then asking the obvious is not necessary. A simple, "How's it going?" works fine.

TOP 13 IMMEDIATE TURN-OFFS

From what I witnessed through the various messages and emails sent to the fake profiles, it's apparent that guys have many common characteristics. Because most men possess similar characteristics, they often think—and, more importantly—act the same way. Here are the top 13 immediate turn-offs many of these men used online and in person. Understanding how most men act and how women respond to them will make it clear what not to do. This will ultimately give you an advantage in knowing how to differentiate yourself, too.

1. *Lying*: The truth eventually comes out. When meeting in person, they'll know whether the picture was old and whether you lied about your height, weight, etc. The same is true for your work, family, and anything in the past you may not be forthcoming about. It's not worth it. If she feels you're deceiving her, you're wasting your time and hers.

2. *Talking about past failed relationships*: Nothing good will come from this topic, and it will immediately shift the focus to an ex. This will distract her from any interest in you, or productive conversation with you, and hurt your connection with her.

3. *Asking why she's single*: This shifts any possible connection you two may have had in the works or the opportunity to meet. It distracts her attention to past letdowns and upset feelings. This question will make her think back to every failed dating relationship she has had. There's nothing good for you or her in going there.

4. *Asking her about her measurements (bra and waist)*: These are immediate turn-offs; they're inappropriate. This will make you look shallow and superficial. Never ask these questions.

5. *Avoid sex talk*: When talking online don't mention sex in the first conversation, even though many guys surprisingly think this is acceptable. If you do, she will view this as if you're a guy looking for one thing. I would be cautious using any sex talk unless she brings it up first, but this is a very slippery slope.

6. Clinginess: Telling her how much you miss her and can't wait to see her again is a no-no. This makes you appear over-anxious and could raise a concern about your becoming too clingy, annoying, and most importantly, easy for her. Remember women want a challenge.

7. *Touchiness*: Touching her a lot, holding hands, and having your arm around her, especially at the beginning, can be too much too soon. Most women see this as a way for a man to mark his territory, which can rub her the wrong way. This can also make her uncomfortable and suspicious of your intentions since she may not be comfortable with you yet.

8. *Possessiveness*: Needing to know what she's doing all the time, with whom she's doing it, and where she's doing it raises immediate concerns. This could lead her to stop talking to you immediately. Two words come to their minds: insecure and controlling. Neither are traits you should want a woman to label you with.

9. *Seeming desperate*: Giving her your whole life story and how badly you want or need to be with someone makes you appear damaged. Women want a strong man and want to feel as if they're someone special and the guy they find is a good catch. If the woman feels as though other women have passed on you and she's one of the few interested, she will view your value as poor, and when a woman sees little value in you, your chances with her are slim.

10. *Don't be over-anxious*: Never seem over-anxious by extending an invitation to her to hang out right away. If you just started talking or chatting with her and are inviting her over already, that's going to be a red flag to her. She'll question how many times you've done this before, and her guard will go up. Ease up.

11. *Fake*: Don't try to be someone you're not. Any uncomfortable actions or jokes can make you come across as creepy and odd. Remember, most women will see through this. Fake men attract fake women.

12. *Avoid negativity*: Women feel attracted to men they enjoy being around. Being negative is a turn-off. Any negativity you convey leads to negative thoughts for her. Once she goes down the road of negative thoughts, she'll think of times she felt bad, past failed relationships, being used, and all that negativity brings. You don't want this. Remember, you achieve positivity by making progress toward comfort and rapport so there isn't awkwardness, and this leads to an enjoyable time for you both.

13. *Never blame*: Some women seem to take credit for any success they could be remotely involved in. Some also blame any failure on someone else, which is why they hate judgment. People don't like to take responsibility, so be careful not to pry into why something went wrong or failed. Simply listen and remember you're not there to solve problems or reach a verdict on whether they were to blame or did anything wrong.

- CASE STUDY -

This case study is an example showing you how giving less attention to a woman can increase her attraction to you and your perceived value in a social setting.

Desiree and Matt had exchanged messages through one of the more popular social sites and spoke once through app messaging. While chatting, they exchanged numbers. He proceeded to send a witty text here and there over the following week. Some of the text messages were in good fun about her job and referencing the complaints she made about it. An example of this was, "I hope you packed two lunches today in case Ms. Lunch Snatcher grabs yours again today :)". This highlighted his sense of humor and kept her interested.

That Friday, she mentioned she was going out with friends from college who were in from North Carolina. In the conversation via text she asked what he was doing, and he told her he wasn't sure yet. She texted him that night to see what he was up to and told him where she was. Matt was out with two friends. He told her the place was lame, and they were thinking about going to another bar, which turned out to be roughly five minutes away from the bar where she was with her friends. In an obvious display of interest, Desiree talked her friends into going to the bar where Matt was.

She didn't mention that the friends she had in town from North Carolina were guys. Though

Matt was surprised, he didn't let this bother him. Rather than getting weirded out or trying to puff out his chest, Matt did the opposite. Upon seeing her in the bar, he said hi to her and hugged her and introduced himself to each of the three guys who were with her. He then went back to talking to his group of friends and made it a point to have as much fun as possible.

I know you're thinking, "Why would his focus be on his friends?" when he has a girl who is obviously interested in him and has made such a blatant effort to see him. The answer is, this was his first time meeting this girl, and he hadn't planned on her being with three guys, so he didn't want to create an awkward situation. Matt understood that the more fun he appeared to be having with his friends, the more attractive he would be to her. He wanted to bring home the point to her, so he smiled and laughed often as she was sure to take notice.

While Matt was clearly having a great time, Desiree literally walked over and stood directly in front of him to get his attention. While standing in front of him, they started talking for a little while before she went to the bar for a drink. Note: This is a way Matt stands out from most other guys. Desiree must have felt taken aback as she dropped numerous hints about needing a drink, and he didn't so much as offer to get her one, let alone purchase one.

This escalated the challenge for her, and most all women love a challenge. While looking in the mirror to his right, which was directly over the bar, he noticed a random guy eyeing Desiree. As Matt saw her walking back, out of the corner of his eye he noticed the guy was still staring at her. Desiree and the random guy made eye contact. However, she continued to walk toward Matt. The random guy walked up to Desiree and started hitting on her while she was roughly two feet away from Matt. He even asked whether he could buy her a drink. She glanced over at Matt, though Matt had already (intentionally) turned his back to the situation.

I know you're wondering why he would turn his back. The answer is he wanted her to know he wasn't worried about the guy in the least bit. After about five painful minutes of a random guy trying to pick her up, Matt felt someone hit his arm. It was Desiree, asking him why he didn't "save her." He smirked and said, "It looked like the two of you were hitting it off."

She responded, "No, he was begging for my attention, offering me drinks, and asking for my number!" He smiled, understanding she was intentionally making it known to him that she had guys interested in her who would buy her drinks. He just smiled as he saw she came back to him (the guy who didn't pay her attention or buy her anything).

She looked back at him and couldn't help but smile. She told him that with the smirk on his face, he reminded her of Tom Cruise's character Maverick from Top Gun. From there, Matt decided it was time to check out the bar across the street. He told her where he was going, and she decided to leave the friends she had visiting her from North Carolina to go with him. They were at the other bar for another 15 to 20 minutes before he and his friends decided it was time to call it a night. He poked fun at her keychain while leaving the bar and told her to have a good night and gave her a hug.

She was dumbfounded and speechless. Most guys would have acted in desperation to invite her over, but Matt didn't even attempt to. When he got to the parking garage, he texted her, saying, "You're more than welcome to come over to watch a movie ;)."

She texted him back, "How dare you!? After not paying me any attention all night, do you really think I am going to come over?"

He replied, "I may be able to pay you more attention in a one-on one setting," and gave her his address via text. She waited a little while before responding she was on her way.

The drive should have taken her 15 minutes, but she went the wrong way on a roundabout twice, and it ended up taking her 35 minutes. When she finally arrived, she was beyond frustrated. Matt could sense this and hugged her once she walked in the door. This helped her relax a little and took away some of the frustration she had from the drive. He then proceeded to show her around his house. While upstairs he offered her a sweater because the night had become cool. She declined and teased, "The guy at the bar said I was hot, so a sweater is the last thing I need."

The mood had settled, and Matt turned on a movie. They sat on his couch under the covers and enjoyed the rest of the night together.

From the outside looking in, it's obvious she was much more attracted to Matt than the random guy interested in her at the bar because of Matt's lack of attention and the challenge he presented. Think about it, the other guy was complimenting her, offering to buy her drinks, and giving his complete attention to her. Through her eyes, he was nothing more than another guy. Through her eyes Matt was not another guy, he was different, he was a challenge.

CHAPTER 7:
IDENTIFYING THE TYPES OF WOMEN

"All women have common characteristics, such as confidence, insecurities, jealousy, and desire. The men that experience most of the success with women are those who can identify which characteristics are most evident in the woman to successfully appeal to her."

—Michael Anthony

TYPE	HIGH MAINTENANCE	NORMAL	LOW SELF ESTEEM
HIGHLY ATTRACTIVE	Selfish, conceited, rude, inconsiderate, judgmental, and highly critical. She has more opinions and options so will typically reject most men she encounters.	Likeable, humble, enjoyable to be around, and not judgmental. She is a rarity to find. She is not demeaning to others because she's attractive.	Insecure, hesitant, shy, uncomfortable, and continually seeking approval. She is easily embarrassed with a compliment and most likely has had a bad experience in her childhood or past relationship directly impacting her self-esteem.
AVERAGE	Not a "natural" beauty, has to work at it, on the surface may appear tough and confident, though still insecure as she remembers how life used to be for her and is still a bit vulnerable behind a "bitchy" persona.	One of the "best" core girls you could find, easygoing in most aspects of life, content in relationships, trustworthy, has substance and good character.	Rarely achieves happiness because she doesn't strive for it. Prefers security and oftentimes settles to feel secure. Ends up regretful since she never lived to be happy, scared of change and prefers to play it "safe" and be okay rather than being happy.

TYPE	HIGH MAINTENANCE	NORMAL	LOW SELF ESTEEM
NOT ATTRACTIVE	Perhaps the worst to be around, resembles a dictator, likes to be in charge, will sacrifice a good guy for one who bows to her every command, and thinks she is much better than she is. Men are responsible for creating this monster by the attention they give her.	Because looks aren't on her side, she gives attention elsewhere. She's typically an intellectual, a deep thinker, a dreamer, and she's intelligent. Tends to be more loyal because she doesn't have as many options and does not want to ruin a good thing.	Very indecisive and insecure. Attracted to more decisive men who will make decisions, and she is typically obedient and quiet - often leading to unhealthy relationships because of her weak nature and allowing people to walk all over.

HIGHLY ATTRACTIVE:

High maintenance:

She knows she's very attractive because men tell her how hot she is regularly. Oftentimes, she completely blows guys off by acting as though she doesn't even know they exist. She may do this by ignoring a compliment given to her or by turning her head or body to avoid acknowledging the guy is attempting to talk to her. If she does choose to acknowledge a guy's presence, she can come across as being very short and not talkative. This is typically intentional. She acts this way because she doesn't have to be nice to get what she wants. Once she blows off one guy, there's another guy right around the corner waiting to compliment her. (We will cover this later in the book on how important it is to stand out.) She can come across as inconsiderate because she doesn't need anyone's attention or approval; she knows she already has every guy's attention.

Analysis: This girl typically falls for the "asshole" guy who doesn't pay her any attention and doesn't treat her as well as you or a perfect gentleman would. We see this all the time, don't we, fellas?

Normal:

This is a rare breed. This is an attractive woman who still has tact. She treats others with respect, is well mannered, is very likeable, and is a very decent person. This woman acts the same with the dorky guy as with the popular guy in almost any situation.

Think of a woman who comes to your mind that most closely resembles the "normal" woman. Think of how she not only treated you with respect, but how she made you feel as though you were equals. Now that you have this woman in your mind, understand this is how you should feel when approaching all women. The confidence and positive feeling you have after talking with her is how you should feel at all times with any woman. That feeling is how the successful guys feel with every woman they meet, regardless of how hot or high maintenance they are.

Analysis: This woman is the total package and is who you should strive to end up with.

Low Self-Esteem:

There are few hot women with low self-esteem out there. The reason for this is eventually they're told how "beautiful," "amazing," and "hot" they are. They start believing this as men continually shoot themselves in the foot, elevating this woman into a position of superiority. In time, women grow to understand the power they have over many men and use it. She catches the attention of most guys since she's hot, stunning, or has the "it" factor. She doesn't see herself as being that attractive or being a sought-after commodity, though. This is the type of woman you may have seen something in or have been interested in at one point in your life. You may have been hesitant to pursue her, only to find out she had started to date or hang out with a guy that confirmed you could have had a shot. You must identify and go after this woman early.

Because she has low self-esteem, the attention she receives may be a bit overwhelming to her. Physically, she's more of the natural beauty, so she doesn't overdo the make-up or outfits. She doesn't show much cleavage, either—that is, until she feels she needs to. When she's at the point of "needing to," she's no longer the woman you may have once liked.

Analysis: This woman typically ends up with whoever fits her life stage. She has no direction, and her future ultimately depends on which guy is willing to commit to her first. Her low expectations follow her instinct to settle with whoever commits first.

AVERAGE:

High Maintenance:

She is average in appearance, although she appears better than average. Though she may appear better than average, inside she knows she must work at it. She is not the "natural beauty." She dresses well to show off her body, tans regularly, and works out to stay in shape. These are, of course, features most guys feel attracted to. She may show a little cleavage, wear tight clothing, and appear impeccable with her hair and nails done at all times.

This is the woman who remembers what being "average" felt like and has experienced the benefits of appearing better than average first-hand by enhancing her appearance. She will not let herself go back to feeling "average" ever again. This woman is often extremely self-conscious. People may repeatedly tell her how great she looks, though inside she still may feel a bit uncomfortable in her outfit and/or appearance. She needs the reassurances guys give her and is never fully comfortable with men perceiving her as hot. She can come across as though she believes she's amazing, though if insulted she's quick to crumble because her inner doubts lead her to second-guess everything regarding her appearance. A confident woman will never let anyone else see her vulnerable; she will do everything possible to seem unflappable and certain with her appearance and confidence.

Analysis: This woman typically ends up with a guy like herself who works on his appearance by tanning, dressing nicely, and so forth since they both want similar physical characteristics in their match.

Normal:
She's the girl who can become a best friend. She's down-to-earth, understanding, and more even-keeled. She's the best candidate to act as your liaison with the opposite sex because she can see the situation with any woman from a woman's perspective. This is important because her judgment is more accurate because she isn't the "high maintenance" or "low self-esteem" woman and can give you insight from what she has seen with other women who are her friends.

She is the type of woman who seldom—if ever—dresses up. She typically has her hair in a ponytail and is a bit more athletic and spontaneous. She's always up for a road trip or an adventure. This is the woman who fits the country-girl profile: low maintenance, easy-going, and not afraid to get dirty. Additional characteristics to watch for with this woman are wearing make-up, high heels, dressing up, and going out with a skirt on, which doesn't happen regularly. If she feels comfortable enough to alter her appearance, consider that a bonus because many of the "normal average" women feel uncomfortable doing that because they lack the confidence to pull it off. Confidence is a mental trait, though a lack is visible.

You can observe their physical appearance and how they handle themselves. Examples of this include having difficulty walking in heels, not sitting properly in a skirt (legs not crossed), and not having proper posture when wearing outfits that can make a woman appear hunched or lacking confidence.

Analysis: This woman typically ends up with a guy who is like herself: easygoing, likes the stability of contentment, and is down-to-earth.

Low Self-Esteem:
This woman most likely has a reason for her low self-esteem. She's typically very shy and rarely makes eye contact. Someone has most likely belittled or made fun of her, and that sticks with her to this day. She doesn't have the confidence to dress or act sexy.

She lacks confidence, which is obvious by looking at her posture. She typically hunches her back, keeps her head down to avoid eye contact, and, to avoid confrontation, rarely voices her opinion.

This personality type is most common in women who do not have a good relationship with their fathers. Another type that fits this mold is a woman who was cheated on or was put down and made to believe she has little to no worth.

Analysis: This woman typically ends up with a guy who isn't good enough for her. She stays with him because it's easier to stay with him than leave him. Note: She's not happy, though she feels secure enough to be content in the relationship.

NOT ATTRACTIVE:

High Maintenance:
This is the worst type for most guys. She is the woman who isn't attractive to 75 percent of the guys out there, though, as the saying goes, "Every dog has its day." This couldn't be truer for this woman. She typically tries to keep up with the latest fashions, likes to get herself dolled up with makeup and jewelry, and is big into celebrity gossip.

She typically shows off her body intentionally. Whether it's showing her breasts off by wearing very low-cut shirts, wearing short skirts, short shorts, dresses, or tight pants to show off her legs and butt, she has one goal, and that's attention. She will do almost anything within reason to get the attention she desires. She loves every bit of it. For her, all attention is good attention.

The biggest enabler for this type of woman is us. Men are the problem. Rather than not giving her the attention she craves, they do the opposite.

This woman mistakes good attention for bad attention. She typically ends up bouncing around from guy to guy. She misplaces her own worth by dating men who don't respect her. Most of these guys don't even so much as call her back after the initial encounter, which then further diminishes her own worth and puzzles her about what she did wrong. She is not the type to learn from this since she continually does this on a regular basis. She's also known to get clingy quick, so beware.

Analysis: This woman typically ends up with whatever guy is willing to settle down with her and obey her commands. She is very high-maintenance and would rather be in charge than happy.

Normal:
This is the woman flies under the radar. She's typically the most loyal and solid woman because she's kept her head on straight. She doesn't go from guy to guy and has morals. She's normally a very good and disciplined worker. She understands what she has to offer. Her understanding of what she has to offer is based on a mental and intellectual level. She does not see herself as a person who has a lot to offer in the appearance department and as a result doesn't try to connect much on a physical level.

Analysis: This woman typically ends up with someone who appreciates what she has to offer as a person and connects with her on an intellectual level more than a physical level.

Low Self-Esteem:
This woman is not someone who many men approach or talk to Watching friends and other women have men talk to them and ask them out compounds her lack of confidence. Rather than making changes, she's truly clueless, and it isn't her fault. Friends and family should offer to help but have let her down. For this reason, many consider her hopeless. She may be a great woman and have a lot to offer but the problem is someone must engage with her to know. She doesn't stand out with her clothing or personality. She's not a follower in social settings. Her perfect match is a dominant male leader. If you have ever watched a talk show that has the show centered on makeovers, this is the "before" version.

Analysis: This woman typically ends up with someone who has a more dominant personality. This is a good setup for her; she can follow his lead and allow him to make most decisions.

Through my studies, I have found that most women feel more attracted to men who are with other women or other women pursue. The reasoning for this is a combination of scarcity and challenge. The concept of scarcity creates a much more desired state when there's very limited supply. The challenge part is just that, a challenge. A woman likes the concept of pursuing a man who may not be interested in her. In fact, women will work harder for a man's attention, simply to prevent another woman from getting it.

Furthermore, many women are competitive by nature and like to win. You can use this information to your advantage by hanging out with multiple women at a time. Women want what they perceive as most desirable. If other women like you, they will want you more. Use this to your advantage.

CHAPTER 8:

LEARNING ABOUT THE DIFFERENT TYPES OF WOMEN

"Women want a challenge. Men want something easy."

—Unknown

Now that you understand the different categories of women's personalities, it's important to understand how you can streamline the process of identifying her type. It's equally as important to understand how you should pursue her type.

This is simple. In fact, it's so simple most men never dare think to do something so painfully obvious to understand women. **Put yourself in the woman's shoes.**

What would you feel attracted to? If you were a woman, how would you respond to the way you approach a woman? How does what you say stand out compared to the other men who approach them? This is such an elementary level of thought, but it sits at the PhD level in intelligence efficiency.

Imagine how a woman must feel if men compliment her daily by stating:

- "You're beautiful."
- "You look great!"
- "You're so pretty."
- "Wow, you're gorgeous!"
- "Your outfit is hot!"
- "Damn! You look good."

Let's take it a step farther: Imagine what it's like for her when she always feels men staring at her, feeding her compliments left and right, offering to buy her drinks each night, and is consistently asked out. Pretty powerful, isn't it? Now, what do you think happens once she feels a guy has ulterior motives? Answer = the guard goes up!

The goal is to avoid making her feel as if you have ulterior motives. You want to make her feel comfortable. Don't act like the other guys, and she won't treat you like the other guys.

Note: If you ever come across a girl who seems to be too good to be true, be cautious. If she's available, there are reasons. If you catch a glimpse of any sort of shady behavior or she acknowledges any past shadiness, avoid her at all costs. That's a dangerous combination, and excuses for their actions are just that, excuses. Those are often the most scandalous women. They can be a lot of fun, but be careful because if you start liking them, you're setting yourself up for heartbreak. Chances are you've experienced or seen a friend deal with a woman like this before. Use caution or avoid these women altogether, despite the temptation.

Remember, a woman who likes to "have fun" understands the game. She's the equivalent to the male player.

Fact: Few women are truly naïve.

Fact: Many women pretend to be naïve and use it to their advantage.

Fact: The reason women pretend to be naïve is to control a situation covertly.

Fact: Controlling the situation in such a stealthy manner enables her to credit you, though she is really the one in charge.

Fact: Most women understand it's a game and know exactly what's going on.

Fact: Women like a challenge.

Fact: Women like to have a good time as much as guys do.

Fact: Women have as many, if not more than, sexual urges as men.

Fact: Women are not as proper and innocent as we were led to believe growing up.

If you give them too much attention, they'll play you. Often, women will act out or dress in certain ways just to get a reaction from you. Most guys will give them the reaction they expect or are looking for.

However, if you don't give them the reaction they're expecting, they'll feel taken aback and will seek you out as a challenge. This leads to their interest becoming a pursuit to getting women to want you. The following pie chart confirms this.

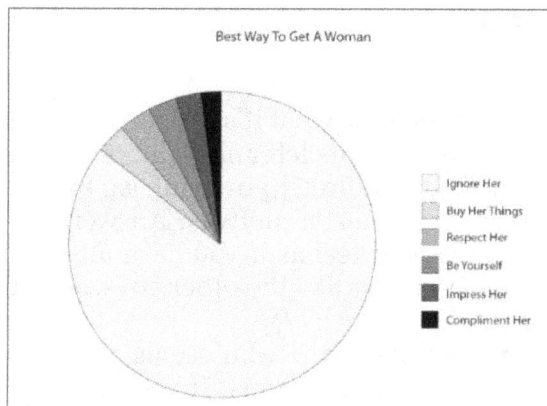

Best Way To Get A Woman

- Ignore Her
- Buy Her Things
- Respect Her
- Be Yourself
- Impress Her
- Compliment Her

CHAPTER 9:

How to Be the "Right" Guy

"Nice guys don't finish last, boring guys do."

—Leo Durocher, manager of the Brooklyn Dodgers

Now that you understand what a woman experiences and can see things from her viewpoint, you must now highlight your attractive qualities. Consistency and authenticity breed trust.

We as humans tend to gravitate to those who are a lot like us. Think of the friends you have. Chances are they possess characteristics you like, which may explain why you enjoy being around them. For instance, when I reflected on a list of my top friends, I could identify the main characteristics I liked and respected about each of them.

My friend Jason has a sense of humor that I find hilarious; Brent has a confidence about him that's contagious; Charlie is an athlete who enjoys sports; and Nick is the level-headed one in the group who keeps us all grounded and in check. As Robert Cialdini stated in his book *Influence: The Psychology of Persuasion*, "Consequently, those who want us to like them so that we will comply with them can accomplish that purpose by appearing similar to us in a wide variety of ways." [5]

Now, I'm not friends with a guy named Mike. Mike is very bland, has a dry sense of humor, and is overly dramatic and very emotional. Upon reflection, it's easy to understand why I'm not friends with Mike. We're drastically different. Additionally, I see nothing of value in having a friendship with him. This may sound direct or even harsh because it is. We're selfish about whom we surround ourselves, whether that's friends or women. People want to be with other people they feel enhance their lives and in whom they see value. We avoid hanging out with people who drag us down or bore us at all costs.

In the dating scene, this is more evident than ever. The key is to find out how to be the "right" guy. Consider this statement, "You can't be the answer to someone's prayers until you know what they're praying for." Short but insightful, right?

When preparing for a job interview, the best way to wow the interviewer is to do some research that will enable you to ask questions and cater responses to what the interviewer wants to hear. (The same thing is true when talking to women; you must cater to the woman.) Asking the interviewer what they're looking for can yield answers such as, "I want someone who answers their phone," "I need someone who is tech savvy," "I must have someone who thinks outside the box and is motivated." From these answers, a good interviewee would respond, "I'm easily accessible and always have my phone with me. I'm very proactive with adapting to new technologies. I'm an outside-the-box thinker and am motivated to do the best job possible for you."

Because you know exactly what they want, you can be exactly what they wanted and be the "right" guy.

Now apply this to dating. When you speak to a prospect (woman), identify her likes and dislikes. Cater to her likes. If she's adventurous, play up your adventurous side and experiences, such as the time you went whitewater rafting or something that fits. If she loves sports, casually mention a time in which you attended a great sporting event.

Don't be afraid to go into detail on these experiences because she'll instantly feel more of a connection to you. Furthermore, she'll be sitting on the edge of her seat becoming more enamored with each word that comes out of your mouth. Nothing is more effective than a story that captivates the other party.

One of the most effective techniques in dating I've witnessed is called "mirroring." As described by Noelle C. Nelson, PhD, in her book *Winning! Using Lawyers' Courtroom Techniques to Get Your Way in Everyday Situations*, "Mirroring: A dynamic technique lawyers use to set the stage to persuade people. Mirroring is a technique whereby you reflect physically and vocally another individual's physical attributes and vocal characteristics." [6] Mirroring body language is based on the same principle as mirroring dress: reflection, not imitation. [7]

The details are what separate Mr. Wrong and Mr. Right. Be sure to pay attention to details; it's equally as important not to be Mr. Wrong as it is to be Mr. Right.

It's much more of a challenge to figure out what a woman likes than what she dislikes. Humans tend to identify their dislikes more quickly and convincingly than their likes subconsciously. For example, if I were to ask you what you don't like about your job, chances are you could quickly rattle off a list.

In contrast, identifying items you like about your job may take more time. The reason it may take more time to identify what you like is that the mind internalizes what someone dislikes faster than what she likes. Furthermore, any acknowledgement of liking something is a much greater commitment to your internal thought process and to your mind.

I'm sure you've been in a situation where you have heard someone state exactly what they do not want. This could be about hanging out with a person of the opposite sex, a vacation, plans for the day, or what they don't want to drink. The reality is they know what they want, they just need direction. One common sales technique used is the question, "I know you don't know what you want, but if you did know, what would it be?" The salesperson is sending a message to the customer's brain that requests a clear answer to the customer's wants.

You'd be amazed by how many people can answer this question. The irony is the question is essentially reframing the question they couldn't answer by asking them what they want. You simply approach the process backwards to get them to clearly identify their answer. Once you have the answer, you can then implement the knowledge you now possess to be the right guy.

Allan and Barbara Pease, authors of *The Definitive Book of Body Language*, have studied the nonverbal messages people send for years. Here are the nine tricks they believe can make someone more attractive. **These play together to separate yourself as "Mr. Right."**

NINE BODY-LANGUAGE TRICKS TO BECOMING ATTRACTIVE

1. **Appear confident on a date even if you're nervous inside**. People who project confidence stand erect—shoulders up, chest out. Confident people also walk slightly more quickly than average, taking medium to long strides and swinging their arms slightly like they're in a march. A subtler thing is not to blink very often. The average blinking rate is eight to sixteen blinks per minute. If you slow yours to four, you give the impression you're cool and in control.

2. **Show someone you're interested**. With people we like and admire, we mirror their body behavior. If the date goes well, mirroring is something you'll do naturally, but you can also intentionally mirror the other person's gestures and posture. It may feel weird, but the other person will just think you're getting along really well.

3. **Recognize the signals that indicate someone is interested in you**. Look for preening signals. Preening is what animals do to make themselves more attractive. In humans, some basic examples would be arranging your clothes, touching your hair, or stroking your arm. These signs may seem obvious, but people miss them all the time in a dating situation, especially men.

4. **Avoid signals that turn people off**. In studies, if a speaker crosses his or her arms, the audience recalls 40 percent less of what the person says and has a more negative attitude toward the individual speaking. They can't even say why; they'll just say they had a bad feeling. Also avoid any scratching or touching of the face. When you hide your face, we feel like we don't know you, and we don't think you're telling the truth.

5. **A woman should smile and maintain eye contact to catch a guy's attention**. It goes back to the preening signals I talked about earlier. She might twirl her hair or touch her thigh. The thing I tell women is that you can't be too obvious. Subtlety is lost on men. When a woman wants to pick up a guy sitting across the table, often she'll lift her eyes and gaze at him, then look away. Women think it's an obvious sign, but men think she's not interested because she looks away. On the other hand, if a woman holds a guy's gaze and gives him a big, perky smile, then he gets it.

6. **A confident man will catch a woman's attention**. When it comes to body signals, men don't have a great range of options because in traditional courtship, women give the green lights and men make the approach. The best thing a guy can do is dress right, look confident in the ways I've mentioned and keep an eye out for a woman's "green light" gestures.

7. **Be careful when initiating casual physical contact; you don't want to look desperate or clumsy**. Men should brush the point of a woman's elbow while they're talking. Just give it a light touch, not a grab or a squeeze. Leave it there for no more than three seconds. She'll be aware of it and her response will tell you how she feels. If she's not enjoying the date, it will feel like you're touching an electric wire. Women, on the other hand, should target a man's hand and lower arm to capture his attention.

8. **Keep your hands busy so you don't fidget during the date**. The best resting posture is anything with your palms vertical or facing up. Turning your palms down looks pushy or arrogant. Don't hold hands with yourself or interlock

your fingers; that means you're reassuring yourself because you're not confident. When you gesture, keep your hands below your chin and keep your fingers together. People who are nervous spread their fingers really wide.

9. **Learn to harness some control over your own body language through role play**. We actually recommend that people take home videos and role-play situations with friends. A lot of people don't even know what they're doing until I show them on film. Once you see what your habits are, you can make a determined decision to unlearn or improve them. [8]

CHAPTER 10:

How to Have *"It"*

"Whatever he has, I want it."

- Samantha from the hit show Sex and the City

We all have heard someone say how much they like someone, even though they don't know them very well or may have just met them. One common response these people offer to justify their feelings is that there's just "something" about them. That "something" is the "it" factor. Most would agree there's an undeniable likeability in the person who has the "it" factor. What this person has is charm, and everyone likes charming people.

CHARM + LIKEABILITY = IT

While listening to my friend's sister continuously complain about a guy she was dating, I asked the obvious question—why was she with him?

I then asked myself, "What has to be true for her to stay with him?" Despite all his negatives, she did stay with him. There must be a reason why she did. So, when I questioned her, she went on this long, exhausting rant about how bad he was and about the terrible things he recently did.

However, she came full circle by the end of her rant, saying he was just so charming, everyone liked him so much, and finally, there was just something about him. As you can imagine, I was beside myself. What is this "it" that keeps her around, that earn so many girls' infatuation? Hell, *she* couldn't even put her finger on what "it" was, but he sure had "it."

From that moment on, I was on a mission, and that mission was to find out what this "it" factor was and more importantly, how to have "it."

I then went on a rampage, reading book after book, researching case studies on personality types, watching movies that starred actors I thought had the "it" factor (while taking notes on their mannerisms), interviewing friends I thought had pieces of "it," researching the great hypnotherapist Dr. Milton Erickson, and monitoring psychology sites to gain a better understanding of the characteristics and mannerisms of people who have the "it" factor.

Also, I traveled for further research. I attended an elite training program in another country to learn more regarding the psychology and physiology of how people think, organize their thoughts, and ultimately make decisions.

Once I had the characteristics and mannerisms defined, I then began analyzing people and their interactions all day, every day, everywhere: at the local mall, in a restaurant, at a bar, and even in the work environment. You name it, I analyzed it.

What I specifically looked for were groups with a good man/woman ratio. These groups consisted of as few as two people. The reasoning for this was to identify how the woman reacted in public to the man she was with, how she handled their interaction, and to ultimately determine who was in control.

I also identified larger groups of men and women, ranging from three to a group of eight. While analyzing the larger groups, I set out to pinpoint the individual who was the leader of the pack.

I observed the characteristics the leader possessed in each setting and compared those characteristics to the person in control in the one-on-one setting between the man and woman. What I discovered was that both the leader in the one-on-one setting and the leader of a group larger than three both had similar characteristics and mannerisms. Their mannerisms, such as their body movements, matched their words, and they always maintained eye contact. Maintaining eye contact is a dominant characteristic. When someone doesn't make eye contact, it makes them appear timid and lacking in confidence. Leaders have confidence. Followers are looking for confidence to follow.

As psychologist Ann Demarais, PhD, and founder of the executive coaching firm First Impressions said, "People normally make eye contact 70 to 80 percent of the time. If you fall below average, you come across as shifty or lacking confidence. People who make less eye contact often aren't aware of it, so ask a friend if you're unsure." [9]

I then realized not all communication is verbal. Once I saw this, I began to dig deeper, identifying the differences that various influencers have and how the people surrounding them respond to their physical demeanor. Note: It was unrealistic to eavesdrop on each group's conversations, so I had to pay close attention to their nonverbal communication and body language.

In a seminal study of communication conducted by Dr. Albert Mehrabian of UCLA concluded that 55 percent of the message you send in a face-to-face conversation is through your body language, 38 percent in the way you speak (paralinguistic), and the words themselves only 7 percent. [10] Taking this into consideration gave me valuable insight into understanding what the differences were between the individuals, as well as the common characteristics each possessed.

I also began to research the work of Tonya Reiman, who has popularized the field of body language. She emphasizes the importance of sending positive messages with body language. She stresses techniques such as mirroring and smiling because these techniques create a sense of familiarity and attractiveness. [11]

Trial lawyers do this regularly. They decide how the jury, judge, and courtroom think and are most likely to perceive the information and what their responses are. The lawyer then tailors the display of his message (often through mirroring) to appear like them which, in return, yields trust as they establish commonalities.

Incorporating this knowledge with Dr. Milton Erickson's research gave me a distinct advantage in my pursuit.

Dr. Milton Erickson was a hypnotherapist who studied human interactions on a minuscule level that proved invaluable. He learned the importance of body language; mirroring another person's posture, breathing patterns, tonality, facial expressions, and gestures can speed up rapport and trust.

Being able to communicate with people at a level outside of verbal communication works on the subconscious part of the other person's mind, which leads them to believe, based on the signals from their subconscious mind, that this person is all right, likeable, and someone they can trust.

"While the words work on a person's conscious mind, the physiology is working on the unconscious mind." [12] Being able to communicate on this level is much more efficient and eliminates time constraints and possible hesitation. The reason for this is the mind is telling them and reaffirming to them this person is okay. Remember that the subconscious mind is always listening, while the conscious mind may not be.

I took the information I learned from the elite international training program, books, case studies, examples, interviews, and real-life observations and made a conscious effort to incorporate these hand-selected mannerisms and characteristics into my everyday life. Armed with this valuable information, I decided I would implement certain characteristics and mannerisms prior to a meeting and gauge the feedback from others. After each meeting, I then added an additional characteristic and mannerism I wanted to expand on to use in the following meeting.

From there, I could grow, building momentum, little by little. Once I saw immediate results, I determined that if I could master these mannerisms and characteristics, I could train myself to be likeable. But most of all, I would have the "it" factor I desired so much.

The biggest challenge was the sheer amount of information I had compiled. I had taken so many notes and defined so many concepts I had to simplify them. I decided to break all the information down by chunking it, so it wasn't as overwhelming to learn. This also made it much more realistic for me to master. One of the best things about chunking is you can track the feedback on a much smaller scale. Being able to track the feedback helps to get a more detailed understanding of what works most effectively. I could do this by focusing on and incorporating only a couple of mannerisms and characteristics at a time.

I also had to be careful about the information I fed my subconscious mind. As Napoleon Hill wrote, "The subconscious mind makes no distinction between constructive and destructive thought impulses. It works with the material we feed it, throughout thought impulses." [13]

With a clear understanding of my objective, I committed myself to a very strict discipline to continually improve. Through this unwavering commitment, I accomplished my goal of mastering the "it" factor. In fact, I've experienced an unbelievable amount of consistent success in the form of feedback from others. This is evident to such a degree that as I was writing this book, I had three different women smile like blushing school girls and tell me there was just something about me they liked; they couldn't put a pin on it, but I had it.

THE FIVE-STEP ACTION PLAN I IMPLEMENTED TO HAVE "IT"

1. **Smiling** at someone is such an easy gesture and doesn't take any additional time. A smile can go a long way. From the people I've observed, when someone

receives a smile, they immediately return the smile. The simple act of smiling can also change a person's state of mind for a brief second, which could affect their day and attitude. If a person is having a bad day and you smile at them, they smile too and instantly stop being upset to feeling better/happy/upbeat. They can also associate the smile and happiness with being around you.

2. **Saying hello** to a stranger was a challenge at first for me. I was raised to mind my own business and not to talk to strangers. I understand you may be the same or just shy. However, saying hello makes you feel better about yourself and helps you decrease your shyness. Saying hello can also open the door to a conversation, a friend, and, potentially, a phone number.

3. **Making time** for a little small talk here and there doesn't take nearly the amount of time we all fear it will. Small talk can be a quick, 30-second conversation about the weather being beautiful, and nice weather puts you in a better mood. Once you understand the minimal amount of time you must invest in small talk, you'll realize the response from the other party and the feeling you leave with is a great return on the small investment of time.

4. **The innocent compliment** I geared, in my case, toward the elderly. The reason I did this was because they give the most sincere and appreciative responses. Their responses made me feel great and I hope I made them feel better too.

5. **Laughing** is contagious and gives the immediate perception of fun, which results in a smile or laugh from the other. It immediately creates comfort and lightens the atmosphere.

It was easier to incorporate giving a smile, saying hello, making the time for a quick conversation, and giving an innocent compliment into my daily routine than I expected, and I want you try each of these ideas when possible.

Two additional items you can do that will enhance your "it" factor is to match the other's body language (mirroring) and speak to them at the same speed they speak to you (slow/slow fast/fast). If they spoke quickly, I spoke equally as fast. If they had their hand on their hip, I had my hand on my hip.

I made my goal to do little things to brighten an otherwise normal day for the average person. For example, I complimented the older greeter at the local grocery store. She may need the job, but I doubt she enjoyed standing on her feet all day greeting people, when she should be enjoying her later years. I feel it's important to compliment, smile, and make time for a brief conversation as the elderly are, in my opinion, the most genuine demographic.

You need to realize that complimenting a woman about her looks is different from complimenting her shoes or hair since a woman interprets these compliments differently. When you compliment a woman on her clothes or on physical items such as shoes or a bag, it shows you're paying attention. She most likely spent time picking the outfit, shoes, or a bag, and your attention and compliment about it means more to her than if you were to compliment her on her looks. There's a way and time to compliment a woman on her looks, though I'm not recommending complimenting a woman on her looks at this point.

Furthermore, you should not compliment or make any sort of comment about her appearance in the workplace. This is a hot topic and is not worth the potential blowback.

The overall goal of this five-step action plan is to make someone else happy and create a warm, inviting atmosphere. This will yield your "it" factor.

When in sync, these five steps will go a long way. The icing on the cake is the fifth and final action, laughing. Don't be afraid to laugh. It will make you feel better, regardless of the moment. If you feel better, it will make others feel better, too. Laughing is also something many women love to do. If she laughs with you, she will not only enjoy your company but will also want to hang out with you in the future. The reason for this is that she viewed the experience with you as worthwhile and fun, in large part due to your charm and likeability ("it").

SECTION III:

CREATING AND SHOWCASING THE NEW YOU

CHAPTER 11:
DIFFERENTIATING YOURSELF THROUGH STYLE

"If you look average, you will attract average."

—Dax Bell

To stand out in a crowd, you must be different (better) in some way, shape, or form. The most noticeable differences come in the form of physical appearance. After all, women can't notice you're different intellectually; you must pass the physical appearance test.

Many men can stand out without any effort. It ranges from being more attractive, physically fit, or taller. While these are great, they don't guarantee anything.

Style is the one element you can control and can be a game-changer, helping you stand out and be more intriguing. Taking care of yourself shows others you respect yourself, which then yields respect from them, so even if you aren't more attractive physically, you can still stand out.

You can use outfits and accessories to differentiate yourself. Your style should be your own self-expression since it's such a key factor to getting women. A woman will form an opinion of you before you have a chance to talk to her. Having a definitive sense of style makes it easy for others to comment about your outfit or accessories, which then initiates a conversation.

I consulted with the head buyer and stylist for one of the largest men's clothing stores in the country, and she confirmed that appearance and style are half the battle; women love a guy who looks put together. The biggest downfall for most men according to her is men notoriously buy a size that's too big for them. Wearing clothes that fit right makes a monumental difference.

You may not have paid much attention to what you've worn in the past, wearing whatever was comfortable. That's cool, and there's a time and place for that, but to be better, you must show better. Better = positive attention.

The following pictures are examples of various styles men wear. Take note of the style highlights. As you can tell from these examples, the good ones stick out in a positive way, which plays a pivotal role in getting results.

GOOD EXAMPLES

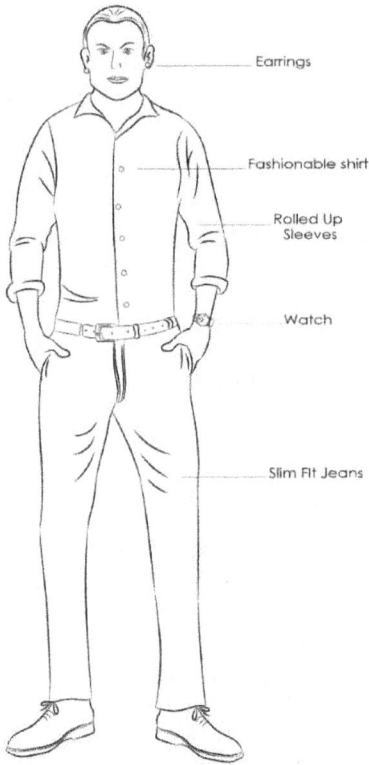

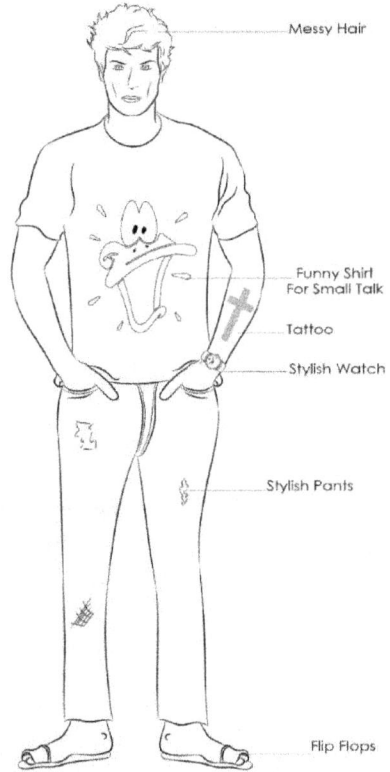

Earrings

Fashionable shirt

Rolled Up
Sleeves

Watch

Slim Fit Jeans

Messy Hair

Funny Shirt
For Small Talk

Tattoo

Stylish Watch

Stylish Pants

Flip Flops

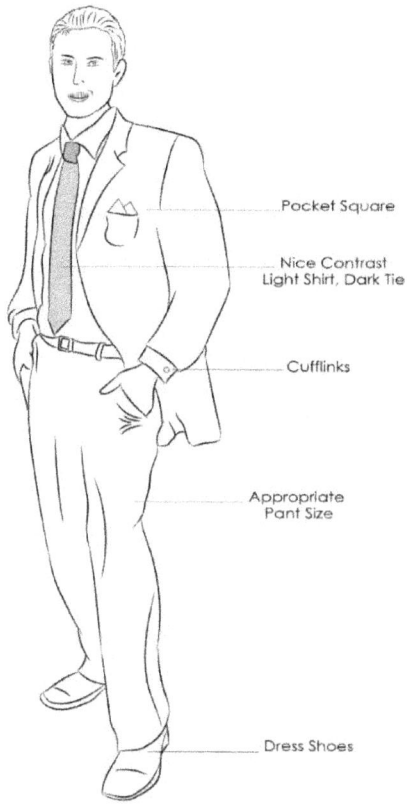

Pocket Square

Nice Contrast
Light Shirt, Dark Tie

Cufflinks

Appropriate
Pant Size

Dress Shoes

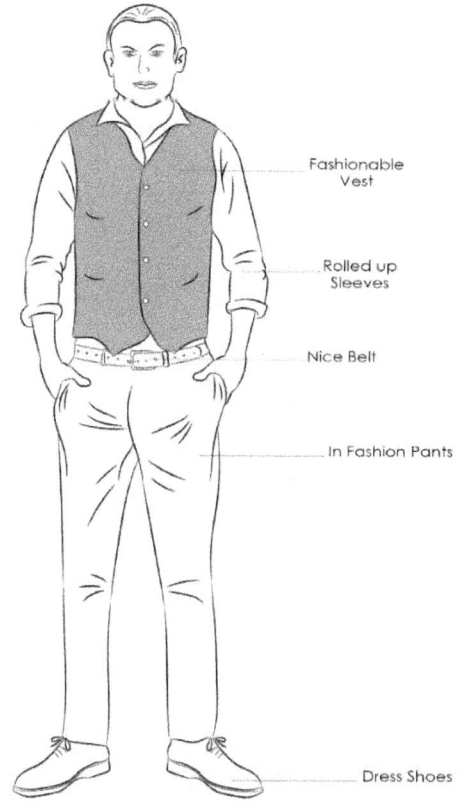

Fashionable
Vest

Rolled up
Sleeves

Nice Belt

In Fashion Pants

Dress Shoes

Well Groomed
Haircut

In style v neck shirt

Stylish Watch

Fashionable
bracelets

Hat

Conversation
Starter

UCLA
BRUINS

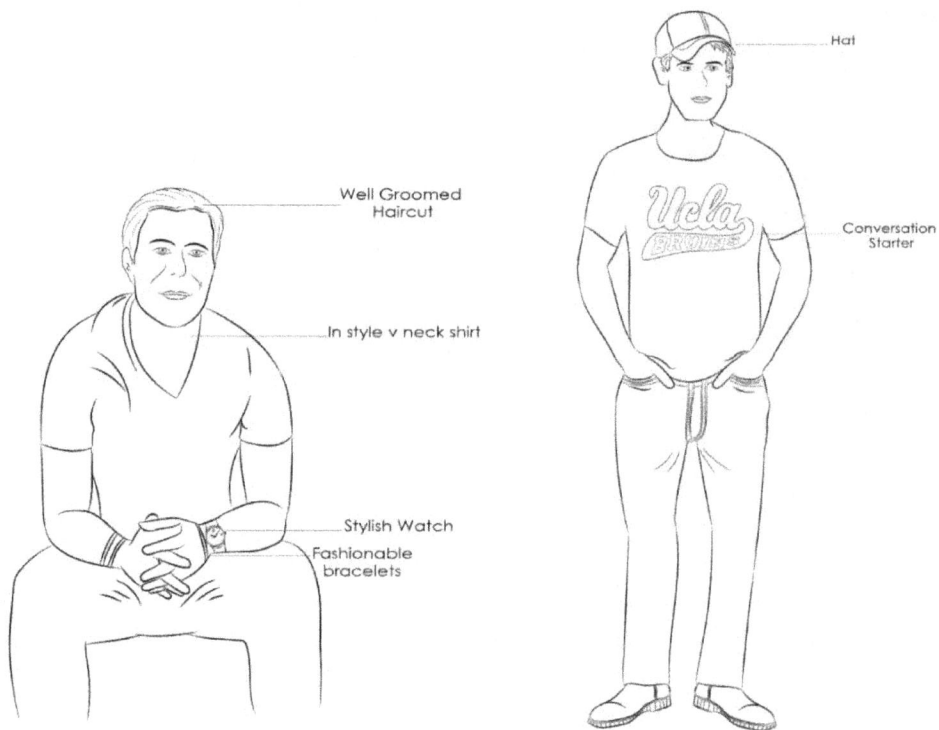

The illustration above on the left shows off style with a watch, rolled-up sleeves, slim-fitting shirt and jeans, and a stylish belt. Shoes are also important if you're trying to dress up an outfit; a nice pair of dark brown or black dress shoes with jeans can really enhance your appearance.

My rule of thumb for shirts is that they should always be pressed, and you should wear a shirt that matches your eye color. This will make your eyes stand out and enhance your appearance tenfold.

The details truly make a difference when it comes to standing out and being unique. These style suggestions will not only differentiate you, they will lead to comments, which lead to conversations and more if there's a connection.

Though the illustration above on the right is a rather plain outfit, wearing a hat is another way to stand out. When wearing a suit, simply adding a pocket square or wearing cufflinks can enhance the outfit to garner attention and be conversation starters.

Just think of how much better you feel when you dress up in a suit. Imagine receiving compliments throughout the night regarding how sharp you look. It's safe to say your confidence will increase. This is what happens when you differentiate yourself for the better: Your life becomes better.

BAD EXAMPLES

While it can be good to stand out by displaying your style through outfits and accessories that can initiate communication with women, it's important to understand the difference between cool and tasteful that yields good attention and bad attention. Not all attention is good attention, and there's a difference between good attention and bad attention. The following examples show what not to wear and brief explanations.

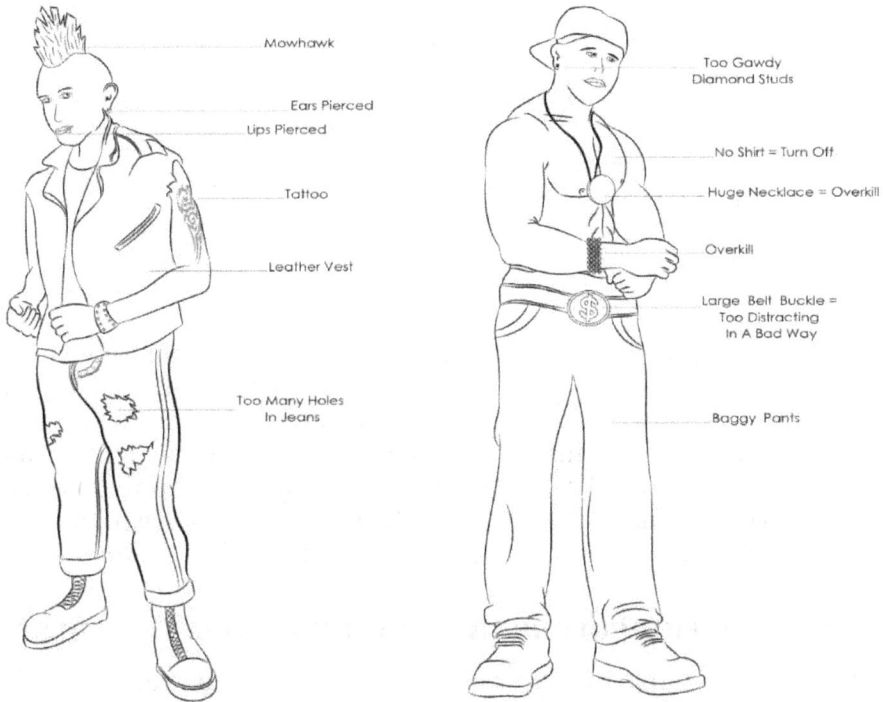

Mowhawk

Ears Pierced
Lips Pierced

Tattoo

Leather Vest

Too Many Holes
In Jeans

Too Gawdy
Diamond Studs

No Shirt = Turn Off

Huge Necklace = Overkill

Overkill

Large Belt Buckle =
Too Distracting
In A Bad Way

Baggy Pants

The illustrations above show two guys who look as though they're trying too hard. The guy on the left looks as if he's begging for attention. Rather than simply having tattoos, he has a Mohawk and piercings all over his face. He's wearing combat boots, and it all amounts to way too much. This is simply overkill and not what most women are looking for. The guy on the right is also trying too hard. The dollar sign on his belt, combined with the gaudy watch and necklace scream tacky and fake. Most women see right through this and know the odds are he's the opposite. For both examples, "too much" is an understatement.

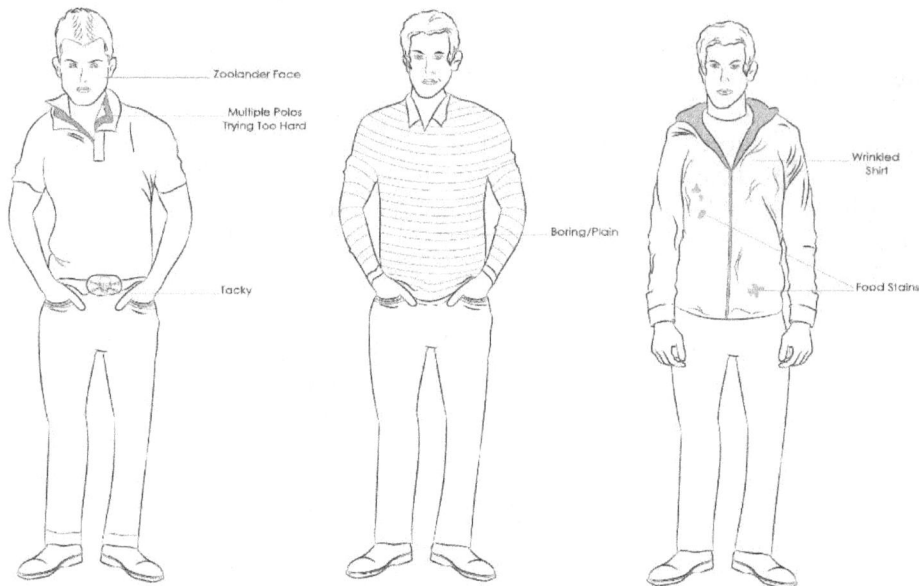

In this group, the guy on the left looks as though he's trying to be a frat guy. The multiple popped collars will not yield the attention he's hoping for nor will the skull belt buckle. The guy in the center is plain, which comes across as boring. There's nothing exciting about him or his outfit. It's easy to see how a woman would overlook him while searching online. The guy on the right appears sloppy. The wrinkles and stains on his shirt make him appear unkempt, and most women will think if he cannot take care of himself, he won't take care of others, either. That's a total turn-off.

HOW TO PICK COLORS THAT MAKE YOU LOOK YOUR BEST

A quick rule of thumb is to have your main color be a neutral such as black, gray, navy, or white for your pants or shorts. From there, pick a color that will compliment your skin tone, hair, and eye color for your top. Think about the colors women like. A woman will never say brown is my favorite color; she will say purple, pink, or blue is.

If you pay attention to what she's wearing or any comments she makes, she'll tell you what attracts her. Show you have confidence and style by appealing to what she likes and stand out. You'll be surprised at how often a woman will compliment *you* (which will be new and different). This fits the goal of the book: to get women to want you.

"Listen to your patient, for he will give you the diagnosis."

—Sir William Osler Canadian Physician from the 1800s

Pay close attention to the compliments you get from women regarding your outfits. You'll realize that a certain color will become your power color based on the response you receive. This should become your go-to color to mix and match outfits with. If you still can't figure out your color, try wearing different ones to work or to family events and ask the women in your life for their opinion. You'll quickly learn that their insight is usually spot on when it comes to what looks good on you. If you don't feel comfortable asking, go to your favorite clothing store, and ask the women working there what colors would look best (pick someone who has good taste).

If you really want to be fashion forward, Pantone is a color company that details what the color of the year is, any new color trends to follow, etc. All the major retailers follow Pantone, and you'll be ahead of the trends if you do, as well. www.Pantone.com

CHAPTER 12:

HOW TO DEMONSTRATE ATTRACTIVE QUALITIES

"Trust is decided within 1/10 of a second, when meeting someone for the first time."

—Alex Todorov, Princeton University psychologist

Social psychologists have demonstrated repeatedly that attractive people are viewed more favorably and are more often automatically granted credibility than those perceived as less attractive. To be attractive means to have the power to attract; to be able to draw people to you, to be pleasing and inviting to others. "Attractive" has a great deal more to do with how you present your physical person than it does with sheer beauty. [14]

The goal of this book is to help you improve yourself in various ways, ranging from appearance to communication, while not changing who you are at the core.

To maximize your potential and demonstrate your attractive qualities, you should smile often, appear well groomed, and be the type of person you'd want to be around. Looking your best requires minimizing your flaws as much as maximizing your positive features. Below are general grooming tips to help you eliminate any potential items that may distract you from getting women to want you:

1. Facial hair—Scruffy is in, beards are popular, ingrown hairs with white heads are not. One of the most overlooked advantages of a little scruff is that it makes a chubby face look thinner. Scruff looks nice but still needs trimming to have length matching throughout. A long straggly hair stands out in a bad way. Go over the facial hair every two days at a minimum.
2. Skin—Moisturize; smooth skin is attractive. As noted above, you're more likely to notice a flaw than something positive. The same rings true for skin. Dry, flaky skin is a distraction, regardless of anything positive.
3. Skin color—Pale guys, get some sun outside. Having a little bit of color will make you look healthier, feel better, and can make you look thinner. Not everyone wants to go tanning, but a simple walk outside to get sun can do your body some good.
4. Body—Look over your body once a day to verify nothing is standing out in a negative way. This can range from loose hairs to unkempt grooming. One common item is having your neck line get out of control. You should have your

66

neck "blocked," meaning shaved on each side and below the line every week to two weeks to give an kept-up appearance.

5. Private grooming techniques—Go with the grain when shaving. Maintain grooming; trimming or shaving a minimum of once a week. Use moisturizers and pay for a better razor to eliminate razor burns and ingrown hairs.

6. Plucking is painful, though necessary. A unibrow is not attractive, nor are potential hairs on the face. Pluck to remove it and check each morning to maintain. This includes eyebrows and any random hairs that may arise on your face, cheeks, forehead, chin, upper lip, etc. Be sure to check your entire body for random dark hairs, some of which can grow out of moles, as well.

7. Acne—Depending on the location, outside of using products to help treat, avoid having hair or hair products irritate these areas. This was more prevalent when men had their bangs down over their forehead, so this shouldn't be an issue for most.

8. Body odor—Be self-aware. Every morning and evening, you should put new deodorant on. Additionally, carry a stick with you in your car or when you're on the go. Be cautious of all-natural deodorants; few seem to have the longevity, so test by trial and error but always be self-aware.

9. Breath—Bad breath can kill any deal. We've all been around someone with bad breath due to not brushing the night before or after eating a bag of Fritos. Yuck! Always carry floss with you and a toothpick and mints/gum. You should make it a habit to check your teeth after any meal and eating any snack to confirm you don't have anything in your teeth, followed by a piece of gum or mints.

10. Nails—Keep your nails neatly trimmed and clean. Dirt under the nails gives the appearance of being a dirty person. Even if you work outside, clean under those nails. Avoid having bitten nails; it looks unkempt and unattractive.

11. Teeth—Straight teeth are a must. Whatever you choose, Invisalign or braces, your teeth are one of the first impressions anyone will have with you in business and in life. Do what it takes to get them straight; your confidence will improve once you notice the impact it has on your appearance.

Now that we have the maintenance items out of the way, we can focus on the substance, which you can implement to really grow as a person.

One of the biggest secrets people fail to acknowledge once they "grow up" is modeling. How does someone learn to dance? How does a child learn to speak? How does someone learn a second language? How does someone learn to throw a ball? The answer is through modeling. Model the characteristics of someone you admire. The reason for this is as Tony Robbins stated in his book *Unlimited Power*, "If you duplicate the exact same actions, you can duplicate the results that a person produces."

I personally admire the quiet, George Clooney-type of persona. There's no need to go overboard with trying to prove you're funny, smart, in good physical shape, or that you have a good job, etc. That reeks of desperation and a lack of confidence. Let's make sure you understand the previous points:

- Do not dress in shirts that are too small for you to show you have a good physique. A slim fitting shirt is fine. A shirt that looks like spandex glued to your body will not gain the attention you want.

- Do not wear clothes that are too big for you. A shirt that's too big for you will make you look boxy and unkempt. If you're not sure, go to a fashion-forward store (popular in fashion styles). While there, try on a shirt and ask for feedback from one of the employees who seems to have a good sense of style. From there, they can direct you to what size fits your body best.
- Don't discuss or refer to money or physical belongings you have. This will bore a woman and turn her off because it looks as if you're trying to prove you're worthy of her attention, when you already have it. Anyone who's impressed by this is a gold-digger. Your goal is to get women to want you, not use you.
- Don't make offensive jokes. You don't know her yet, and this may turn her off and cost you points before the game begins.

Think of a time when you stumbled upon finding out how successful someone was. You may have suddenly had a "newfound" respect for them, didn't you? Now compare that with an individual you may have encountered who bragged about his home, how much money he made on his last deal, the car he's driving, or how expensive his watch is. Total turn-off, right? This is a turn-off to everyone. Don't be that guy.

Your goal is to be the guy who flies under the radar. Think of how much more impressed you are when you learn something about someone and what they've accomplished, when they don't brag about it but rather stumbled upon through questioning. Be that person who doesn't brag, but who impresses many when questioned directly—in a humble, tactful way, of course.

CHAPTER 13:

THE IMPORTANCE OF YOUR SCENT

"Nothing is more memorable than a smell. One scent can be unexpected, momentary and fleeting, yet conjure up a childhood summer beside a lake in the mountains."

—Diane Ackerman

Few people realize just how powerful the five senses are to trigger our memory. Sight is the most obvious one because someone can reflect upon an image, recalling when they originally saw it and their feeling in that moment. This could be an image of your sister falling while rollerblading, your friend surfing in the ocean, your first kiss, etc. However, it's important to realize the role the other senses play in how we experience our reality. For example, if you close your eyes while taking a bite of food, your taste buds create a much more powerful effect on what your tongue feels and how the food tastes because your focus intensifies. With your sense of sight closed off, the other senses are at an elevated level.

Smell is one of the most powerful of all our senses. Some say that more than 75 percent of taste comes from smell. Additionally, smell is the most powerful sense we can use to recall a past memory. We can elicit any past memory through closing our eyes and imagining how the air smelled. Crazy, right?

<u>Must-do exercise</u>: Try thinking of a time you were lying on the beach. Close your eyes to get the picture in your head, take a couple of deep breaths, and remember what the smell was— the salty air. Don't just read this sentence; do the exercise. Not acting this out won't help you in your understanding; acting this out will, and you want to learn this.

Now that you've done this, you have hopefully realized just how powerful your mind is. If you analyze Neuro-Linguistic Programming, you'll understand that each sense offers a different representation to the brain. As soon as you hear something, it registers a thought and a reaction in your mind. The same is true with an image you have in your mind from something you saw; the recollection you have is based on your senses' registry to your brain. The same is true with other senses, such as smell. Understanding each sense is powerful in its own way; you can use great-smelling cologne as an anchor for women to remember the smell, hence remembering it as *your* smell whenever they encounter it.

Great-smelling cologne is priceless, while a poor-smelling or overly popular cologne is extremely damaging. Having bad body odor is a sure-fire way to lose a woman's interest.

If your cologne is a very popular type, it could bring back a past memory for her. However, a good-smelling cologne that isn't as well-known could imprint your scent on her brain for a very long time, if not forever. Avoid wearing cliché colognes such as Curve, Aqua Di Gio, etc.; you want to have your own distinct smell. If you're struggling with finding a signature scent, go to your local department store such as Nordstrom and try on several. Ask the salesperson which scents can combine to create your own unique scent. Combining a couple of different colognes can differentiate you since very few people do it well.

A good, sweet smell is preferable to the overbearing heavy musk smell. I often combine a couple to amplify the smell, while still not being overbearing. If cologne is not your thing, a refreshing soap, shower gel, and/or deodorant are musts. The goal is to create a smell they attribute to you, one they wouldn't connect to someone else. The importance of having a good and distinct smell cannot be overstated.

CHAPTER 14:

CREATING AN AURA

"To reason rightly one must be neither in love nor in anger; for those two passions reduce us to the level of animals; and unfortunately, we are never so much inclined to reason as when we are agitated by one or the other of them."

—Casanova

We all have experienced being out in public where there's a person who seems to light up the room. This same person garners all the attention through presence alone—not with words or obnoxiousness. This person has an aura. You want this. You want to have a presence about you. You should strive to walk in a room and compel others to notice you and to sense your *presence*. You have arrived.

As Dale Carnegie wrote in his book *How to Win Friends and Influence People*, Charles Schwab (yes, that Charles Schwab) told him a smile had been worth a million dollars to him. To gain a further understanding as to why the smile had been so valuable to him, we must understand how he used the smile and how it could be valuable. This value often comes in the form of likeability. People tend to work and surround themselves with people they **know, like, and trust.** [15]

Women look for men they enjoy being around, and a smile is a great start. They are subconsciously going to smile back, which gives you an *immediate* head start.

Smile often, walk with good posture, and make sure your pull your appearance together. (Dressing nicely and being clean-cut makes you feel good, which, in turn, makes it easier to be self-confident.) While out in public, be sure to smile often, make eye contact with everyone you greet, create small talk regularly, and wave to anyone who looks your way. Others will perceive you as a very popular person who knows everyone, which will increase your value and everyone's perception of your importance and popularity.

CHAPTER 15:

HOW TO BECOME CHARMING

"The more a woman feels as though she impresses you, the more impressed she'll be with you."

—Michael Anthony

Chances are you may have wondered at some point in your life how some people come across as being so likeable and have so many friends. It's difficult to explain why a person is so well liked and can engage almost anyone. It's equally as difficult to determine what the difference is between the people who have "it" and those who don't.

As stated in the book *How to Marry a Multi-Millionaire: The Ultimate Guide to High Net Worth Dating* by Ted Morgan and Serena Worth, "Being charming, sexy, and flirtatious is an important tool for getting what you want from another person." [16]

The person who has "it" has charm. Charm is many things. Charm is an aura, though you can create it if you have the proper ingredients. Having charm means being a good listener, speaking eloquently, having strong mannerisms and gestures. Charm is not one sole ingredient. It's a mixture of several ingredients, which are all needed for the perfect recipe. Some people will like you for you, for only a couple of your attributes. But the goal of this chapter is to educate you with the necessary tools to charm anyone you encounter, from the woman who already likes you to the standoffish, difficult woman trying with all her might to not like you.

As Brian Tracy and Ron Arden say in their book *The Power of Charm: How to Win Anyone Over in Any Situation*, "Women love men who are charming. They want to be with them constantly. To be charming you have to understand how they think and feel." [17]

Below are 10 actions to create charm immediately. These have played a paramount role in my life for additional sales, stronger friendships, new friendships, and, most important to you, women.

10 ACTIONS TO CREATE CHARM IMMEDIATELY

The 1st Action—Confidence: Holding your shoulders back, wearing a nice outfit, being neatly groomed, smelling good, and smiling will give you the confidence needed to create a level of charm that will change your life. You'll learn more about each of these later in the book.

The 2nd Action—Maintain Good Eye Contact: This is the most obvious way a person can tell you're paying attention to them. If you were to look away, they'll question whether you're paying attention or may even question you about what they just said. (We've all been there.) Looking away while they're talking is also a dead giveaway you're distracted or not paying attention. It's simple; make eye contact with them while they're talking; they don't have to know you're spacing out as long as you're looking into their eyes.

The 3rd Action—Shift Your Eyes: To not come across as weird or too intense, an eye shift is worth implementing. This is the simple act of shifting your gaze from one of their eyes to the other while listening to them talk. This will also seem more genuine, make them feel more comfortable, and eliminate prolonged staring that can create discomfort.

The 4th Action—Smile: Smiling to someone makes them feel more at ease with you and typically generates a smile in return. This will make both parties feel better and is the first step to being on the same page. When you smile, practice having your top row of teeth showing only. Having a smile in which both your top and bottom rows of teeth are showing can come across as a little over the top. When you smile, do it genuinely; a fake smile is easy to spot.

The 5th Action—Nod Your Head: The head nod shows affirmation of your agreement about what they're speaking about. The head nod also shows you're engaged in the conversation and not sleeping.

The 6th Action—Positive Body Language: Position your entire body facing the person you're talking with. Be sure to keep a fair distance, sitting and standing distance should be roughly two feet apart to avoid invading their personal space. Your body facing them shows you're giving them your undivided attention with your body language.

The 7th Action—Avoid Negative Body Language: While sitting, avoid having your legs crossed and having your knee on your top leg point away from the speaker. Also avoid having your face and body facing opposite directions. While standing, be sure to keep your arms at your sides; crossing them will look as though you're closed off and avoid having your hands behind your back or in your pockets. You also should keep your distance in a conversation. If you're in someone's personal space, they'll find you too abrasive and not charming at all. If someone feels you're too close for comfort, they'll tilt their heads back away from your direction and may either step back or create a barrier with their arm between the two of you.

The 8th Action—Verbal Reassurances: The following phrases are great examples of verbal reassurances as they develop rapport, while not standing firm in agreement with their statement or beliefs. Examples include "Interesting," "That makes sense," "I understand," "Got it," "I see," and "Seriously?"

The 9th Action—Vocal Reassurances: These actions are little noises that don't say anything, though they mean a lot to the person talking. You will notice that good, active listeners always make little noises like "Uh-huh," "Aah," and "Mmhmmm," or other assorted sounds. These are what we call "vocal reassurances." [18] These are clear indicators you're in tune with their conversation.

The 10th Action—Tilt Your Head: Tilting your head to either side gives the appearance that you're taking in the conversation with deep thought and attention. Though a slight tilt of your head seems like such a small detail (which it is), it's vital to your success. Think of a time when you've watched a movie, and you sympathized with a character. You most likely tilted your head to show sympathy. We have a tilt for sympathy when they show us they need it. The head tilt is also useful when there's an engaging story, a funny joke, etc. The goal of the head tilt is to create an in-depth connection.

Dr. Albert Mehrabian of UCLA conducted a seminal study of communication that concluded that 55 percent of the message you send in a face-to-face conversation is through your body language, 38 percent in the way you speak words (paralinguistic), while the words themselves represent only 7 percent. [19]

Author Ray Birdwhistell used the word "kinesics" in the title of his 1970 book *Kinesics and Context: Essays on Body Motion Communication* to describe and explain the movement of the human body when it uses all its senses. This was a groundbreaking observation since it's the basis of all the research that has been and is still being performed on nonverbal communication, i.e. body language. [20]

Body language is the single most powerful communication channel. Communication research has demonstrated repeatedly that when body language and the content of communication disagree, body language is *always* believable *over* words. [21]

Here's an exercise for you to do. I do it all the time. It's amazing how well you can dissect a person or a relationship without hearing them talk. While out to eat, look around the room and make judgments about couples you see eating together. Judging only their body language, you should be able to tell if they are on good terms, fighting, or if one has little to no interest in the other. From the tips listed previously, you now have unbelievable social identification power in your hands. However, it's only useful if you use it.

You should be able to identify the level of interest the person you're with has in you in a very short period. It's very important for you to identify their interest. In doing so, you can decide whether she's a good fit or someone you're interested in. Additionally, you can evaluate the likelihood of any advancement or future.

Last and most important, one of the easiest ways to charm a woman, or any person for that matter, is by finding mutual interests and what she's passionate about. Through dating sites and apps, you already have an advantage because you can simply view her profile and read the detailed information she provided about herself and what she likes. If you would like to expand further, you can. Do this by searching social networking sites based on her name, location, or email address. These sites typically go into detail regarding her likes, dislikes, photos, and more. You can use this information to get a competitive edge over others vying for a woman's attention because you'll have a leg up on her interests, dislikes, etc. Having this information is important because you can then cater your conversations with her to common interests, such as your favorite band and eating sushi, which she just so happens to like, as well.

There is a fine line between having things in common and coming off as a stalker. You don't want to creep her out by being too coincidental; she'll see right through it. Also, you never want to admit to looking her up because it could rub her the wrong way. However, once you locate a common interest you both thoroughly enjoy discussing, the rapport will lead you to further attraction.

- CASE STUDY -

The following is a sample conversation online establishing common interests.

Guy: I can't believe it's raining outside again! I am sooo ready for summer!
Girl: Me too, I am not a fan of the rain at all. Though it gives me an excuse to visit Petland and play with the puppies!
Guy: Are you serious? I love playing with the puppies at Petland!
Girl: Yes, it's pretty much my favorite thing to do...ever!
Guy: I remember having dogs growing up, and the best part is when they're puppies...real soft fur, just sitting and sleeping on your lap.
Girl: Aww..that is so cute. What kind of dogs did you have?
Guy: Saint Bernards!...I wish they would stay puppies forever!
Girl: Like Beethoven!...I had a retriever!
Guy: Now you're making me want to go play with the puppies at Petland, lol!
Girl: I think I might!
Guy: There is no thinking for me...I'm ready to go play with some puppies. It's 1:30. I'm heading to the one at Broad Street, be there in 30. You should stop up...I bet they may even have a retriever ;)
Girl: Maybe I'll see you up there ;)
Guy: Maybe I'll let you play with the cutest dog in all of Petland when I'm done playing with it ;)

CHAPTER 16:
HOW TO SHOW YOUR SENSE OF HUMOR

"Humor is mankind's greatest blessing."

—Mark Twain

It's important that you aren't just a teller of funny jokes. Telling a joke that you've heard more than once is a good way to start, but you don't want to come off as Dustin Hoffman's character, Raymond, in Rain Man, continually reciting jokes; it will look to her as if you have a comedy routine lined up, and she's the audience.

The goals you should have when showing your sense of humor are to:

- lighten the mood
- show you can connect on a humorous level
- see if you have any similarities
- make sure she's having fun

Friendly pokes at her outfit or an observation of an item sitting nearby can be innocent enough. However, you must be aware that this can be like playing with fire. Women can stand for hours in front of a mirror before a first date, primping and trying to figure out the perfect outfit. Making a joke about it could be disastrous if it's taken wrong. You must gauge the woman. Never make a poke about something which involves her physical features (face, body, teeth, hair, etc.). There's a difference between joking about an article of clothing and insulting someone. (Helpful female hint here from our editor.)

In this chapter, you'll see pictures of various items that a woman may be wearing for you to comment on. An example of a comment you can make to a woman wearing a pair of crazy shoes is simply, "Nice shoes." With the comment should come a little sarcasm with a facial expression such as big eyes. This is sure to warrant a response (which is the goal—to initiate conversation/break the ice/put you in the position of an equal or above rather than that of a lesser trying to get her attention). Following her response, you can state how you were being serious and how thankful you are you're not a woman and forced to wear shoes like that since dress shoes hurt your feet enough.

Following this paragraph, you will see various illustrations of women, with highlights for you to note. The items noted are for you to use as conversation starters and for you to display your sense of humor. For instance, a comment such as "Those are great shoes" leaves the woman to question if you were being sincere or not. The reality is, though, you couldn't care less about her shoes; you're just keeping her on the edge of her seat by making a random comment, which is sure to warrant a reaction. She may question what you find wrong with her shoes, and you could respond that they don't match her outfit or something outlandish to create further dialogue. Eventually, you can admit you don't know anything about women's fashion.

However, since your appearance is put together (with the information you learned on how to style yourself in this book), you'll appear to know something about fashion and any comments made will carry some weight. Your one comment alone will create a little challenge for her, which all women are sure to react to. This will get her going as she reflects on the original conversation and ends up laughing about getting angry in the first place. **Note:** The only reason she responded angrily is because she cared about how you viewed her.

Despite the tough persona many women portray, women *do* care about what you and others think. Making innocent comments and friendly pokes will play to your advantage. Below are labeled items that you can comment on.

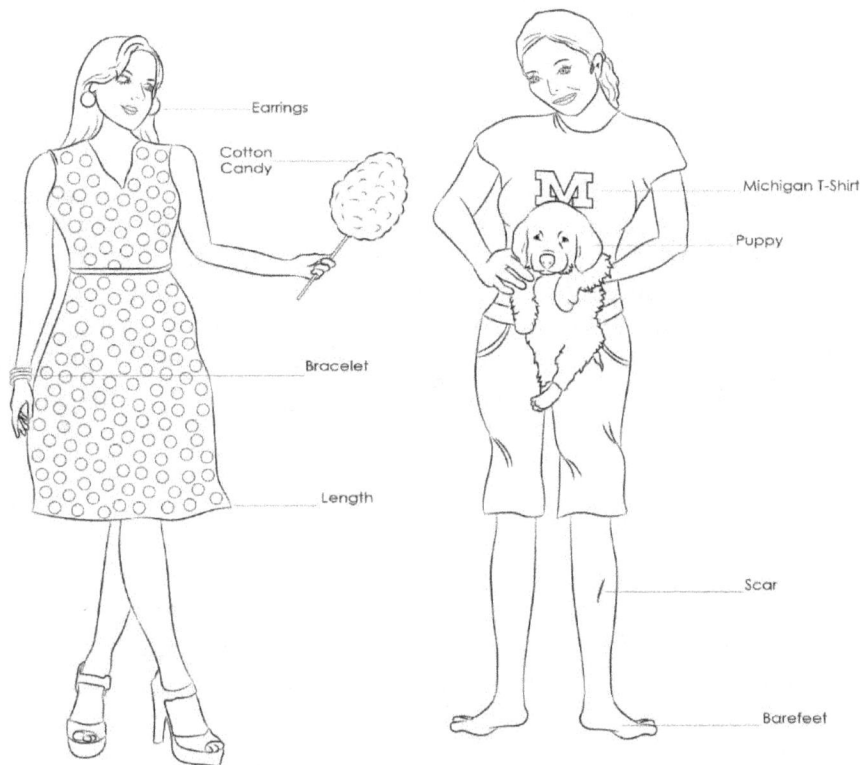

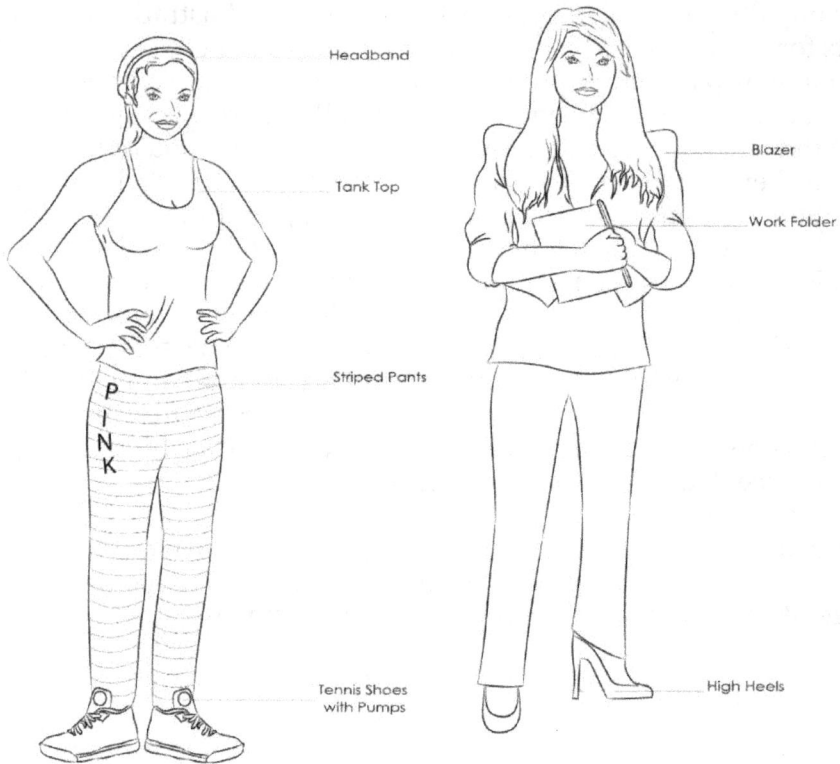

Headband

Tank Top

Blazer

Work Folder

Striped Pants

P
I
N
K

Tennis Shoes
with Pumps

High Heels

What you're doing is standing out from other guys. You're calling her out, which she most likely hasn't encountered often, if ever. Once you call her out, she'll look at this as being different from anything she has ever experienced. This is good; when you receive a reaction, you can confirm that what you're doing is working. The play after her reaction determines the winner of the game. If you show her you can keep up intellectually with humor and intelligence, you'll use this more often than you ever thought possible because it will be that effective.

CHAPTER 17:
THE ADVANTAGE OF ORIGINALITY

"The truth isn't the truth until people believe you, and they can't believe you if they don't know what you're saying, and they can't know what you're saying if they don't listen to you, and they won't listen to you if you're not interesting, and you won't be interesting until you say things imaginatively, originally, freshly."

—William Bernbach

Improv (**Improvisation**): the practice of acting, singing, talking, and reacting, of making and creating, in the moment and in response to the stimulus of one's immediate environment and feelings. [22]

The best ways to learn how to further display your sense of humor is to be quicker on your feet and become more comfortable in a one-on-one or a social setting is by studying improv. Some of the easiest ways to study improv are to take an acting class, watch a live comedy show, or search "improv" on YouTube. If you have ever caught an error on *Saturday Night Live*, you have witnessed actors and actresses acting and reacting on the spot to the error, which is improv. If you have ever watched a rerun of *Who's Line Is It Anyway?* You have seen a group of people, or perhaps as few as one person, given a scenario, and they must think quickly to create humor and run with whatever scenario or idea they encounter. This is relatable to life; we never know what we may experience. A quick comment in an awkward situation could lighten the mood or create attraction or comfort. The first rule of improv is to agree. **Progress is much more certain when in agreement compared to disagreement.** Use this rule and continue the path of least resistance for the quickest way to establish rapport.

Think of an episode of *Sportscenter*. The analysts you tend to like the most are those who put a little twist on typical sports announcing. For instance, when an announcer makes a comment or coins a new phrase or word to describe an exciting play, it creates additional excitement. It catches our attention. Where do you think the basketball phrase "slam dunk" came from? The answer? From the legendary former Los Angeles Lakers announcer Chick Hearn. He left fans everywhere with a well-known phrase that played a major role in turning him into a legendary announcer. What about the football phrase "POP! What a hit!" and "Boom"? The answer? Legendary Raiders coach and Hall of Fame announcer John Madden. Watch an episode of ESPN's *Sportscenter* and you'll notice each sportscaster displays a little personality in the highlights, hence the reason it's called color(ful) commentary. These analysts are using improv to make what could be the typical reading of a teleprompter or paper more exciting, unique, and original.

Never underestimate the value of a personality. Improv can help you find yours or display it further. Improv is great and can be a true resource for you with women and in life. You can spot a phony miles away; originals stick out and stay in your mind. Improv helps bring out your originality. Everyone has a sense of humor and wit; some just display it more than others. Improv helps you not only find it, it helps you become comfortable using it.

Also, don't hesitate to be engaging, excited and enthusiastic when you're describing an experience you had relating to a dislike she has or a pet peeve she may have. She'll become more engaged in the conversation and you as a person.

- CASE STUDY -

Originality = Bonus Points. A good friend of mine is very witty and doesn't follow what everyone else does—he's original. He has had unbelievable success meeting women on Facebook. You can search each one of his 3,000+ friends' pictures, and I will guarantee you that he has left some sort of random comment under most of the pictures of any somewhat attractive woman. The random comments are witty and often leave people laughing out loud. This is what he does. He plays the numbers and has had *a lot* of success. Fortunately for him, he's found his niche. Unfortunately for the other men out there, they still compliment the girl on how hot she looks in the picture and get nowhere.

The following is an example of a picture a woman posted on her profile and the various comments other guys posted regarding the photo, followed by the one in which our case study male posted. The comment posted by our case study male is an example of how to stand out and catch a woman's eye in a typical setting, such as this.

Random Guy: Wow, you look so hot!
Random Guy: Beautiful ☺
Random Guy: You'd be smiling more if I were there
Case Study Guy: Tweety looks a little too excited for this photo shoot...
p.s. I would put the kid to bed before you take a pic like this

- CASE STUDY -

My friend Brady and I were at a bar. He goes to pay his tab and gives the bartender his credit card. I glance down and see that it reads: Dr. Brady Kennedy. I question him on it, and he responds with, "You can put whatever you want with your name on your credit card, bro." As he showed me, this is a great conversation piece. Anyone who sees this card is sure to ask about it. Some even smile and assume he is a doctor. If anyone questions it, he simply replies, "I'm working toward my doctorate, and this is a consistent reminder of where I'm going—motivation, so to speak." He's very calculated in his use of the card, playing it as his ace in the hole. He typically uses the card to pay for his bills with any bartenders or waitresses he feels attracted to. He also uses it when there's an attractive woman who's nearby and can see his card when he sets it out to pay for a bill. Now that's originality.

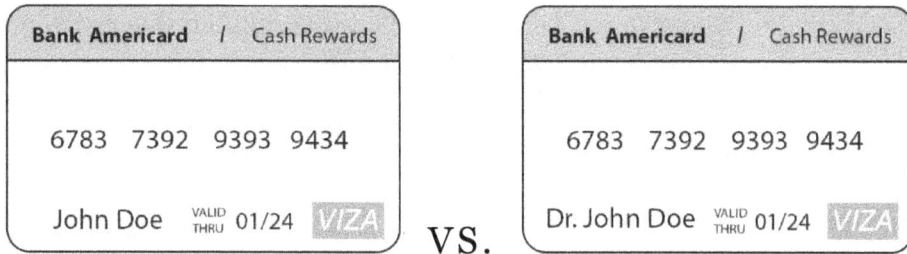

Bank Americard / Cash Rewards		Bank Americard / Cash Rewards
6783 7392 9393 9434		6783 7392 9393 9434
John Doe VALID THRU 01/24 VIZA	**VS.**	Dr. John Doe VALID THRU 01/24 VIZA

- CASE STUDY -

Another example of originality is a friend of mine who made sure his area code on his cell phone was from the other side of the country. This friend is from the East Coast, though his area code is Los Angeles. I asked him why. His response was, "Why not?" That's how you should be thinking, without limitations.

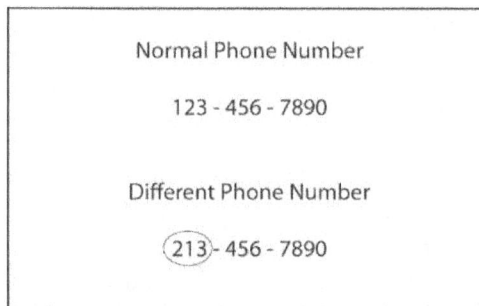

Normal Phone Number

123 - 456 - 7890

Different Phone Number

(213)- 456 - 7890

CHAPTER 18:
HOW TO CREATE CONFIDENCE

"You can't be the answer of their prayers unless you know what they are praying for."

—Hayden Dwight

$$CONFIDENCE = \frac{\text{Mental Clarity Defined}}{\text{Physical Clarity Action}}$$

Your confidence processes in your mind through your actions and appearance. Actions that lead to success are the most surefire ways to increase your confidence in your ability. Your appearance can give you confidence in your physical appearance and mental state. Others who meet you will notice this, too. Enhancing your appearance is one of the quickest—if not the easiest—ways to increase your confidence.

If you're looking to dramatically increase your confidence, tan a few times and go to the gym regularly. The reasons for going to the gym aren't to become a bodybuilder, but rather for the impact it will have on you mentally in addition to improving your physical health. Simply going to the gym will increase your confidence, regardless of the weight you may lift or exercises you may do. You'll feel healthier and be in overall better shape. Tanning is one of the quickest transformations you can make to your physical appearance. It makes you feel healthier, and it's widely accepted that people look better in the summer when they're tan. Conventional and spray tans are both great options if you don't look orange. These examples are just a few of the most effective ways to create a change in your confidence in the quickest amount of time.

As the book *The Rules: Time-Tested Secrets for Capturing the Heart of Mr. Right* by Ellen Fein says, "Look your best! The better you look, the better you will feel and the more desirable you will become." [23]

Translation: As you enhance your appearance, your confidence will increase from the attention you receive from others, and that attention yields more attention and creates momentum for your confidence.

It's important to remember, though, that going to the gym one time will not yield an instant six-pack. However, the direct effect on your mindset, combined with the new activity your muscles will experience is sure to yield more energy and an increase in your confidence immediately. The most important part is the invaluable help it will give your mindset.

Once your appearance increases your confidence, the next step is to increase your confidence through your actions. You can do this by saying "Hi" when you walk into a bar, waving to anyone who looks in your direction, and smiling at others who make eye contact with you and greeting them. Perform these actions with anyone and everyone, even if you don't personally know them. It will give you the appearance that you're *the* man.

You want to walk around like you own the place and the perception will be that you do, making you seem much more important and powerful to others. You'll believe you can take on the world. For the full effect, it's important to cover all these bases.

Real Life Example:

While visiting friends in Vegas, I convinced a few of them to drive to Los Angeles to check out an LA Lakers basketball game. We arrived about 15 minutes late, and I lucked into some great seats—front row, actually. The only better seats in the gym were courtside. About 20 minutes into the game, the two courtside seats directly in front of me, roughly five feet away, were still empty. As luck would have it, Adam Sandler and Steven Spielberg came in and sat directly in front of me. As you might imagine, I was stunned. I immediately decided to use the surroundings to my advantage. Hell, everyone in LA is someone, right? I looked over and saw Adam Levine, the lead singer for Maroon 5 courtside, and not far from him was actor Kevin James, actor David Arquette, model Diane Cannon, and the list goes on.

It was clear this was a once-in-a-lifetime experience, and I told myself I belonged there. Though guards were everywhere, ranging from Staples Center personnel to personal security guards, I acted as if I not only owned the place, but I also acted as if I belonged. As I took in the scene courtside, talking to celebrities, I had a couple of strangers reach out to shake my hand. After the game, I stayed behind and hung out with the players' families and friends, as well as the actual players themselves. No one questioned who I was or whether I was allowed there because I didn't let the opportunity come up.

I'm willing to bet accomplishing this at a Lakers game is a bit more difficult than what you might encounter online. It all starts with taking that chance. You miss every shot you don't take.

CHAPTER 19:
DIFFERENTIATING CONFIDENCE FROM ARROGANCE

"No one is more arrogant toward women, more aggressive or scornful, than the man who is anxious about his virility."

—Simone de Beauvoir

We all know someone who exemplifies power. We can not only sense their confidence, but we also admire it. We wish we had it. This is the confidence that's imperative to your ultimate success with women.

A person with this type of confidence does not boast about the power they possess or make threats to prove what they have to offer. If you're loud and obnoxious, you will cross the line from confidence into arrogance, regardless of the success you may experience.

One person who exemplified confidence to me was Hugh Hefner. The man routinely appeared with multiple girlfriends in their early 20s (young enough to be his great-granddaughters), when he was in his 80s. Rather than being audacious about his widely known success for having the most gorgeous women in the world by his side at any moment, he carried himself in a very humble, respectful manner.

Imagine if you owned a mansion with the most beautiful women in the world living there with you 24/7. Would you have parties and invite young, attractive, very physically fit, and famous athletes, actors, and musicians to come "hang out" at your place? I can tell you most would not; they would be worried some of these women may leave the mansion (or him personally) for these younger, more attractive, more physically fit, or wealthy athletes, actors, or musicians. Hef didn't worry, which would show insecurity. He did the exact opposite. He invited the cream of the crop and partied side-by-side with them.

He knew how old he was, but the 24-year-old football superstar didn't dare take his woman because the mansion was his domain, and if the woman does leave, Hef would have another one in line to take her place. Talk about self-confidence. This is comparable to a woman feeling attracted to her boss. Her boss exemplifies power and earns respect from others, which elevates her opinion of him. There's no doubt that Hugh Hefner's power was on an elevated level as his confidence was a quiet one without arrogance. This explains why he was successful with women and was likeable to almost any woman who watched a show he has been on or sees him in person. From the outside looking in, almost every other woman would be quick to classify an 80+-year-old man dating girls a quarter of his age as a dirty old man and would even classify him as a pig for not being with one exclusively.

However, by the time people finished listening to him talk and seeing how he humbly, respectfully, confidently, and quietly carried himself, they can't help but like him. The X factor with Hef was he was always very humble and not arrogant. **People like humility**.

We all know someone who's confident in an area where they excel, whether it's an athlete who's very talented in his sport, a salesman who consistently exceeds his sales goals, or a coach who has his team on a winning streak. Others have taken notice of these people because of the results they've achieved. Think of the expression, "Confidence is contagious." Often, people accomplish this unintentionally and strictly through their persona—body language, attire, and reputation. Without being aware of it, they influence others to believe in them without saying a word. This is very valuable when things aren't going your way as they don't always do.

"You are going to make a ton of mistakes, you won't be judged by that."

—Steve Jobs, founder of Apple

Now, let's look at the opposite end of the spectrum. You may know someone who's very good at what they do, though they come across as arrogant and self-serving. This person brags continuously and rarely listens to anyone or anything other than himself talk. He considers himself to be God's gift to the world. This person's success streak is often short-lived because people don't want to be around this type of person. Most people prefer to be around the confident person who helps their morale and is more enjoyable to be with.

Take a moment to compare a person you believe is confident and you enjoy interacting with and someone who's arrogant and self-serving, whom you dislike. Write the name of the confident person on the left line and the name of the arrogant person on the right line:

_____   _____

Confident Person vs. Arrogant Person

Isn't it amazing how a simple comparison can create a much more in-depth analysis of your thoughts of the person, their mannerisms, and the past experiences you remember them by?

Being arrogant with women is a surefire way to a man's demise. Another way is being arrogant to others you meet on a regular or semi-regular basis. The case study to follow regards a younger kid I took under my wing. I showed him how to experience immediate success with women, as I'm showing you now.

- CASE STUDY -

Zack was a somewhat normal high school kid, yet at the same time, an everything but normal high school kid. He was socially awkward, going through puberty, and his hormones were going crazy. Underclassmen and upperclassmen often picked on him in the hallway as an easy target. An upperclass girl even humiliated Zack in front of a large crowd. Talk about feeling low, right? One day, Zack reached out to me to ask why everyone treated him differently and why no girls would give him the time of day. Since I had helped others have success with girls, I decided to make him a project and a challenge to test the knowledge I felt I possessed.

I coached him and took him through the step-by-step process. The transformation was an unbelievable image makeover to those who knew him and to himself. The girls he met who didn't know him before, had no idea how he was before. He was doing so well, he was talking to three girls at one time. Before, he had never talked to three girls in his entire life, let alone have girls seek him out. His confidence was continually increasing as he was learning the ins and outs for success with girls.

The first thing I did with Zack was change everything about his appearance. To feel different, he had to get out of his old reality. It was like a makeover you'd see on TV. His hairstyle went from long and down to short and up. His clothes went from wrinkled and oversized to form-fitting, pressed, and fashionable. We parked his typical jokes and conversation starters and adopted new ones. We spoke with each other on how to talk to women, how to approach new women, and how to respond to rude ones. Learning how to respond to the rude ones was important for Zack since he was going to meet the people who remembered the old Zack and would treat him as such. I changed his reality by changing his surroundings.

Just as online provides you a fresh start, Zack needed a fresh start. Zack began to go to hangout spots outside of his old small town, which exposed him to new girls, most of whom had never met him before and never knew the old Zack. He had a new reality; he could be the person he always wanted to be, just as you can online.

After various people from school saw him out with different girls at the movies and at different restaurants, word spread quickly. Zack had new friends come out of nowhere. Many of these new friends were stuck in the same rut he was in and couldn't figure out how he changed his life so quickly to get these girls. They all wanted to know the secrets to this sudden change and quantum leap in his success with girls.

This was the turning point for Zack. For the first time, he stepped back and reflected on who he was before the transformation and who he was after. He then thought about his past rejections and his current reality. Rather than being humble and thankful for the change he had experienced, he became the direct opposite. He became arrogant and brash, which yielded the exact opposite results. From that moment on, his confidence became arrogance, and things changed quickly.

Zack started to treat people they way he once was. This new *arrogance* lost him many prospects who had previously expressed interest, including girls he had hung out with as recently as the week prior. He told a girl to her face she needed to lose weight. He told another one she was one of many he could have and then forced himself on another. This behavior leads to self-destruction. Remember, if the words or actions are powerful enough, people will not forget them.

Other women decided to cancel on him and stopped all communications. The news of his arrogance and the way he treated others spread like wildfire. Before he knew it, he had isolated himself from friends and girls and fell back into his old self. I have since received numerous calls and emails from him reaching out for friendship as he has done with many others. He even went so far as to apologize and expressed how much he wished he could go back to what he was for that brief period, but the damage was already done.

Now mind you, this guy had lived through 16 years of hell and experienced a short period of glory before returning to where he was originally. He experienced what the good life had to offer when you can get women to want you. Once he lost it, he was forever remorseful for the arrogance and the missed opportunities because of it. In fact, he ended up moving to another city to get away from it all. The biggest mistake he acknowledged making was losing what everyone liked about him, confidence and humility and becoming what he felt he deserved, arrogance.

You must be careful, not only at the beginning, but throughout your life with this fine line of confidence or arrogance. Age is not important, the substance is. This can relate to your getting a promotion at work or a new job, which completely changes your life based on the income you now make. You must stay confident but remain humble and respectful to all. It takes a much shorter time to destroy your reputation and what you have built than it did to build it. Furthermore, if you have a rough day or experience a rut, if you're humble, others will be there to support you and restore your confidence. If you're arrogant, you're on your own, and some may even be rooting against you. Be humble. It's better in every way for all involved, especially you.

THE FUNDAMENTALS OF ONLINE DATING DEFINED

CHAPTER 20:

WHY ONLINE DATING IS BETTER THAN ANY DATING OR MATCHMAKING SERVICE

"Being busy is a form of laziness—lazy thinking and indiscriminate action."

—Timothy Ferriss, author of *The 4-Hour Workweek*

Why do people hire matchmaking or dating services? The common answer is that they have a hectic schedule and do not have time. The secret behind this answer is that the guy is lazy and is hoping for everything to fall into place with as little inconvenience and work as possible. The reality is the opposite. This guy is walking into a complete trap.

You see, when a guy signs up for a dating or matchmaking service, he's at an immediate disadvantage. He's placing his trust in a service that only knows him based on his answers to a questionnaire or what he wants relayed to women. Essentially, he trusts someone to make judgments on his behalf. The problem is that he doesn't know the person or the service making the decisions for him well enough to give them that power.

Think about it: The dating service or matchmaker only knows to search for what you tell them to search for. The reality is that you sometimes don't know exactly what you want, and what is attractive to you can vary based on the day or your mood. These services cannot learn everything about you in a quick phone conversation or a sit-down meeting. And let's be honest, who knows you better than you?

Because you know your likes and dislikes better than anyone else, it makes far more sense to join an online dating site or app without these services. The setup is already favorable for you since you can access the sites around your hectic schedule to save both time and money. Now that everything has gone mobile, you can access it on your phone at any time, so time is on your side.

Most important, it builds on the idea that you decide for yourself. Only you know whether you're attracted to something or someone outside of what you may have written down. Despite an attraction to brunettes, there may be a blonde who catches your eye or even a redhead, for that matter. Frankly, the **biggest** problem with hiring a matchmaking service is **you're not in control**.

Most of these services have a woman in charge. This woman *thinks like a woman* and *is subconsciously going to be looking out for the woman.* The issue with this is that women strive for a quick Cinderella story, which hardly ever happens. They attempt to force things, rather than letting things happen naturally. They coach the girl to hold off on sex to move the guy toward being in a committed relationship quicker. The matchmakers' intention is to get paid (which she typically does regardless of the outcome; otherwise, she'd be out of business).

Your intention may not be to "settle" down with just anyone. Settling implies taking less than you want, and we don't agree with this approach, nor should you.

The woman's intention is to "make" you wait to give them the control. You don't want this. These dating and matchmaking services' "goals" are to have everything happen quickly as a whirlwind romance. These types of romances are based on lust and not love. All of this can happen so quickly and can be overwhelming to most guys since their guards are down, and this is not what they signed up for or even expected. I can say with almost absolute certainty that many of the women on these services go in expecting this type of romance. In the midst of this whirlwind romance that these services push for, you should also expect an intense rush on kids and marriage. If the woman's biological clock is ticking, you should expect the rush to be even more intense. These are absolutely wrong reasons to commit further.

Don't take getting married and having kids lightly. Sure, you may eventually want to get married and have kids, though you're reading this book to learn how to get women to want you. This book provides tools for you to meet and interact better with women, resulting in finding the right fit, if that's what you ultimately choose. Both getting married and having kids are expensive, and each can tie you to the other person for the rest of your life. This isn't in the best long-term interest of either of you or the potential kids.

The divorce rate is so high because of cases like this. I call this leverage for women, power over your once-flexible life; the marriage can end in a divorce settlement, alimony, and the kids will require child support. The reality is the honeymoon fades. It's natural for everything to be exciting when you first start hanging out with someone. There's no need to rush anything ever, which is another reason that online dating and apps are far superior. These dating and matchmaking services brag about their conversion rate. However, the rate they publicize is typically based on their members eventually *dating* the woman they set them up with. *They do not publish the breakup and divorce rate.* That's because it's not good for business.

High-end dating services are the most obviously flawed. The foundation is based on a woman landing a wealthy guy. Perfect, let's allow some money-grubbing woman to enter a dating service when her only clear intention is to nab a wealthy guy, not find her soul mate.

Suppose the two hit it off, and the matchmaking service's goal comes true: the two fall head over heels for each other, the woman holds off on sex, they decide to make things official, shortly thereafter they're engaged, and she's pregnant. After the pregnancy, another kid comes. They're now married, and they live happily ever after.

This is not reality. There's a reason for the high divorce rate: everyone wants to have a whirlwind romance and loves the idea of being married more than actually being married.

See the statistics below to confirm that statement.

Percentages of Divorces [24]		
Age	Women	Men
Under 20 years old	27.6%	11.7%
20-24 years old	36.6%	38.8%
25-29 years old	16.4%	22.3%
30-34 years old	8.5%	11.6%
35-39 years old	5.1%	6.5%

Percentage of first marriages ending in divorce: 41%
Percentage of second marriages ending in divorce: 60%
Percentage of third marriages ending in divorce: 73% [25]

The real question is: If you're going to be married for the rest of your life, why rush it?

As I conducted my research, I couldn't help but see the irony that the matchmaking and dating service consultants helping others find true love are either single or divorced.

CHAPTER 21:
THE DO'S AND DON'TS OF CREATING YOUR ONLINE PROFILE

"When you got my kind of stats, it's hard to get a date

Let alone a real girlfriend

But I grow another foot

And I lose a bunch of weight every time I log in."

- Brad Paisley, lyrics from the song Online

Now that you've learned about identifying the types of women, how to have "it," changing your appearance to look your best and improving your mindset, this next part will detail how to implement what you have to offer to get women to want you online and on dating apps.

Your online profile is like a resume. Since women are taking in information rapidly and make instant decisions to discard a profile based on pictures and information provided, you must be on point with what to include and not include.

Do's

- Have more than one photo
  <u>Reasoning</u>: Many people may be suspicious if you have only one picture and may wonder if it's a fake; they may also wonder if you have something to hide.

- Create a witty, eye-catching headline that's in good taste.
  <u>Reasoning</u>: First, the headline sticks out and shows that you have class and an education because you're not speaking in slang and don't have words that are misspelled. Remember, your headline conveys a message. A good sample heading is "Giving this thing a shot!" It tells girls you're new and a little hesitant, which they can appreciate. It also shows you're new to online dating, and they may be, also.

- Post pictures of yourself that show fun, excitement, and something for everybody.

Reasoning: Women will hold you in higher value if you describe exciting things you have done and fun things you enjoy doing. It will also make for easier conversation. Examples include photos of yourself playing sports, attending a sporting event, surfing, skydiving, racing, etc.

- Post pictures of yourself alone.
Reasoning: Having additional people in photos increases the odds that you'll have a mutual friend with women who are viewing your online profile. They may ask this friend about how you know them, which is not the attention you want. If the mutual friend has a bad reputation, you will be guilty by association, which can lead to awkwardness if friends or family catch wind of your being on a dating site. If you're a more private person, this is more reason to post pictures of yourself alone.
Additionally, if your friend is more attractive, you look less attractive in comparison.

- Post tasteful pictures if you're showing off your body.
Reasoning: It's not as tacky. A picture of you in a cutoff shirt while you're playing a sport or at the pool is better because it doesn't look as though you went to great lengths for this photo. If the photos are in good taste, they leave something to the imagination.

- Be likeable and non-discriminatory with your opinions or statements. Essentially, be politically correct.
Reasoning: Women are sorting through profiles. They narrow down profiles based on what they dislike, not what they like.

- Emphasize commonplace interests as your main interests. Remember, the goal is to be universal.
Reasoning: When you have very specific interests that only 10 percent of the people share with you, you are eliminating 90 percent of your possibilities. Instead, state the specifics that include items most people can relate to. Recommended interests include vacationing, comedy movies, the beach, local sports teams, exercising, volunteering, etc. Being very vague with a little spice (here's a chance to add a sense of humor) is a surefire way to differentiate yourself further.
Example: "One of my favorite things to do is vacation! I enjoy escaping to the warm weather, and my dream would be to ultimately visit Hawaii. There's just something about the warm weather that puts you in a better mood. And to be honest, I'm sick of the snow, cold weather, and people who can't drive in snow."

- State one generic like you have that's popular.
Reasoning: This will increase the percentages of women who can relate to you.
Example: "I also am a big Ben Stiller fan. Though the movies are usually about nothing, it is a nice change of pace from the typical stresses of life to relax and get a good laugh!"

- State something that tugs at the heartstrings.

<u>Reasoning</u>: It shows you're a decent person, and that holds a lot of weight with women, especially in the online dating world. This also gives you a distinct advantage over other guys and may make the woman lower her guard quicker. <u>Example</u>: "In my free time I enjoy volunteering. There isn't a better feeling than helping those in need. It makes you feel grateful for all you have."

- State the somewhat regular activities you enjoy.
  <u>Reasoning</u>: It shows you're active and provides additional items they can relate to.
  <u>Example</u>: "When I'm not working, I like to stay active by going to the gym four times a week, play in a kickball league, camp, and catch a football game on campus."

- Highlight why you're better than most guys without bragging and without coming off as an arrogant asshole.
  <u>Reasoning</u>: If you have followed the examples above, you're already showing why you're better than most guys.

- Show your tattoos, piercings, and body in good taste.
  <u>Reasoning</u>: The goal is to be tasteful and not appear desperate. You must leave something to the imagination, as well.

- Include pictures with any pets.
  <u>Reasoning</u>: It provides another way for a woman to relate, like your profile, remember you. Not to mention, if your pet is important to you, you don't want to attract someone who can't stand your pet(s).

- Monitor your settings. Some dating sites allow far too much information, specifically social networking sites, and allow others to write on your profile, which others can view. We recommend editing the settings so you can see the comment before allowing or disallowing it on your wall for others to see; have these requests sent directly to your email.
  <u>Reasoning</u>: You never know what someone may post and taking this precaution protects you. You don't want tons of comments on your profile page, nor do you want to be a person who's the favorite of a lot of people. The reason for this is you don't know what someone may post on your page. Imagine one of the girls you're interested in writes on your wall about how excited she is to hang out that night. By changing your settings on common social networking sites, you can limit what others can see.

Example:

EMAIL BOX

NEW	FROM	SUBJECT	DATE
☐		Request to Approve	Apr 14
☐		RE: Checking in	Apr 10
☐		RE: Checking in	Apr 8
☐		RE: Checking in	Apr 8
☐		RE: Checking in	Apr 5

1 -10 Results   1 2 3 4 5 6 7 8 9 10 11 12

THE KEY

- Make it appear that you live life to the fullest. Who wouldn't like that?
- You always have a great time!
- You're comfortable with yourself and don't need anyone else in your life to be happy.
- You're very likeable and have a lot to offer as a person.
- Appear as if you're a "catch," leaving little doubt that other women would be interested in you. The goal of this is to create a buzz about how great you are without saying it.

Women will ultimately want to hang out with you and feel attracted to how you live life, how much fun you must have, how likeable you are, and, most importantly, women will find you even more attractive if they think (or know) other women are interested in you.

The best part of coming across as the confident, self-assured guy is that your attractiveness to women will increase because you don't come across as needing them. This plays to their subconscious mind and increases their attraction to you, creating a challenge for them—they will want you to need them.

DON'TS

- Don't post a photo of yourself with someone who is better-looking than you.
  Reasoning: Obviously, if they're better-looking than you, it's going to make you less attractive to the person viewing the photo.

- Don't have your name anywhere in your profile. This includes your screen name, user name, and email address.
  Reasoning: You do not want to have your personal information available for anyone and everyone to see. There are crazy people in the world.
  Example: MedicalDoctorDave and DaveMD@aol.com
  Example: Hello, dating world, my name is Dave.

- Don't ever mention exes. Period. This includes your profile write-up, any email correspondence, why you joined the site, or photos you cropped them out of, etc.
  Reasoning: There's nothing positive that will come from talking about an ex and why they're an ex. Focus on the future, and women will appreciate that.

- Don't have a tacky headline.
  Reasoning: Few people have a quirky sense of humor, and your goal is to appeal to the majority, not the minority.
  Examples: "Looking for my Cinderella," "Will you be my Mrs. Robinson?" "In search of the one," "Are you my other half?" etc.

- Don't post a photo of you and any baby or kids.
  Reasoning: This comes across as exploiting the kid and is creepy. Despite what most men think, this does not attract women.

- Don't ever post pictures with an ex or any females for that matter (no matter how good you think you looked in the picture).
  Reasoning: It isn't worth your good picture. You most likely have other photos, so use common sense. If you don't, you know a question will arise as to who the girl is in the photo. You do not want to go down this path.

- Don't post close-up pictures of your face.
  Reasoning: It's not necessary, and if you do, it may come across as if you're trying to hide what you're not showing. Additionally, a close-up of your face comes across as creepy and makes it easier to find imperfections and reasons to discard your profile.

- Don't ever take photos or post photos of yourself at work. This is a common mistake nowadays.
  Reasoning: Privacy. A photo can tell a lot about someone, and taking one while you're at your desk can show items in the background that many would overlook. See the example in the following chapter of the guy sitting at his desk.

- Don't ever have shirtless photos, especially mirror shots.
  Reasoning: This makes you look like you're the Don Juan of profiles and have no depth. The goal is to fly under the radar. You want to leave something to the imagination, as well.

- Don't write anything about being a nice guy. Furthermore, don't say that anyone you know will say the same. Nor should you say that if they don't agree that you're a nice guy, they're lying.
  Reasoning: If you are a nice guy, you don't have to tell anyone you are; they can tell. Furthermore, being confrontational regarding people lying and not agreeing with you is a turn-off and shows insecurity.

- Don't ever acknowledge any shortcomings in your life or bad luck you've had.
  Reasoning: It will come across as negative and depressing. People want to hang out with those who are positive and contribute in a positive manner to their life.

REITERATING THE CRUCIAL PICTURE PITFALLS TO AVOID

PICTURE WITH FRIENDS

Reasoning: A picture with friends increases the odds that a prospect will know someone you know, too. Depending on the mutual friend's reputation, this could be a negative.

Furthermore, you want a clean, new start and not to be associated with others.

PICTURE WITH AN EX-GIRLFRIEND

Ex - Girlfriend

<u>Reasoning</u>: Why? Nothing good will come from this, and it will appear as though you still can't get over your ex.

PICTURE WITH A BABY OR A KID

<u>Reasoning</u>: This spells desperation and appears creepy. This has the exact opposite effect that many hope for—a nice, well-rounded guy who's good with kids.

PICTURE AT WORK

Reasoning: This jeopardizes your safety and eliminates privacy. A photo can tell a lot about someone and taking one while you're at your desk can show items and reveal information about you such as your location, name, company, award(s), family photos, etc.

PICTURE WITH YOUR SHIRT OFF/MIRROR SHOT, OR ANY OTHER COMPROMISING PHOTO

Reasoning: If the photo is not one you would be comfortable with your business associates coworkers, and family members viewing, don't take it, let alone send it. When things don't go well, people will blackmail you. Think first and protect yourself.

* Remember you're marketing yourself to women as a company would market a product to consumers. While many companies market to specific clientele, your goal is to appeal to all women. You do this by avoiding any reasons for someone to eliminate you from the mix. Most women out there would discard you because of a photo like this. Women will discard a profile before clicking on one they're interested in since it's far easier. Eliminate these bad pictures so they don't have the option to discard you.

THE REALITY OF ONLINE PROFILES

- People will post old pictures.
- People will lie.
- This is essentially your online job interview snapshot.
- Each person puts his or her best foot forward.
- Privacy is important for your safety.

CHAPTER 22:
HOW TO DESIGN YOUR PROFILE FOR MAXIMUM RESULTS

"Humans strive to be liked. Hence, the shock and awe that many respond with, upon hearing the news that someone dislikes them. Being liked by all is much easier than being disliked by any."

—Unknown

Attention spans are at an all-time low. For this reason, advertisers and companies are trying to catch your attention as quickly and powerfully as possible. It may be an image or an outrageous tag line, but it must be quick-hitting information. It must catch your attention and then resonate. This is also true for online dating and apps. In this chapter, you'll see pictures that fit this thinking, and content to get women to want you.

"YES" PICTURES

The following are types of pictures to have on an online profile. The goal with these photos is to show off various aspects of your life, which can include hobbies, adventure, and other activities. Those are tasteful ways to show off your body without coming across as tacky or trying too hard. The goal is to appeal to the masses and to appear an exciting person who enjoys life.

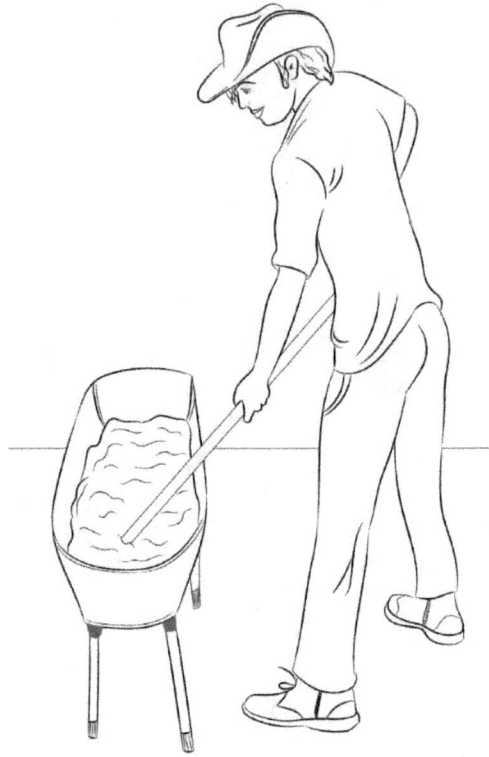

"No" Pictures

Do not post close-up shots in the bathroom mirror (weird and awkward). Additionally, you should not post partially clothed pictures in an unnatural setting—the beach is acceptable; everything else is not. No exceptions. For further clarification, not only are you not to take partially clothed photos, you should absolutely, positively, never send any partially or fully nude pictures. If you're not sure, ask yourself whether you'd mind if the picture you're about to take or send would be plastered throughout your workplace for all to see.

Do not post any pictures with friends, especially not with anyone who's more attractive than you. Instantly, anyone viewing the photo will look at the more attractive person, which will, in turn, make you appear less attractive. Think of a picture you see with a group of girls. Your eyes gravitate toward the most attractive girl, which diminishes the interest of those who surround her. This is exactly what you don't want. Your safest bet is to not have pictures with anyone.

Do not post close-up photos of tattoos. I'm sure there's a meaning to it, but save it for when she asks about it. It can also appear as though you're trying to hide something if your face and the rest of your body are hidden. Your tattoo can be visible in a full body shot, no need to zoom in.

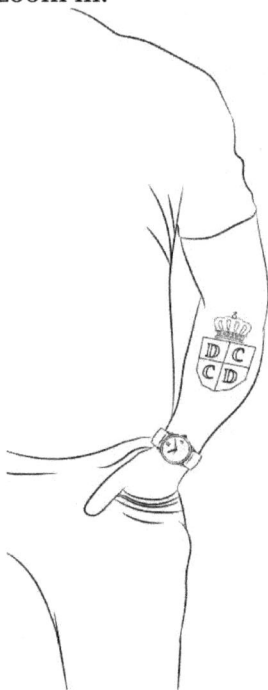

Do not post pictures with friends. Pictures with additional people increase the odds that someone viewing your profile will know someone else in the picture. This can lead to guilt by association if any of those people don't have the greatest reputation. Remember, your goal is to take advantage of online dating and start fresh.

Do not post pictures of yourself drinking alcohol. Drinking in high school and college may have been an easy way to fit in. Having pictures of yourself drinking in your dating profile is not. The goal is to be a guy a woman wants to hang out with, not someone who just wants to party and may come across as immature. A picture holding a beer is also not recommended. Stand out and be better.

Do not post pictures with ex-girlfriends. If you post a picture like this, a question will inevitably come up about who the woman in the photo is. As soon as you reveal her identity, it will make it look as if you're not over her or just odd that you chose this picture. If you choose to not reveal her identity, you're blatantly lying. Just avoid this issue altogether; there's no reason to have this in your profile, period.

Do not post pictures that appear as though you're trying to show off. These pictures can make you come across as insecure and trying to "prove" something. Women will view this as if you don't have enough to offer on your own, so you're overcompensating by showing off your belongings. Step up and be confident; you have every reason to be once you finish this book.

GOOD PROFILE

Look at the following profile from a woman's perspective and tell me how she couldn't be interested in this guy. He comes across as a person who is easy to relate to. He mentions enjoying the nice weather, traveling, driving with the windows down and joining the site after his close friends urged him to and because he was tired of the bar scene. These are all very generic statements, yet all very relatable and agreeable.

His pictures are not ostentatious and leave women wanting more. The pictures display a person who's adventurous, has an edge, is stylish, and seems fun to be around. What's not to like? Remember, women are not looking for a boring person who has nothing to offer them, they are looking for something exciting or enticing = attractive.

He says he's looking for dating or a relationship. Really, he may only be interested in dating, but by including he's interested in a potential relationship, he appeals to so many more women, and he may change his mind later.

He also has a wide age range, from 18 to 40. Talk about hitting on all cylinders to maximize potential matches. This profile is spot on; he doesn't want to limit his exposure and options with women of all ages.

Live&LoveLife

Giving This Thing A Shot!

Active within past 3 Days
28 - year old man
Houston, Texas, United States
Seeking women 18 - 40
Within 60 miles of Houston, Texas

Interested In: Dating, Relationship

Relationship Status: Single
Have Kids: No
Want Kids: No
Ethnicity: Italian
Sign: Aquarius
Body Type: Athletic
Height: 6'1"
Religion: Agnostic
Profession: Sales
Smarts: Some College
Do You Smoke: No
Do You Drink: Yes
Do You Drugs: No
Do You Have A Car: Yes

<< Previous Photo   Next Photo >>

More of My Photos

In My Own Words:

My Job: Sales

My Ethnicity: Italian American

My Religion: Agnostic

My Education: Some College

Favorite Things: Sports & Traveling

About Me:

I am new to the online dating world. I enjoy traveling,
hanging out with friends and family, and working out. I
decided to join this site after enough urging from close
friends, as I tend to work a lot and don't get out as much
as I would like! I think online dating could be a good fit,
as I am over the bar scene. I'm easy going, positive,
confident and try to make the most of any situation! I
love the beach, warm weather, listening to the radio, and
singing with the windows down! I am not looking for
anything as it never happens when you do, though am
going in with an open mind and to live life to the fullest!

Do you Match?

See more like him

Add him to favorites

Forward him to a friend

Block from contact

Block from search

Report a concern ?

Click on a word to see more profiles with
the same word. Click in a "+" to add that
word to your profile.

MatchWords are a way of finding people
with common interests. Add your own
MatchWords to your profile and get in
the excitement now!

Things You Are
Both Looking For

Comparing your profile side by side is a
quick way to calculate chemistry.

Yes	Age	Yes
Yes	Height	Yes
No	Eyes	Yes
Yes	Body	Yes
Yes	Smoking	No
Yes	Drinking	Yes

3 Favorites

BAD PROFILE

If you're asking yourself what's wrong with the profile below, then this is going to be very enlightening for you. There are many issues with this profile, so let's begin.

Your dating profile is not the right place for a picture with a kid—ever. It comes across as if you're exploiting the kid for your own benefit. The profile name reveals his real name, which threatens your privacy. The title is cliché and not original: "God Fearing Guy, Looking for the Perfect Girl" for many reasons. First, referencing God in your title is not tasteful; second, there are no perfect women and saying that is sure to scare someone away since you're realistic.

Photos in a group setting are not a good idea as detailed previously. Stating in the profile that you're interested in sex is an immediate turn-off for most women. Also, don't list that you're divorced. When you meet with someone, tell them early before anything may develop out of respect to them. Don't eliminate a lot of the potential matches you may have by giving too much information to start. Also, the pictures show you're not a bodybuilder. Don't embarrass yourself with your inflated ego by being inaccurate and stating your body type as a bodybuilder. This will raise concerns regarding your profile's accuracy and your sense of reality.

Listing your profession with specific information, including your company name, spells disaster. You don't want any woman to stalk you, gather more information about you, or have access to pertinent details that don't favor you.

The "About Me" section has many items I don't recommend including, such as referencing your daughter (even including her name) on a dating site is not appropriate. Acknowledging you have been on and off the dating sites puts thoughts in the woman's head that you're a player who has been around and for some reason you're still single—and for a reason.

DanTheMan

God Fearing Guy Looking
For The Perfect Girl !!!

Active within past 3 Days
33 - year old man
New York, New York, United States
Seeking women 18 - 40
Within 60 miles of New York City

Interested In: Dating, Sexual Encounters

Relationship Status: Divorced
Have Kids: Yes
Want Kids: No
Ethnicity: Irish
Sign: Aquarius
Body Type: Bodybuilder
Height: 6'1"
Religion: Agnostic
Profession: IT Verizon Wireless
Smarts: Bachelors Degree
Do You Smoke: No
Do You Drink: Yes
Do You Drugs: No
Do You Have A Car: Yes

<< Previous Photo   Next Photo >>

More of My Photos

In My Own Words:

My Job: IT Wizard

My Ethnicity: Irish

My Religion: Agnostic

My Education: Bachelors in Computer Science

Favorite Things: Basketball and Football

About Me:

My name is Dan, I am a God fearing guy who loves to have a good time! I have a daughter who means a lot to me and I try to see her as often as I can. I love you Elizabeth! I work hard and like to play harder. I have been on and off of these dating sites and am just trying to find someone who is a good down to earth person and doesn't do drama!!

Do you Match?

See more like him

Add him to favorites

Forward him to a friend

Block from contact

Block from search

Report a concern ?

Click on a word to see more profiles with the same word. Click in a "+" to add that word to your profile.

MatchWords are a way of finding people with common interests. Add your own MatchWords to your profile and get in the excitement now!

Things You Are
Both Looking For

Comparing your profile side by side is a quick way to calculate chemistry.

Yes	Age	Yes
Yes	Height	Yes
No	Eyes	Yes
Yes	Body	Yes
Yes	Smoking	No
Yes	Drinking	Yes

10 Favorites

SUMMARY

Follow the outlined do's and don'ts, and be sure to understand the reasoning. If you understand it, you'll become more aware of your actions. Remember your profile should be brief, though still interesting. As you begin your search online, you'll understand why: Avoid information overload.

CHAPTER 23:
UNIVERSAL DATING TIPS DEFINED

"Creating a universal understanding is like being given a cheat sheet for the game of life."

—Michael Anthony

In this chapter, you'll learn the "Universal Dating Tips" to improve your success; using them will streamline the online dating process for you. By incorporating the tips into your behavior, you can expect the online scene to appear simplified and easy to navigate. This will put you in the best position to meet women and, ultimately, get women to want you.

TOP 17 UNIVERSAL DATING TIPS

1. Create a quick default search. This will save your settings for your main search, including specifics such as age, distance from a ZIP code, interests, etc.
2. Create more detailed searches. Many sites and some apps will allow you to set up multiple searches, which you can save. Take advantage of this. For example, rather than setting up a search for 18- to 35-year-olds, expand this into searches for 18 to 21, 22 to 25, 26 to 30, and 31 to 35 years of age. Having other searches set as additional defaults eliminates the need to change your search criteria repeatedly and helps you be in tune with new sign-ups.
3. Edit your custom search options. Only list or mark the deal breaker items. There are many options: marital status, education, height, weight, location, language, ethnicities, kids, drinking, smoking, salary, occupation, astrological sign, and pets, though you must step back and determine if some of those items are not complete deal breakers if she has many of the other characteristics you want. The goal is not to eliminate someone before checking out her profile. Create a top four and marking the others "no preference" to keep your options open. The more specific you are, the fewer matches and results you'll get. Be vague, then evaluate.
4. Decide if you would like to activate the reverse and the mutual match features. This gives women the option to get an alert to your profile if you have similar likes and characteristics as they do.

5. Decide if you want your profile to appear private or not. If your profile is private, you can access profiles when you search, though others will not see you unless you contact them. This is a great option if you're hesitant and don't want to be seen on an online dating site or app just yet.

6. Identify the option to hide your profile so others can't see you unless you initiate contact (stealth mode).

7. Decide if you want to activate the "online now" status. If you do activate it, you can use instant messaging features to contact others if they're also online. You can also search specifically for women who are online.

8. Some sites offer daily notifications such as the "Daily 5 Results," which is a daily matching feature. Though the titles vary, they're all identical. You can select "yes" or "no" if you're interested in a person the site has paired you with. If you choose "yes," the site will email the woman directly showing you have interest, and she'll have the opportunity to respond.

9. Identify the options and account settings on your account. This is very useful to block anyone you don't want to contact you.

10. Make notes of past conversations or screenshot any interaction if anything is important to know. **Note**: Be careful doing this; there's always the chance someone will get their hands on it.

11. Don't give out too much information (including your full name) when chatting online. There's little good that can come from giving your full name or work email address—anyone can research you with that information.

12. Be cautious when adding any women from an online dating site or app to a social networking site. A lot of your personal information is available on the social networking site, and they can access your network of friends and family.

13. Never ask a woman out on a date directly. Joke around and make it more casual, such as hanging out. Once a woman feels she's asked out on a date, she'll go into the "dating evaluation process" in her mind. This process begins with determining whether she likes you or not, if she sees anything in you and what the future may bring, and as scary as it sounds, she may mentally combine her first name with your last name "just to see how it sounds." You don't want this, so don't go this route.

14. Have all email correspondence and search results sent to a personal email account, not a business one.

15. Be 100 percent truthful in your profile description. This includes your body type, height, and weight. Your goal is to meet the person, and if you're lying, you're wasting your time and theirs.

16. Never list any range for the salary field. Whether your salary is high or low isn't necessary and won't help; the woman will judge you on this either way.

17. Don't hesitate to pay for premium member benefits. Start with the shortest paid option to see if the results justify it. If you notice results, keep it.

Chapter 24:

A SITE AND APP FOR EVERYTHING AND EVERYONE

"Well, dating has become a sport and not about finding the person you love."

- Rashida Jones

Technology has connected everyone and everything as never before. It gives us the ability to learn, interact, and find exactly what we want or need at a moment's notice. This also holds true for dating sites and apps.

There's something for everybody. From the person looking for someone with a prestigious degree you can go to TheLeague.com; for those looking for a farmer, you can go to FarmersOnly.com; if you're looking for a Jewish person, you can go to JDate.com; or if you're looking for casual sex and nothing more, there's AdultFriendFinder.com. There are many other sites that center around common interests, whether it's religion, animal lovers, or even marriage.

Despite these specific and targeted sites, I still view the larger member-based sites as superior. Who's to say there isn't a farmer, Jewish person, or animal lover on any of these other sites? I can tell you with certainty there are. Additionally, you should open yourself to as many members as possible. We men tend to value some features more than others when looking for a woman.

I would stick with the biggest and best sites and apps. Sure, you can join a smaller site or app too, but don't miss out on the larger ones with the highest number of members.

As important as it is to choose the right site, it's more important not to choose the wrong ones. Some sites cater to lining up arranged marriages, having an affair, meeting an inmate, and paying for sex.

You're not the type of person needing to resort to these types of sites. Put yourself in the best position to succeed, which is not these sites.

As you can tell, there really is something for everyone online. There are thousands of other sites online and more added regularly. Go with the more well-known sites because there will be more prospects for you with a larger member base. The higher the number of members, the more options you have.

CHAPTER 25:

DISTINGUISHING BETWEEN THE MOST POPULAR DATING SITES AND APPS

"You must have the right map to assure you'll get to where you want to be. If you're driving to Florida, but the map you're using is to California, you can't reach your destination. The same is true for being successful with women. This book is your compass and map to success with women. All you have to do is follow it."

—Michael Anthony

As stated above, the same is true for online dating. You must realize that your past dating successes or failures do not translate to online success or failure. It's a different map. This is the first step in your growth. The key is to establish a universal map to produce results. At that point, you'll discover how online dating can be much easier than traditional dating.

Below is a breakdown of the most popular online dating sites and apps for you to review. Ultimately, you must determine which ones fit what you're looking for.

WWW.MATCH.COM

- Founded in 1995; helped pioneer the online dating industry
- More than 20 million users
- 49% to 51% men-to-women ratio

Match.com is one of the, if not the, most popular dating site today in terms of quality. Match.com has made acquisitions of competitors in the past to further strengthen their customer base. It's a dominant player in today's online dating world and controls Chemistry.com, BlackPeopleMeet.com, OurTime.com for the 50+ crowd, SingleParentsMeet.com, Christian Dating through LoveAndSeek.com, and Personals.com, among others.

While Match.com has had notable successes in the dating world, the percentages favor those looking to date. Though some hope to find "the one," the odds are not in favor of this, so joining Match, where the selection is greatest, can yield the most options for you. Match.com is a step above PlentyOfFish.com in quality because there's a fee associated with membership. The members on Match are typically younger in comparison to the members at eHarmony.com.

Site-Specific Tips:

- You can track and reset the number of times people have viewed your profile for your own viewing.
- The site will keep a running tally for you regarding the number of winks and emails sent and received.
- With the Daily 5, Match will connect you with five people you may be interested in.
- You simply click interested or not on each of the Daily 5 prospects, and they'll receive notifications only if you're interested. If it's a match, they connect you two.
- Typically, there's a trial period. I recommend taking advantage of this, so you can decide, based on the prospects, if it's the right site for you to invest your time in.

WWW.EHARMONY.COM

- 33 million members in the U.S.
- In nearly 200 countries around the world
- Harris Interactive states an average of 542 eHarmony members in the United States marry every day.

eHarmony is a site focused on creating long-term, lasting relationships. The site requires members to complete a questionnaire totaling more than 400 questions for compatibility. The site requires its members to complete many steps to ensure the members are, in fact, serious about finding "love." According to Quantcast, 71 percent of users are women. The odds are in a man's favor; however, you need to remember this website is for those looking for a relationship.

After completing the profile and the questionnaire, members can't search the site for women. eHarmony provides matches to you via email. This takes the control out of the member's hand, which is not good for you since it imposes limitations on your search capabilities and how many women you can contact. This is good for members looking for serious compatibility. The matches provided to you are based upon the answers you gave on the questionnaire as well as the information you provided regarding what you're looking for. eHarmony matches that information with women who seem compatible with you based on their answers on the questionnaire and criteria such as age and other specifics.

Site-Specific Tips:
- eHarmony provides hints on completing your profile assessment. Mainly, the hints are to give as many details as possible.

- Depending on your membership level, you might have the option to have your ID verified for protection, a deeper analysis of your personality conducted; you might be able to request photos from matches, see who has viewed your profile, and send/receive communication requests.
- Members can control preferences on potential matches sent to them based on their distance from your ZIP code; if you're interested in someone who drinks, smokes, or has kids; religious preferences; and education.
- eHarmony basically controls the access to its members. It isn't as open as their competitors, which most likely helps its members find someone on an emotional level.
- Most people online want to search and view their potential matches' pictures. eHarmony focuses more on connecting on an emotional level.
- Go through a free trial period so you can decide, based on the prospects, if this site fits what you're looking for.

WWW.PLENTYOFFISH.COM

- More than 4 million people using it daily
- 70,000 new sign-ups per day
- More than 10 billion page views every month

Plenty of Fish is a free dating website and app. The site is one of the easiest to navigate for its popularity. The site is open to everyone, so there are people from all walks of life—from the best of the best to the worst of the worst. The quality prospects may be mixed with a large quantity of those who don't have the qualities you want. Often, you'll see the same people on other dating sites who are on Plenty of Fish. Don't let this deter you. This is one of the, if not the, best sites to meet women quickly for free.

The site offers a chemistry test and a test to discover your relationship needs. The site also offers a "Relationship Chemistry Predictor" questionnaire. As stated in the universal Do's and Don'ts sections, don't get too sentimental with details; your goal is to appeal to everyone. Then, you can decide whom to proceed with.

Site-Specific Tips:
- At the bottom of each profile there's a number next to "favorites." The higher this number is, the more likely the prospect has been on the site for an extended period (and isn't a desirable prospect for you).
- You can check out who has viewed your profile from your homepage.
- You can also make your profile private and access additional features such as specifics on profile views so that no one can see whether you viewed their profile or not.
- It's possible to see someone's last log in. This lets you know whether they're an "active" member. If they haven't been online for a while, you know they're not active, and you can save yourself the time of contacting them.

- This site has alternative names, POF or www.POF.com.

Now that you have the universal map you need to succeed in selecting the right dating sites, navigate around them, perform searches, design your profile, start messaging, and see what works for you.

CHAPTER 26:
MOBILE DATING APPS ANALYZED

"The only advice I can give you is to expect anything you type or send from your phone to be viewed by everyone you don't want to see it."

—A father handing his son his first cell phone

New apps and online dating sites are being created daily. Many will come, and most will go. The strategies, insights and analysis provided within this book are universal. They have stood the test of time and are currently working today.

Just as traditional dating has shifted online due to the convenience and efficiency needed for our hectic lifestyles, mobile dating has taken the reins from online dating through apps. In doing so, people can check their phone throughout the day, receive notifications in real time, and talk anytime using their phone.

With our attention spans at an all-time low and expectations of getting what we want now, the mobile dating market through apps have taken the dating market by storm.

The larger online sites have taken notice and have their own apps, too. A smart phone is all you need to experience online dating today.

To help you gain a better understanding on the best apps to use and universal tips, read below for a detailed cheat sheet:

14 GENERAL TIPS FOR DATING APPS

1. When viewing photos or profiles, you simply swipe your finger across, and it directs you to the next photo/profile.
   Despite the appearance that pictures are all you see, most apps, as with actual dating sites have profiles with information such as age, height, weight, about me section, headline, etc.
2. Do not merge your dating site with your Facebook account, even if the site is pushing for you to appear as "verified" for other users.
3. If you must merge your Facebook account, check your privacy settings on both the dating app and Facebook, since not doing so can lead to your personal information, friends, photos, work info, and more being available to any and every person you come across.

4. In contrast, a woman who has her account merged is great because you a) know she's real b) can do some research on her to get more information

5. Don't bite on profiles with only one photo if the site allows for more. Quantity in terms of information and photos is important to validate, while not sacrificing your quality expectations.

6. Use the settings to show if someone is currently logged-in or online. This is the best type of person to reach out to since they're an active user. More importantly, the timing of you both being on at the same time is great for interacting.

7. Keep an eye on any New Sign-Ups. If interested in a woman who's new, you must act quickly before she feels overwhelmed.

8. Adjust your settings and pay the fee if there is one to see who's viewing or has viewed you. This is important to see because you can reach out to them after they view you, since they were intrigued enough to check out your profile.
Check regularly, if anyone looks promising, you should message them quickly.

9. In sales, lead conversion (success in making a sale) directly connects to the response time. The longer it takes to respond, the less likely the customer will be as interested. This is the same with dating profiles online and messages. Keep their attention while you have it. The longer you wait, the lower the odds of connecting or hanging out.

10. Set up a new email just for dating sites and apps. It's much easier to organize and reduces the possibility of mixing work with fun or revealing personal information.

11. Create a system for organizing the experience. You can do this by grouping based on site, labels in your phone as detailed in this book of pertinent details such as age, location, profession, name, and or interesting fact about them.
It's easy to get overwhelmed and distracted since there's so much to sort through. By organizing, you can limit missing a woman you may be interested in.

12. Attention spans are shorter than ever. For this reason, pictures and quick-hit information such as a witty headline or title is more important than ever before.

13. There's a time to be cheap and time not to. The features many apps offer to highlight your profile, view who has viewed your profile, and certain messaging capabilities are worth it. As a result, you will talk to more women and meet more and higher quality women.

14. While online dating sites and some apps may differ with various features, the fundamental principles are the same for you to experience success in getting women to want you.

TINDER

This dating app has taken over. With its popularity at an all-time high, the number of members is continually increasing. The more the members, the better for you. It's free to start and is very easy to navigate. Both parties must agree to a match. This eliminates a lot of the guesswork before talking. Below is a quick breakdown of features Tinder offers:

- Logs in with your phone number or Facebook.
- Uses the swipe technology to view pictures and profiles.
- You can "Skip the line" and be the top profile for 30 minutes to get more matches.
  - Highly recommended, it will increase your exposure, interest, and odds of meeting women.
- You can "like" a profile, "super like" it, or discard it.
- For a fee you can get Tinder Plus, which gives you unlimited likes, one free boost a month, control what others see about you, and choose who sees you, and you can customize your setting to see only those you liked, etc.
- When you're a paying member, you can "rewind" to go back to profile you mistakenly swiped too quickly. This is a great feature.
- The profile focuses on your main picture although beneath it gives a location and various other information.
  - Features include the listed distance away (two miles away), which can prove beneficial if interested and both members have their location settings on. It allows them to see how feasible it is to hang out if they're already near one another.
  - Despite not having as much weight, a bio/about me section is still there. Use this section with three to four sentences to stand out.
- Tinder allows you to link Instagram pictures and connect on Instagram.
  - Do this cautiously because many have personal information, including family photos, work photos, pictures with friends, etc. on Instagram.
- You can recommend a profile to a friend
- The premium feature of "Passports Plus" allows you to swipe around the world. This is great if you're traveling or may travel to an area soon.
- A paid membership offers additional features such as no ads.
  - Not showing your age
  - Not showing your location
  - Eliminating the annoying advertisements

ZOOSK

Zoosk started as a Facebook app in December 2007 and is now available in more than 25 languages and more than 80 countries. Zoosk can pull up your information from your social networking account to help create your profile if you decide to link it. Keep an eye on your settings and what you're sharing—with and without your permission. Once you start to send and receive messages, a popup appears that says, "You must be a subscriber to send messages" If you choose to proceed, they have subscriptions ranging from monthly to three months at a time and six months at a time. This is a great strategy by Zoosk because it allows you to send and receive a message, and then you either must subscribe or lose the capability of sending further messages. Before Tinder, Zoosk was dominant. Below is a quick summary of Zoosk:

- It has more than 35 million members.

- Zoosk provides a tutorial to make it more user friendly, which is great for a new member.
- Swipe to see profiles.
- You can send messages and emojis under their profile picture (recommended).
- It has a "smart pick" option, which is a feature to match you and others.
- The radar function allows you to see who's currently around you, based on your distance specifications (within 5, 10, 15, 20 miles, etc.)
- Zoosk builds a messaging service into the site to chat directly.
- It allows you to see who has viewed your profile and whether you viewed theirs.
- All members can reply to emails premium members send.
- Premium members are the only ones with access to any member.
- Ads do appear to generate revenue.
- Credit on the site uses the term "coins"
- There are options to get coins free:
  o Invite friends to join Zoosk
  o Become a fan of the Zoosk Facebook page
  o Install the Zoosk Dating Application on your iPhone
- There are additional options at a fee, using coins
  o Capability to go invisible (which can be good for privacy)
  o Purchase "Boost Profile" to increase your profile views through increased visibility by having your profile highlighted and at the top of search results (the more people who see you the better for getting women to want you).
  o Delivery confirmation: You can find out if the person has read your message.
  o Special Delivery: You can make sure she sees your message before all the others through this option
  o You can send gifts. (This is not how you want to get her attention.)

POF

POF, also known as Plenty of Fish is the largest free site or app out there today. As with anything in life that's free, it may not always yield the best quality, but the quantity is there. It's the world's largest dating site with more than 4 million people using it daily and more than 70,000 new members every single day. This translates to more than 1 billion messages per month. Below are some quick facts and pointers for using POF:

- It has the option to see whether the attraction is mutual by simply expressing your interest in a member with a single click.
- You can hide your profile, which may be necessary at times.
- Popups with tips and facts do appear.

- One which was alarming was "Income is the single biggest predictor of relationship failure and of relationships starting. Please select your income range."
  - This can lead to a temptation to embellish. Use your best judgment.
- As with any free site or app, there are add-ons for a better user experience. These include:
  - Upgrade to 1st Look, which highlights your profile and puts it at the top of search results. It also puts your messages first in the line of messages a woman may receive. This is huge because you'll have an advantage of being seen. (highly recommended).
  - The Ultra-Match, which is a personalized service of the Top 50 matches
  - The Top Prospect presented to you
  - Seeing who has viewed your profile (great feature since you can message them, and you clearly caught their attention to click on your profile).
  - As with all sites that offer a paid option, you will pay less for the longer length of your commitment, for instance, 12 months is less than six months and six months is less than three months and three months is less than one month.
- Plenty of Fish is now holding socials for singles to meet. This could be a great opportunity; all the attendees are clearly single and ready to mingle.

OK CUPID

OK Cupid has recently attempted to differentiate itself from the other sites and not compete with the POF and Tinder markets. It does this by marketing the site as superior to its competitors by "getting to know the real you" through a more detailed questionnaire, helping to arrange matches through its proprietary algorithm and help you find authentic connections. While the approach is a less crowded space, with only eHarmony and Match as similar competitors, it's not different enough from the sites and apps it attempts to separate itself from. Below is a condensed outline to get familiar with OK Cupid:

- You can keep your personal information private by not having to sign in using Facebook unlike Tinder or Bumble.
- The questionnaire can be cumbersome but necessary to answer some of the questions to proceed.
- You can gain more insight into a potential partner based on the long quizzes and surveys.
- In between your searches, facts do appear as popups from OK Cupid. From my experience, most of the facts were sex-related. Examples include the following:
  - 24 percent of men and 62 percent of women want their partner to take charge in a sexual ncounter.
  - Those who tend to like scary movies like pain.

- I found these distasteful and unnecessary. It completely contradicts the stated approach.
- Additional questions appear, including those involving politics. This may be a good tool to connect those with similar beliefs, but I'd avoid answering them. The questions I experienced included a host of topics such as:
  - Thoughts on the death penalty, guns, and raising taxes on the wealthy
    - If you answer any of these, you're reducing your exposure, which is not a good idea.
- "Quick match." This will bring up a list of users with just their profile pictures.
- It can also search based on who was online last, best match, mix (Great feature— highly recommended).
- Percentage match feature allows for the site to connect you based on questions and information provided.
- Remember, less is more. Listing too much information can give someone looking at your profile a way to find something wrong with you.
- You can message people and "like" other profiles.
- The site restricts your ability to see who likes you until you pay for the website and become an "A-list" member.

BUMBLE

Bumble is a unique site because it has a feature unlike any other, which allows only the woman to send the first message. An ex-Tinder employee created Bumble to give the woman more control in the dating world. This is great for any man, as long as he receives messages. If you can implement the tools and strategies provided within this book to get women to want you, this is a great site. If you're still new to online dating, we highly recommend you start with this app. It reduces the pressure of what to say, and you can get a behind-the-scenes view of what women say to crack the ice. However, this may also be a site to use after you have confidence in your use of other sites to get women to want you. Below are some details on the site:

- Most login through Facebook.
- View profile using same swiping method as others.
- You can share a profile or person to a friend if you think they may be of interest or to get their thoughts.
- Bumble provides a connection guide to assist with matches
- One of the best features is the "Back Track" technology. As you'll find out, it's very common to swipe quickly while viewing profiles and accidentally swiping past a potential match or someone who caught your eye. This technology allows you to literally shake your phone and it goes back.
- Clicking on the name shows their location.
- Option to share or block/report someone to an admin (can be helpful if you run across a bad one).

- Since the site is free, it also offers additional services at a cost such as:
  - See who has liked your profile.
  - Access old matches.
  - Unlimited "Extends" on previous matches or conversations.
  - You can extend the time for them to send the first message, because your connection expires in 24 hours.
  - You can rematch with the same person your connection fizzled out with if they don't send a message.
  - "Bumble Boost" increases more exposure to women searching profiles.

CLOVER

Clover is a different type of app; it reminds you on an old-school message board. The format allows for members to post on a common board, though the members can take the conversation private. It offers a short free trial period of seven days and baits you with many great features to convince you to join. It does this by having groups to help members identify the right fit for them. Below are some of the details you should know when using Clover:

- Log in can be through email or Facebook.
  - Use email. You don't need to have all your personal information linked for strangers.
- You can't start free trial period without entering your credit card information.
  - After your trial period, the membership starts immediately thereafter at $29.99 per month, though can be canceled at any time.
- Allows members to see if anyone read their messages.
- Quick interest options include a heart if you like them, an x if you don't have interest, or an option to message them directly
- Groups created, though they're always evolving:
  - Girls that want relationships
  - Nice guys
  - Socially awkward
  - Tall girls
  - Pet lovers

MATCH

Match is the gold standard for online dating. With its massive online presence, it's a clear-cut winner. It has continually acquired competitors to assist with this growth. With such a powerful database, the launch of an app was an easy decision and seamless transition. It has a large user base and requires members to pay, so the quality is arguably the best in terms of people. Most of the app features mirror the online site, though are still relevant and useful:

- You can log in using your email.
- Membership options are most expensive for the shortest duration.
- It has options to save profiles.
- Messages do not disappear.
- Daily matches are based on similar interests you and someone else provide in a questionnaire.
- The ability to send emojis such as a smile or wink is a nice feature to break the ice without having to send an actual message. Plus, it's quick.
- Search options based upon your current location, ZIP code entered or distance.
- Photos are prevalent, though profiles have depth with information.
  - This is important, so you can learn more about the woman you may want to talk to. Having this information can make it easier to start a conversation based on something listed in her profile.

SKOUT

Another site that has and will continually make a splash in the mobile market is Skout. Skout is a location-based app on your cell phone and is in more than 100 countries in 14 languages. It identifies where you and the other users are within their network. For safety purposes, the exact location is secret, though it identifies the area. Users can see those who are near and view their profiles. If an interest is there, you can use the instant messaging feature to contact the other person. Skout prides itself on the users' having complete safety. However, the app has a zero tolerance policy for bad or offensive behavior, which is a breath of fresh air for many. Below are more features on Skout:

- Skout appears to hold itself to a higher standard with recommendations to members on meeting at public places. This can be good for members who are hesitant online.
- Allows users to see where those on their "friends list" on sites such as Facebook are, aligning with their location on their phone's GPS.
  - While it may not reveal the exact location, this is a prime opportunity for you to connect with someone on their friends' list.
  - This can also be a bad thing, so be cautious. Depending how populated your area is, it may not be too difficult to find the spot to conveniently run into them or where to avoid them.
- Features to connect and share are wide-ranging:
  - Allows for sharing photos.
  - Send messages through the instant messaging format.
  - The option to send virtual gifts such as flowers. (Don't do it.)
  - Capability to send notes if the person isn't online to send a regular message (think emails).

HINGE

Hinge is a dating app that connects you through friends. This eliminates the "stranger" aspect, which may appeal to you if you're looking for something serious. It could also be a bad fit if you aren't looking for awkwardness or potentially ruining friendships over a bad experience, date, or relationship. Join this site if you have a specific person you're interested in. If not, there are many pitfalls to justify it, unless you've exhausted other sites with no success and are looking for commitment.

- Add up to six photos
- Can add captions beneath photos
- iOS users can upload a video in lieu of any of the six photos.
- Can add and edit lifestyle characteristics such as gender, height, location, ethnicity, kids, family plans, politics, drinking, smoking, marijuana, and drugs.
- Can also include some basic information about yourself like work, job title, school, education level, religious beliefs, and hometown.
- Can link your Instagram account

THE LEAGUE

Designed specifically for those who are attending or have attended prestigious universities, the League offers the expectation to meet educated and successful people. The site verifies this when you grant access to both your Facebook and LinkedIn profiles. The site then creates a profile for you from your photos and information you provided on the sites. This is a more targeted site, which is useful to those with very high standards based strictly on academia.

- Wait list for approval of your application
- Pay a fee to avoid waiting
- Protects your privacy by blocking your Facebook friends and LinkedIn contacts
- A handful of matches each day
- If both parties agree, it's a match
- Must stay active on the site or be removed if no activity for two weeks

POTENTIAL PITFALLS

It's easy to wander into trouble because of the convenience of mobile dating since it's readily available anytime, anywhere. The accessibility leaves you much more susceptible to an invasion of privacy because you're likely to access the site from your phone at any moment, without the privacy your home may offer. This can lead to a friend, stranger, boss, or coworker watching you slack off or possibly even catching a glimpse of what you're up to. Additionally, since cell phones today have built-in cameras and video cameras, it's tempting to use them since they're so easily accessible.

It's important to understand everything with your cell phone is **traceable**. Someone can trace the information you exchange directly to your cell number. This information includes any text messages, emails, phone calls, and pictures. Once someone has your cell number, they can research and access your information, such as your full name, address, and employment.

Furthermore, the hacker can use this info against you. If you're willing to take the risk, prepare for anything you say or send in any conversation to be public with your personal cell phone number attached to it. Your safest bet is to expect everyone who you don't want to see it to view anything you type or send from your phone. At some point or another, this will certainly happen, so be cautious.

There's no doubt about it, the dating scene of today is through your phone. Luckily, you have the tools and strategies in your repertoire to experience success in all aspects of dating: in person, online, and mobile. This book can prepare you for anything in all aspects of life; however, we can't caution you enough to read what you type or what autocorrect types before replying.

One aspect which can be funny or humiliating, depending upon your position is the auto correct function on your cell phone. This function is like spell check on Microsoft Word. The only difference is that auto correct changes the word on its own and sometimes doesn't ask for approval to change it. You want to pay attention since things can come across a little different from what you intended. The following is an example of this:

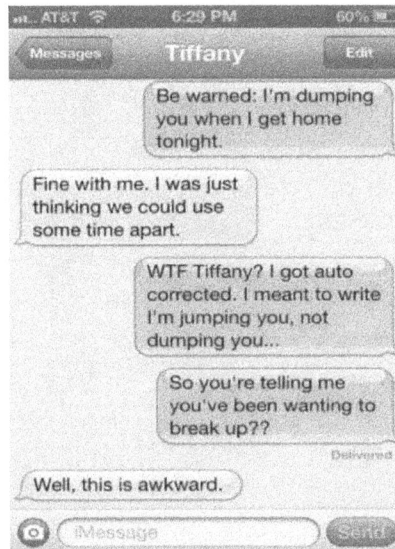

THE GREAT NEWS FOR YOU!

- The information provided throughout applies directly to the mobile dating market.

- You have a distinct advantage since you can work both the online and mobile markets.
- Your knowledge of this information will provide many more options for you.
- All you must do now is act.

CHAPTER 27:

STEALTH SITES: HOW TO FLY UNDER THE RADAR ON DATING SITES AND APPS

"Fair: a place where there is cotton candy and pony rides"

—Kyle Max

Not all dates have to be set up using the conventional dating sites or apps. You can also meet women on social networking sites. They're great places to talk to, meet, and hang out with women.

FACEBOOK

Facebook has become one of the most popular sites online. Number three, to be exact. Facebook's main function is to connect friends online. However, with a huge database of members and a lot of money, it has branched into various other arenas with force.

I have reservations about using Facebook to meet or connect with strangers online because it reveals far too much information (full name, location, photos, friends' list, etc.). While you can hide some of these with privacy settings, Facebook is notorious for changing its policies and settings with little to no notice to their users.

For these reasons, it's better to check your settings regularly and have as much of your information hidden/private as possible. This includes your wall posts. You don't need drama on your wall or your business on the wall, for that matter. Simply put, this isn't the ideal site to fly under the radar.

However, Facebook does provide a great platform to meet women without being on an actual dating site. Adding a stranger as a friend is not as effective as messaging one with a quick note. It doesn't come across as odd and some view it as more normal.

Since Facebook's goal is to connect everyone, it's common for people to succeed in connecting with random strangers, past friends, and exes through the site friend recommendations. This can be good if you're looking to reconnect with someone. Facebook can also be a great resource for those trying to reconnect with past flames, previous crushes, and those you knew though never talked to or pursued.

With its huge user base, Facebook can plug and play almost any idea for a seamlessly quick implementation to see how the users take to it. These have included adding video to the site, business pages to like, messenger apps, and more. The most expected move is into dating. The implementation may take time to perfect, though this is something to keep an eye on.

Site-Specific Tips:
- This is the most personal site; each person provides their full name.
- This site allows searches that will locate people by networks such as city, college, high school, workplace, etc.
- Profile pictures are viewable by all on the site.
- If you do not adjust your privacy settings, searching a person's name through Google can yield a link to your profile.
- Facebook keeps ALL your information, including messages, so be careful.

TWITTER

Twitter is a popular site that gets a message out (referred to as a tweet) in 140 (or now 280) characters or less. You can use it to interact with other users, view their tweets, post photos, promote business interests, and state your own personal opinions. Many celebrities enjoy using Twitter to control the messaging of an event or item of importance, rather than the media inaccurately reporting it. You can use this website uniquely and break the status quo by having the intent of engaging with women for dating purposes.

You can like others tweets with a heart or send a direct message. Research the chapters on what to say to stand out and use this to your advantage. If the person has a large following, it will be difficult to catch their attention due to the overwhelming number of likes and messages they receive. With everyone treating it as a social networking tool and not a dating avenue, you can turn this into a distinct advantage in separating yourself.

Site-Specific Tips:
- The more people you follow, the more followers you're likely to have in return.
- Retweeting a tweet is a good approach to contact someone, since they get notification.
- Keep direct messaging short and to the point.
- Post valuable content to gain exposure and more followers.
- The more followers you get, the more people you'll ultimately be exposed to.
- Don't be obvious and only follow attractive women, they'll see through that.

INSTAGRAM

Instagram is another very popular social networking site that people use to post pictures or videos and even a timeline of their day within the past 24 hours. People will post their travels, new purchases, or other things they find significant in the moment. You can "like" the photo or comment on it and they'll get notification. You can also directly message a user, and the site will tell you when they read the message. This is another great avenue to test your wit and post something that may catch a woman's attention.

Do not simply create a profile with the sole intention of meeting women. Remember to give and take. You should post pictures, too, which can display your exciting/interesting life. Unlike Facebook and Twitter, this site doesn't force you to post personal information.

Site-Specific Tips:
Facebook owns it.
- The site is based on pictures and videos.
- Timeline story feature is new, and a user can post anything within the past 24 hours for their friends to see before the post disappears. Note: The user can see who viewed their story.
- Groups are prevalent—travel, sports, kids, literally something for everybody.
- The site comes with heavy photo editing and filtering features.
- This site allows the novice to become a photo editor in no time.
- Posting subjects range from travel pics to new purchases, or a funny meme.
- You can "like" a photo or comment and they'll get notification.
- You can direct message a user and know when the person read your message.

- CASE STUDY -

Kevin has done very well strictly through Instagram. While many think this site isn't a site to meet others, Kevin pays no attention to them and continually cleans up. He has a Facebook account too, though he refuses to try any apps or online dating sites. He doesn't see the need since he experiences great results meeting women through Instagram. The number of women he has met on Instagram alone exceeds 200 in a four-year period.

When I asked him why he doesn't go out to meet girls, his response was, "Look, I'm not a good-looking guy; I'm average at best. I'm not in good shape, tall, nor do I have a ton of money. I am quick-witted and fun to be around. Online, I have an advantage, and I don't have to blow all kinds of money and waste time on the "what if" scenario. Using my advantage online with my humor, wit, and intelligence, I focus my attention there because it's my own competitive advantage." Wise words from a wise man. He uses the same techniques you're learning.

Stand out by paying attention to the details (comment on her pictures and in any messages sent; she'll appreciate it), establish common interests by referring to an experience to engage her (for instance, if she has a picture in Times Square, relate with a story about a trip you took there with a cool experience) and be willing to go out of your comfort zone. Sure, you don't know her, but the more information someone has online, the more we're tricked into believing we do know them. Have exciting photos and show your personality, it will make you that much more enticing.

OLD SCHOOL—THROWBACKS!

The two sites detailed below are two sites that were ahead of their time. Face the Jury and Myspace are both now distant memories, but they're relevant; many of the case studies we've used for this book are currently having success on Match, POF, Tinder, Bumble, Facebook, and Instagram also had success on these sites. It was where they cut their teeth and learned the ropes on how to effectively interact online. Their legwork helped shape this book. Enjoy the summary of each site below, as you pay homage.

FACE THE JURY

Face the Jury was a site that allowed you to rate another person's profile from 1 to 10. It was very similar to the site Hot or Not. Each member typically posted one of their best photos for rating. The key was a catchy screen name, a good headline, and pictures to stand out. Because this site was accessible to all regardless of location, the attention you got from people viewing your profile created a viral amount of activity for your profile, and the views quickly added up. With that momentum, messages followed.

Despite the site being small by design (never having more than two employees and three servers), it quickly grew to be one of the top 800 most highly trafficked sites on the Internet with more than 6 million page views per day.

There was a top-10 list on the site, which ranked the most viewed profiles on the entire site. One of the case studies used in this book, Marcus, had in fact climbed to number one on the entire site. He compared it to going viral; once you're at the top of the list, the views and activity jump quickly, and you simply enjoy the ride.

One of our other case studies, Jason, had success with this site, as well. He had two different women drive from other states to hang out. He stated the site "was fun though not as productive as others regarding selection of women and communication."

MYSPACE

Myspace was once the dominant social site to interact. Now it's a site designed for music. It has become overwhelmed with slow-loading pages and advertisements. It's a shame to see how Myspace fell out of relevance so quickly but welcome to technology.

Many of the characteristics Myspace possessed were and still are valuable to meeting others online, while flying under the radar. Today's sites and apps center around linking your real name and Facebook accounts. The beauty with what Myspace offered was creating your own persona. People could create their own name for others to see and play music and customize their page. It gave you complete control. Most sites today that require linking to your personal information cater advertising to you.

IN CLOSING

We've provided you with the most popular sites used by our case studies for optimum success. Use this information as a cheat sheet in understanding what sites suit your needs best and how to navigate these sites effectively. You now have not only the understanding gained thus far, but you also possess a book to refer to when needed.

There are many dating sites to choose from. In fact, new sites appear daily on the Internet. The universal concepts provided to you in this section will aid you in your success, both in the present and the future with all sites you visit. Just adapt to the woman you're interested in with the information we provided you, and success will follow.

CHAPTER 28:
How to Identify and Classify Women Online

*"I'm learning now what I didn't know then, so I can enjoy now what
I wasn't able to then."*

—Austin Major

While rummaging through various profiles online, you'll notice the variety of women and profiles. Some women will post photos that are more tasteful and may appear conservative, while others leave very little to the imagination. Those are black-and-white profile differences. Deciphering the profiles that fall into the shades of gray will help you determine who wants to date, hang out, or is looking for a relationship. There are four classifications of women you will find online and on apps; these classifications are based upon characteristics they possess and where they are or have been in the online dating scene. Each woman you meet should fall into one of the four following classifications.

THE GOOD-TIME GIRL

This woman will have a high number of favorites listed on her profile (not all sites will have this feature, though). The number of favorites displays how many people have marked her as one of their favorites from the site. She will also likely have risqué photos posted. Risqué photos are on display to generate many comments and messages from men. She wants the attention and isn't shy about putting herself out there for it. Though one dating site can keep a person busy, don't be surprised if this woman is on multiple sites. If she is on several sites, you can assume she's not new to online dating. Typically, someone who's new to dating online will attempt only one site at a time. Being on multiple dating sites gives this woman several avenues to attract new guys and get the attention she craves.

Another surefire way to find out if a woman falls into this category is to discover whether she has been on the site for an extended period. If she has been, she understands the game and is typically not as naive in her beliefs as she is in check with reality. The easiest way to find out is to either ask her directly or to form an opinion based upon profile details and communication. These details can include any past experiences she may mention, such as being back on this site, etc. This girl has most likely already dated at least one or two men and has hung out with more while being on the site. It's typically more difficult to get this girl's attention because she usually receives a lot of messages. This does not mean she's popular; it could be strictly a time thing because the longer someone is online, the more messages they'll receive. It's the law of averages in practice.

Additionally, this woman can act conceited since she associates the attention she receives online with her value. She doesn't realize it's more likely that she's receiving attention because the men are looking for a good time. In contrast, some of these women are direct and will acknowledge they're looking to have a good time and will sometimes even pursue guys. If any of these "good-time girls" act naïve, they're doing it intentionally because they've been around the dating scene and understand how it works.

EXAMPLES OF THE "GOOD TIME GIRL"

- CASE STUDY -

COURTNEY
23 YEARS OLD
EMAIL CORRESPONDENCE

Summary: Drew saw Courtney was a new member on PlentyOfFish.com. Because she was new, he knew he needed to get her information ASAP before she became flooded with emails and messages from other guys when they too saw she was new. She was an attractive 23-year-old and sure to be in demand. He immediately got her email so he could search for her on social networking sites to get more information on her. Yes, you can look someone up based on their email too, not just their name. From there, they corresponded and really hit it off. He could tell she was all about having a good time, and the following conversation shows just that. He quickly identified her as a realistic possibility to come over and hang out with. The two corresponded for a couple of days before ultimately meeting that Saturday night for a movie near her place. After the movie, they hung out, and the rest is history. Below is an example of Drew's game in action.

Email Heading: Do I know you??

Drew: haha:)

Feedback—Joking, haha, in reference to his email heading!

Courtney: lol. okay let's only use one msging system now before this gets confusing. =] i'm done being a creeper now. very nice pictures. ;]

Feedback—Was messaging through a service offered through Plenty of Fish. Once has personal email, emailed directly.

Drew: i like ur style...do u have G Chat?

Feedback—Straight to the point, trying to move conversation to Gchat.

Courtney: that i do not. sorry handsome. ;)

Feedback—Flirting with a compliment, though direct with her response.

Drew: i say you google it, download it in like 5 minutes and get it so we can talk! thanks;)

Feedback—Assumptive close with a direct request for her to download it flanked by the benefit of talking to you = Very nice.

Courtney: you're a bossy one. =] i'll see what i can do do...no promises/

Feedback—Flirting back with her, liking the comment about him being bossy with a little sexual innuendo about being in control, followed by a tease.

Drew: i like to be in control. :) if you stepped up, i may let you take control too....may

Feedback—She's throwing compliments out about him being hot and is playing into the sexual nature, score!

Courtney: hmmm, is that so? well, although it is realllly hot when i guy is in control...sometimes i just can't help myself but to take over. ;)
Drew: hmmm...u like to take over...give and take maybe;) i like that too! see if u had a messaging thing we could talk more in 5 minutes then what we could in an hour of normal messages, haha

Feedback—Again, he's trying to move the conversation to Gchat since emailing back and forth takes too much time and drags out a conversation. Also, it makes it more difficult to talk to more than one person at a time.

Courtney: and why exactly should i go dl g chat.... just kidding...i suppose i can budge on this one.

Feedback—She's still trying to play tough, but she gives in.

Drew: good choice..youre lucky..if u didnt download it and add me and when we hang out...u would be in trouble, haha

Feedback—Nice work!

Courtney: i'm used to be being in trouble...it's more fun anyway. =] what's your sn on messenger?

Feedback—She's definitely intrigued and interested.

Drew: looks like we may get along then...think we could get in a little trouble together:) (email removed for privacy)@gmail.com
Courtney: well, i tried the messenger thing and i must be completely computer illiterate. i thought i had it. anywho, my sn on there is (name removed for privacy).....or maybe (email address removed for privacy)@gmail.com. not sure? well, ttyl =)

The New Sign Up

She's new to online dating and isn't scarred by past experiences nor is she aware of the various avenues guys attempt to use to get women online. In addition, she's most likely to be open to meeting you early and hasn't met the weirdos who come with online dating. She most likely joined the site or app because she hasn't experienced the success she'd like and is frustrated with her current options or lack thereof in the dating scene.

This woman is also your best bet for quality since this could be her last resort because of her busy lifestyle. There are many reasons she might be frustrated: a lack of decent guys she would be interested in, guys strictly pursuing her for one thing (sex), the ending of a recent relationship, her biological clock ticking, or growing tired of being alone. She's joining this site to meet people; don't lose sight of this. Be careful not to let a woman who acts as though she's new to this and doesn't know about this scene fool you. You must use your best judgment to decide whether she's playing the game intentionally or whether she's being honest. If she's a new sign up, act quickly.

The Substance Girl

This woman has substance, a combination of intelligence, wit, and respectability. While this woman may not have "substance" written on her forehead, she's typically easy to pick out of a crowd. When talking with one of these women, her wit and charm will be immediately obvious. The respectability part of her substance will only reveal itself through conversation when she speaks about instances where guys have attempted to pick her up and play her for a fool in one way or another.

She'll bring attention to this intentionally to let it be known she's smarter than that. She wants you to understand she isn't like that, and this is her attempt to get you to realize there's no use in pursuing her if this is what you're about. Respectability will also shine through when you test her, such as when you invite her over or ask her for her number or something personal. This woman will almost always reject an invitation to come over, responding that she's smarter than that, she doesn't even know you, or she might even question your intent.

She will also not reveal any personal information for an extended period. This personal information includes her phone number, where she lives, or her real name. She's cautious and intelligent in her dealings with guys. She wants the guy to prove he isn't like "every other guy."

- CASE STUDY -

CASEY
21 YEARS OLD
MESSENGER CORRESPONDENCE

Summary: Steve was on PlentyOfFish.com (POF), talking to various women at the same time. His game plan consisted of getting one of their Messenger names as quickly as possible to talk directly to her rather than competing with all the other messages she most likely was getting on POF. During their discussions, she provided enough information for him to search for her on Facebook. His reasoning for looking her up, but not adding her or anyone as a friend, was to verify a) they didn't have friends in common or people he knew and b) to gain valuable insight as to the type of person she was by viewing photos, posts, etc. Unfortunately, he had no luck with finding her, so he asked her directly. After doing his due diligence, he felt he had a better understanding of who she was as a person. He encountered some resistance from a respectable woman. Casey had substance and made it known she wasn't like the other women online. Steve recognized that and liked it.

This revealing discussion showed she was still visibly upset due to a guy using her and cheating on her. Knowing how upset this made her and respecting her as a quality woman, Steve chose to not push the envelope by getting into the details, while he may have in the past. He was respectful but wanted to end the direction the chat was going. They connected on Facebook and exchanged phone numbers. From there, they chatted through Facebook's chat service and texted back and forth. They eventually met at a public place, and they decided to go back and hang out at his place. They hung out for the next few months, and both were happy with their arrangement.

> **Steve**: hey i saw u added me as a friend...now how far are you from where I'm at? ps i normally dont add randoms, so im giving you the benefit of the doubt that youre not a weirdo..
>
>> *Feedback—Generic email he had sent successfully numerous times before. He was lucky this didn't backfire since he didn't have this woman properly identified.*
>
> **Casey**: dude ur on POF lol. you gave me your name.
>
>> *Feedback—She calls him out. It turns out he gave her his information and she added him. Lucky for him, she said she was on POF; otherwise, he would have been clueless about what they had already talked about.*
>
> **Steve**: ok..that still doesnt answer how far you are from me..
>
>> *Feedback—He's brushing off her calling him out and is calling her out for not answering his question about what town she lives in. Shift in control of the conversation.*
>
> **Casey**: oh i forgot to type that sorry. I live about 30 minutes away from where you are
>
> **Steve**: so what makes u different than all the other girls on pof..besides obviously being high maintenance and taking alot of pictures of yourself;)
>
>> *Feedback—Attempting to get her to compete for his attention. Also, calling her out since she had a lot of pictures of herself.*
>
> **Casey**: Well, actually im a total sweetheart. I am not high maintenance at all. I dont expect guys to buy me stuff or pay for me. I can take care of myself. I am very smart as well as being good lookin. Im not a slut like MOST girls. lol. need anymore..
>
>> *Feedback—She's eating it up. She's trying to prove why she's different and better. He's in control of the conversation .*
>
> **Steve**: sure lets hear more..

Feedback—She opened the gate, and he's just taking in as much information as she's willing to give.

Casey: I am very honest. I have never cheated on anyone in my life, but have been cheated on recently. I am always smiling. I am very helpful and I care how others feel. Im dependable. well thats enough haha =] Im just me you either like me or not. Im not going to be a bitch until you mess with me or one of my friends basically.

Feedback—Reading between the lines, she's obviously loyal and upset from recently being cheated on; seems to be a "good girl."

Steve: i believe ya..so how long have you been on pof and how has that gone for ya?

Feedback—His comment about believing her is to keep the conversation going while gauging a feeling for how long she has been on POF. The follow-up about how the site is working out for her is to identify what to avoid doing that she may have already experienced.

Casey: actually about 2-3 weeks. Only made an account because i was talking to a boy for over 4 months and my friend saw him on there. I had been hearing stuff about him cheating on me. Well he started hitting on my friend on there, so I ended it. I deserve better

Feedback—Obviously, she's still upset over her ex-boyfriend situation.

Steve: yea, im still new to that site..thinking about getting rid of it here soon...too many weirdos..not too mention when they have options for if youre looking for an intimate parter, encounter, do drugs, dont have a car...little pathetic..but who knows. everything happens for a reason.

Feedback—He's saying very relatable things that almost any respectable person would notice if on the site. Also used a generic comment most women agree with, "everything happens for a reason."

Casey: yeah im going to get rid of mine. he can be on there to look for someone i dont even think half the girls on there are somewhat pretty at all. Obviously hes just a player and tried to blame me, too bad im not stupid and caught him. But whatever. like you said everything happens for a reason. lol

Feedback—She's on to why many use the site.

Steve: you still sound bitter. i just got out of a four month relationship about two months ago too, things fall apart for better things to happen.

Feedback—He's calling her out for not being over it while softening the comment of relating to her and stating better things are ahead for her.

Casey: Not really bitter, I just dont understand when you ask someone if something is true how the lie to your face and how they try to put you in the spot to blame everything on. Thats prob the two things that piss me off haha. Normally, Im always too happy to be mad haha.. Well you have a good outlook on life =]

Feedback—She's still not over it.

Steve: i cant remember the quote off the top my hand..but have it on my Facebook...about attitude..try living by it and its true about how attitude effects everything in life and its one of the few things you can actually control, if you were lucky enough to be a friend of mine on their you could view that quote among others, haha:)

> *Feedback—The "lucky enough to be a friend of mine" comment is a great poke to lighten the mood and the subject. He's putting feelers out to see whether she's legit by looking at her "real" profile while saying he's okay with her seeing his, as well. Give and take.*

Casey: oh wow. well if you were lucky enough to be my friend well you would just be so damn special haha (: betcha wish you were my friend

> *Feedback—She's joking back and connecting with his sense of humor. This is a win.*

Steve: ORRRR you wish you were my friend to look at the quote and stalk my profile..since im in a "nice mood" today and seeing how you found me on here..i could...just could look you up on Facebook if i had your whole name..then we could both kinda sorta be lucky to have each other as friends...just a thought...no promises

> *Feedback—He's trying to speed things along as she seems to be dragging out the conversation.*

Casey: cocky maybe a little bit..lol..Idk if you should know my name yet i dont know anything about you... you could be a weirdo

> *Feedback—She's repeating what he said earlier regarding weirdos online.*

Steve: Ha, cute.

> *Feedback—Not amused! No originality points for her for copying and repeating what he said.*

Casey: Just try searching my first name Casey and for college (location removed for privacy) Technical College in (location removed for privacy) let me know if it works

> *Feedback—She's trying to make him work, as most people have their entire names on Facebook anyway. She did, too.*

THE RIGHT MOMENT GIRL

This could be any woman characterized in Section II: Identifying and Understanding. The quote "timing is everything" rings true for almost any woman or situation, not only in dating but life in general. We all have been in a position where we acted on our emotions or desires, which may or may not have been out of character. When we act out of character, our brains place a higher value on those actions than when we act in character.

Women who act in the moment typically go with the flow because they're easier going and inclined to justify any action mentally to do what they desire. You most likely have known someone who purchased a car that may have been expensive, but they justified it because it gets good gas mileage or it's safe.

Other examples include a woman purchasing a designer handbag because she really "needed" a purse. Though she could have easily purchased a purse at a thrift store, she chose to buy a brand-new Coach bag that cost more than $500. Though these reasons don't make sense to many, the only person it needs to make sense to is the person making the decision. They will justify anything they want to do. This comes into play when they're deciding whether to hang out with you. Your intention is to justify hanging out with you because they like you.

On the other hand, women who typically don't act on their emotions or desires characterize doing so as "out of character" for them are more of a challenge. These women need further justification for hanging out with you, which is why you need to create a desirable setting for them and expand on it with details.

You must time this well for everything to fall into place. You may luck into timing it right if it's a Friday night and they're bored, lonely, or on the rebound. These women will require time. It's not as simple as just messaging them. You must pay attention, be different, and be better.

The case studies provided in this book and examples of quick comments are there to help you show off your sense of humor, keep them on their toes, and show them what you have to offer being different from the other guys online. Many times, this will lead to justifying hanging out with you or acting in the moment. Remember, timing is everything.

REALITY CHECK

It is imperative for you to understand that women aren't going to pick pictures that make them look bad. In fact, they will do the opposite and choose pictures that will likely be better than what they look like in person. Think about it. Do you think they're going to choose the ones that are the least flattering? They will find the best ones to post. Prepare for the worst; get additional photos and information for your protection. Don't request this information immediately; they'll think you're superficial. Remember, this is like a resume, you aren't going to send a resume with anything other than your best information. They're painting a picture of how great they are. You'll be doing the same. Understand this, and you'll be fine.

The pages that follow show examples of both good and bad girl profiles.

GOOD GIRL PROFILE

Note: On this profile, you'll see more wholesome photos and fewer risqué ones. You will find a lower number of "favorites" if she's new to the site. Remember, the higher the number, the more likely it is she's been on the site for a while. She typically will have a thorough write-up about what she's looking for without coming across as desperate. Her writing is direct and honest. She is writing from the heart, not to an audience.

<< Previous Photo   Next Photo >>

More of My Photos

In My Own Words:

My Job: Numbers Gal!

My Ethnicity: Italian American

My Religion: Agnostic

My Education: Associates in Management

Favorite Things: My dog Stanley

NewYorkMacy

Why Not!?

Active within 24 hours
33 - year old woman
NYC, New York, United States
Seeking men 29 - 40
Within 100 miles of NYC, New York

Interested In: Dating, Relationship

Relationship Status: Single
Have Kids: No
Want Kids: Yes
Ethnicity: Italian
Sign: Aquarius
Body Type: Athletic
Height: 5'6"
Religion: Agnostic
Profession: Account Representative
Smarts: Associates Degree
Do You Smoke: No
Do You Drink: Yes
Do You Drugs: No
Do You Have A Car: Yes

About Me:

I think online dating can be a good avenue and hoping for success. I don't want to meet any more guys at the bar scene and I'm looking for a nice guy. I'm an easy going girl who makes the most of all situations. I'm confident, very positive and a boat load of fun!

I want to put it out there, if you're on this site just to meet new people, only make friends, just hang out casually and get some booty please DON'T contact me. That is not what I'm looking for. Although I am not opposed to becoming friends with someone after dating and getting to know them. And I only respond to profiles with pics Esp. those that show your personality.

My main struggle with this e - dating thing is I know I always get a lot more from meeting someone face to face. Emailing back and forth for what seems like forever and never meeting just seems like a waste of time. Either way I think you learn so much more about a person face to face.

Do you Match?

See more like her

Add her to favorites

Forward her to a friend

Block from contact

Block from search

Report a concern ?

Click on a word to see more profiles with the same word. Click in a "+" to add that word to your profile.

MatchWords are a way of finding people with common interests. Add your own MatchWords to your profile and get in the excitement now!

Things You Are Both Looking For

Comparing your profile side by side is a quick way to calculate chemistry.

Yes	Age	Yes
Yes	Height	Yes
No	Eyes	Yes
Yes	Body	Yes
Yes	Smoking	No
Yes	Drinking	Yes

122 Favorites

144

BAD GIRL PROFILE

Note: On this profile, you'll see more risqué photos showing cleavage, partying, etc. You will also typically find a higher number of "favorites" (unless she is newer to the site). She's writing to an audience, not from the heart. There's little depth to her writeup, and she's making it clear she's about having "fun."

<< Previous Photo   Next Photo >>

More of My Photos

In My Own Words:

My Job: I'm very techy

My Ethnicity: Asian

My Religion: Agnostic

My Education: MBA

Favorite Things: Dallas Cowboys!

ArizonaAllie

Just Want To Have Fun!

Active within 24 hours
33 - year old woman
Phoenix, Arizona, United States
Seeking men 29 - 40
Within 500 miles of Phoenix, Arizona

Interested In: Dating, Relationship

Relationship Status: Separated
Have Kids: No
Want Kids: Yes
Ethnicity: Asian
Sign: Aquarius
Body Type: Athletic
Height: 5'3"
Religion: Agnostic
Profession: Management
Smarts: Masters Degree
Do You Smoke: No
Do You Drink: Yes
Do You Drugs: No
Do You Have A Car: Yes

About Me:

I am ready to be swept off my feet. I have been let down so many times. I question why I continue to let myself be hurt. If you are a cheater, keep on looking. I am always up for a challenge! I am a mommy's girl and love to party it up with my girls! I like to go out and enjoy a nice dinner every now and then. I am at the point in my life where I want to have as much fun as possible! I have been in relationships that have taken a lot of my time and am ready to get back to enjoying life!

Do you Match?

See more like her

Add her to favorites

Forward her to a friend

Block from contact

Block from search

Report a concern ?

Click on a word to see more profiles with the same word. Click in a "+" to add that word to your profile.

MatchWords are a way of finding people with common interests. Add your own MatchWords to your profile and get in the excitement now!

Things You Are Both Looking For

Comparing your profile side by side is a quick way to calculate chemistry.

Yes	Age	Yes
Yes	Height	Yes
Yes	Eyes	Yes
Yes	Body	Yes
Yes	Smoking	No
Yes	Drinking	Yes

412 Favorites

CHAPTER 29:
HOW TO ATTRACT YOUNGER WOMEN

"You must differentiate to be different and be different to be better."

—Joseph Michaels

To start, don't try to fit in and be hip. Don't try to mimic the way younger people talk or what you might hear on TV. These will show your age and make you appear as though you're trying too hard to fit in. Using what you believe to be the most current lingo will increase the gap between you and the woman you're pursuing. There's nothing worse than making a comment that's old and sounds tacky.

Many think men feel attracted to younger women strictly based upon their attraction to a younger-looking woman. However, some men feel younger when they're in the company of a younger woman and value this greatly. They see a younger woman and like the setup with kids not yet on their radar. With younger women, commitment isn't as much of an issue, while an older woman may want to have a family and view commitment as necessary quickly to have a family anytime in the near future.

Sure, some of the younger women may feel attracted to an older guy based on what he has, which is why it's important not to go overboard showing off all the "stuff" you have. Posting pictures of an item or two, such as a motorcycle, is fine; taking a picture of every item you have is a turn-off.

The following is an example of a picture that's more attractive to younger women. It's showing off, but it flies under the radar, and they don't view it as trying to fit in and attempting to be hip to make up for the age difference.

This next picture is an example that isn't going to be attractive to any women unless they're gold-diggers. This is not the attention you want. This picture makes the guy appear insecure and as if he's trying to take the focus off him and put it on his possessions.

It's important to identify the type of woman you want to attract. It's okay to acknowledge you're older and that you're not only comfortable with this, you're going to use this to your advantage. Spin the negative perception of being older to a positive.

You should come across as fun and highlight your adventurous side. When a guy adds something to differentiate himself from the others, such as boating, going out on wave runners, skydiving, etc. he'll be noticed. This is impressive and is sure to catch almost any young woman's eye. It also eliminates the negative age association.

DANIELLE
19 YEARS OLD
FRESHMEN COLLEGE STUDENT AT NEARBY UNIVERSITY

Danielle was a freshman in college. She happened to be online on a Friday night and bored.

Marcus: hey
Danielle: hey
Marcus: whats going on?
Danielle: nm, u?
Marcus: just turned on the fireplace...yeaaa!

Feedback—He's creating a desirable image since it was cold out and almost everyone can relate to the smell and warmth of a fireplace .

Marcus: that, the warmness to watch a movie, the smell..just awesome to be in from the cold cuddled up,lol

Feedback—He's using visual imagery again, creating a picture for her to see in her mind.

Danielle: lol bye yourself?
Danielle: by8
Danielle: by*

Feedback—She engages in the conversation with three quick replies in a row before Marcus can respond. She's excited. She expresses interest because she knows the answer is "yes."

Marcus: well...its normally better with someone;)
Feedback—He's playing into it.
Marcus: that's why wedding crashers is in...but it still feels weird watching movie alone...so I still haven't turned it on...

Feedback—Good use of a movie that almost everyone knows and likes.

Danielle: awww..thats so sad :(

Feedback—She didn't invite herself, so move on.

Marcus: lol
Marcus: so WHY aren't u doing anything tonight

Feedback—Because she's on her computer, he's inquiring to see if she has plans or not. He doesn't want to invest time with her now if he finds out she's going to be busy with other plans later.

Danielle: there is nothing going on, absolutely nothing.
Marcus: yea, some people are weak..
Danielle: yea and to make matters worse my roommate is a bore and its my birthday...

Feedback—She's frustrated because she has nothing to do, and she wants to do something to celebrate her birthday.

Marcus: You aren't doing ANYTHING for your birthday?
Danielle: no, there is nobody here to make plans with..

Feedback—She's making clear she wants to do something with somebody = your opening.

Marcus: that's no good
Danielle: I kno!
Danielle: nobody on the floor even knows!
Danielle: is wedding crashers a good movie?

Feedback—She's obviously interested, going back to the previous discussion in conversation. She's playing dumb; 99 percent of people her age have seen the movie.

Danielle: doesn't it have Owen Williams in it?

Feedback—Again playing dumb. Owen Williams? Funny girl, she said the wrong name intentionally.

Marcus: Wilson..yea
Danielle: Wilson
Danielle: that's right
Danielle: lol
Marcus: wedding crashers is GREAT
Danielle: I think I may have seen part of it
Marcus: it is one of the funniest movies ever, haha

Feedback—He makes her want to see it more.

Marcus: It makes me laugh thinking about some of it!
Marcus: well, if ur not doing anything tonight, ur more than welcome to come over and watch it...even wear sweatpants to get comfortable by the fire, lol

Feedback—He throws out an innocent invitation, followed by another descriptive image for her to picture.

Danielle: that sounds really good
Danielle: but, are you sure you don't want to watch it by yourself?

Feedback—She's playing the game now, too.

Marcus: youre right..

Feedback—Two can play that game. Win!

Marcus: lol
Marcus: I think it could be a little better with you;)
Danielle: oh yea?
Marcus: could be..
Marcus: that is if you aren't someone who gets annoying quick..then again its hard to keep my attention, lol

Feedback—He's keeping her on her toes.

149

Danielle: lol..i bet I could

Feedback—She's ready for the challenge.

Marcus: I don't know...I get bored easily, lol
Danielle: lol..well, I could try
Marcus: true true
Marcus: seriously you are going to LOVE wedding crashers..its one of the best movies, ha

Feedback—He's giving an assumption close: Not only will she watch the movie, but she'll love it, also.

Danielle: cool..except there is one problem
Danielle: I am a freshman and I can't have a car on campus..so I don't have a car here... Marcus: ouch
Marcus: so no car?
Danielle: nope
Danielle: that a bad thing?

Feedback—She knows he'll respond that he could pick her up .

Marcus: no worries
Marcus: what time u thinkin...
Marcus: I could pick u up if ur not some weirdo/stalker

Feedback—Again, a little jab for fun.

Marcus:;)
Danielle: lol
Danielle: im not a stalker
Marcus: well that's good
Marcus: so you excited?
Danielle: sry, im on the phone

Feedback—There was a long pause without a response from her (roughly three to four minutes). Rather than acting annoyed with a smart comment, he plays it cool and is patient. She could be testing him. Play it cool. If you lose your cool or act mean, your chances are slim to none.

Marcus: u wanna just text me or call me in a little bit
Danielle: im almost done
Danielle: im sry
Danielle: I am excited though
Marcus: lol
Danielle: are you?
Marcus: its wedding crashers..hell yea!

Feedback—It's obvious she's excited about meeting.

Marcus: well meeting you too... :P
Danielle: lol so what time were you thinking?
Marcus: its like 6 now..so like 730ish??
Danielle: sounds good
Marcus: alright what your number and where exactly do u live

Danielle: (phone number removed for privacy)
Danielle: (address removed for privacy)
Danielle: (city, zip code removed for privacy)
Danielle: easy enough?
Marcus: cant find high st online...
Danielle: do you know how to get to the McDonalds on High Street by the Chipotle?
Marcus: yes
Danielle: where are you coming from?
Marcus: say from the (information removed for privacy)
Danielle: okay go down 5th and turn right on high
Danielle: then you go to Rothstein Drive and turn right
Danielle: tad a! ur there
Marcus: haha
Marcus: u in a house, dorm or condo
Danielle: um...then mine is the first residence hall on (street name)
Danielle: the closest to front st
Marcus: whats it called
Danielle: (residence hall name)
Marcus: alright
Marcus: so u want to plan on 730 or would 8 work better

> *Feedback—He used an option close. He gave her two choices. He was fine with either choice, and she makes the "decision." Stealth precision.*

Danielle: 730 is fine
Marcus: sounds good..ill text u my number real quick so u have it;)
Danielle: okay
Marcus: let me know when u get it
Danielle: I got it
Marcus: alright...ill hit u up when im close...730 it is
Danielle: k...im gonna do some stuff around here
Danielle: ttyl
Marcus: see ya

- CASE STUDY -

JENNIFER
22 YEARS OLD
LIVED ONE STATE AWAY FROM MARCUS

Jennifer contacted Marcus via email. He saw she was from a neighboring state, so he didn't bother pursuing her. He said via email that she seemed "nice" though she was too far away. She seemed offended by his lack of interest and took this as a challenge. He could see she was proud of her current appearance since she had recently lost 65 pounds. Understanding she probably suffered from a lack of attention when she was heavier, Marcus used this as a focal point. Seeing that his lack of interest offended her, he used this to his benefit, as well. The following is the conversation with edits (protecting the phone numbers and actual locations).

Marcus: No offense, but you live in another state...don't wanna waste your time

Feedback—Being direct is sometimes the best approach.

Jennifer: Who says it would be a waste of time?

Feedback—She's appalled! She's probably never received a reply like that before.

Marcus: I think youre an attractive girl, though its not realistic...
Jennifer: Why is that
Marcus: Im not planning on driving to you..

Feedback—Laying down the law; setting realistic expectations.

Jennifer: Well, fine then..
Marcus: How far are you from me anyway?

Feedback—He's gauging distance to see whether she's interested enough that it's not a big deal. There's a chance she could be talked into driving to him!

Jennifer: Idk
Marcus: Type in from where youre at to this address (address removed for privacy)
Jennifer: 2hrs 12 min
Jennifer: That's not too bad
Jennifer: And you were acting like an ass
Marcus: Well still im not planning on driving a couple hours..

Feedback—Again laying down the law.

Marcus: Unless of course you are willing to road trip this way, haha ;)

Feedback—He's putting out a feeler out to see whether she'll bite. If yes, he would take her answer seriously. If no, he should respond he was just joking.

Jennifer: I was chatting with you to see if youre worth the drive, lol

Feedback—She's down. She just needs to feel connected on an emotional or humorous level since she already likes what she's seen.

Marcus: Maybe you can keep up
Jennifer: Lol
Marcus: Then again you may have another strike against you too..

Feedback—He's keeping her on her toes. She's trying to prove she can hang out with him.

Jennifer: Oh yea, whats that
Marcus: Youre only 22

Feedback—He's making the fact he's older benefit him.

Jennifer: And?
Marcus: Probably too young
Marcus: No offense, but you probably aren't old enough to keep up

Feedback—He knows this comment is sure to garner a response. Because he knows it's coming, he's in control and can plan for it.

Jennifer: Sounds like a challenge

Feedback—She's in.

Marcus: I guess you could look at it like that...
Marcus: So whats your story?
Jennifer: Story?
Marcus: Yea, whats your story, what do you do, enjoy and a little about you...
Jennifer: I work at the hyatt hotel downtown ..love working out, have lost 65 lbs

Feedback—Because she's obviously very proud of her weight loss, this is a hot button to gain insight into who she is and what comments will get the biggest reaction.

Marcus: Wow, that's impressive
Jennifer: Thanks
Marcus: You must feel good!

Feedback—Great response to appeal to her feelings since she's letting him know she's happy with her appearance. She's proud of herself and the hard work it took to get there.

Jennifer: I do, its an amazing feeling
Marcus: I like to workout too, what all do you do
Jennifer: I love to run, though the machines have helped me a lot with toning
Marcus: I must say...im slightly impressed :P

Feedback—He compliments her but keeps her on her toes by not overdoing it.

Jennifer: Funny
Marcus: So do you work a lot?

Feedback—He's gauging her availability without directly asking when she's free next.

Jennifer: Yea, but I have the next two days off

Feedback—Great news for you.

Marcus: Nice
Marcus: Well youre in luck

Feedback—Leading her to his next response, two steps ahead.

Jennifer: Why am I in luck

Feedback—He's clearly thinking ahead and has a response ready for her to ask this.

Marcus: I don't have to work tomorrow either

Feedback—He's using a comical assumption close, insinuating that because both are free, they'll hang out.

Jennifer: I don't get it

Feedback—Over her head. She is only 22.

Marcus: Its perfect for you to head this way tonight since we both don't work tomorrow

> *Feedback—He spells it out for her.*

Jennifer: What would we do?
Marcus: Well I could take you to chuck e cheeses and then if youre good you can have ice cream

> *Feedback—Joking about her age and establishing himself as a challenge to her.*

Jennifer: Youre mean
Marcus: Not really, though im good at pushing buttons.. ;)
Jennifer: Yea you know how to push my buttons alright
Marcus: So what do you have going on this evening?
Jennifer: Nothing...worked out earlier and got off early since I worked late yesterday, u?
Marcus: Just getting ready to hop in the shower then want to see the new Ben Stiller movie after dinner

> *Feedback—Mentioning hottest movie out to make her acknowledge she wants to see it too, creating another reasoning for her to come out!*

Jennifer: That movie looks sooo funny!
Marcus: I know, ben stiller is hilarious
Marcus: So what time are you planning on heading this way?

> *Feedback—Assumption close.*

Jennifer: Who said I was heading out that way?
Marcus: Well its 3:25 now, the movie starts at 755...that should give you plenty of time to get here, grab dinner then catch a movie!

> *Feedback—He's laying the groundwork by giving her details she can imagine in her mind.*

Jennifer: I haven't even talked to you...

> *Feedback—Stating she's willing but not comfortable enough yet.*

Marcus: (phone number removed for privacy) call me, im getting off here, gotta shower!
Jennifer: K

SUMMARY

She called, and they hit it off on the phone. She made the trip to his place, and they grabbed a bite to eat and headed back to his place.

- CASE STUDY -
BETH
19 YEARS OLD
STILL LIVED AT HOME

Beth was fresh out of high school. Jason had logged online at just the right time. She was a friend of his on Facebook after he added her randomly one day. He didn't know her, but he added her randomly because a suggested friend ad-listed her, and she was cute. She lived in a neighboring city. After logging on, he noticed she was online and sent her a message through Facebook Messenger. Seeing her online and being able to chat back in forth in real time was important since they were both in for the night and bored.

Beth: Hi
Jason: Whats up
Beth: Not much
Jason: In kinda early on a Saturday night eh
Beth: yea
Jason: Did you do anything fun tonight?
Beth: Went to a party..it was so boring

> *Feedback—She's expressing disappointment and showing she's looking for excitement.*

Jason: Youre telling me all parties aren't exciting with performers shooting fire from their mouth and tons of other cool things going on all at once??

> *Feedback—His humor's shining through, acknowledging most parties are a letdown, including the one she just left.*

Beth: Yep!
Jason: Haha
Beth: Well im just over it, ready to move on with the next part of my life

> *Feedback—She's expressing that she's over the immature party phase and is ready for mature guys.*

Jason: Yea..
Jason: Wait a second, youre 19?
Beth: Yea
Jason: You shouldn't be at a party – you can't drink!

> *Feedback—He's pointing out the obvious, while also making the comment in good fun.*

Beth: ....
Jason:?
Beth: Im a good girl and that's not my scene. I'm over it.
Jason: Got ya
Jason: Don't know if I believe you though..

> *Feedback—He's letting her know in a joking way, but he may be serious.*

Beth: Seriously

Jason: I believe you...

> *Feedback—Keeping her on her toes, by her being uncertain what to think he thinks.*

Jason: You seem believable, I just don't know if you can be trusted to hang out though

> *Feedback—Poking fun at her.*

Beth: Haha

Jason: So youre not denying it

> *Feedback—Poking fun at her.*

Beth: Haha

Jason: So where are you from

Beth: Austin

Jason: nice

Beth: you?

Jason: Fort Worth

Beth: Cool cool

Jason: So do you still live there or just from there?

Beth: No live in Fort Worth now, downtown

Jason: Really?

Beth: Yep

Jason: Wow...youre only 5 mins from me, im right by the mall, if you know where that is

> *Feedback—He's acknowledging how close she is and names a common place she's sure to know. The familiarity increases her comfort as well.*

Beth: Yea, im like 2 mins from there!

Jason: Haha, crazy

Jason: Well if you weren't a creeper, I would say you could come hang out if youre that bored...though I don't want a creeper to know where I live..

> *Feedback—He extends an invitation in a noncommittal way so that he can judge her response. If she says no, he can go with the "I was just joking" angle. "I don't even know you!"*

Beth: Yea I may stalk you

Jason: Promise?

> *Feedback—Humor! Good stuff!*

Beth: Hahahahaha

Jason: Well, im getting ready to hop in the shower as I just came home from playing soccer..you can call me if you want (phone number removed for privacy)...I trust you wont abuse it though;)

> *Feedback—He creates a mental picture for her with saying he's "just getting home from playing soccer," insinuating he's in good shape. He ended it with leaving the ball in her court and followed by closing with a poke of fun so it's not too serious an invitation.*

Beth: Ok

SUMMARY

She called, they talked for a few, laughed at one of the outrageous signs a homeless panhandler has at a main exit ramp and developed good rapport. There were no definite plans, but she accepted his invitation to hang out. When she arrived, he showed her some of the paintings he had since she was the artsy type, and they had fun.

IN CLOSING

It's important to understand and identify where the fine line is when poking fun and flirting so that you don't come off as offensive. If you come across as too strong and offensive, it will turn a woman defensive and against you. You must determine her type. Remember, it's always better to play it safe than be sorry. Stay attentive to her body language when you're with her in person. Online, you must gauge her typed responses and be extra-cautious. Remember, however the woman sees you is how she feels about you.

CHAPTER 30:

HOW TO ATTRACT OLDER WOMEN

"Older women are beautiful lovers. Older women, they understand.
I've been around some, and I have discovered that older women
know just how to please a man."

—Singer Ronnie McDowell from the song "Older Women"

In this chapter, you'll to learn how to attract older women. If you're a younger guy who's generally attracted to older women, this chapter is for you.

Simply review the following case studies; they'll dissect actual chats that resulted in meeting older women. Mason was in each of these case studies. I interviewed Mason, who is in his 20s but attracting women ranging in age from their late 20s into their early 50s.

He has even gone as far as having a woman drive from a couple of states away to enjoy his company. This was not a lower-tier woman, either, fellas. She pulled up in her new S Class Mercedes and was a career woman who had her act together.

The following are summaries and actual excerpts from chats he had. It's important for you to understand that women don't hit their sexual prime until they're in their mid-30s to 40s. [26] For this reason, older women may be more direct and spontaneous in their approach.

- CASE STUDY -

REBECCA
41 YEARS OLD
PARALEGAL
LIVED TWO STATES AWAY

This case study features a very respectable and conservative 41-year-old business woman named Rebecca. She has sole custody of one child. Her ex-husband has visitation rights every other weekend. They divorced roughly two years. She has limited time for herself because of her hectic work schedule and because her child was younger and demanded a great deal of her time. Because her personal time was limited and because she had the need for companionship, she joined Plenty of Fish to get back into the dating scene. She was from a smaller town, and her selection was scarce. Furthermore, in her small town everyone knew everyone and all their business. She lived roughly six hours away from Mason.

Usually, this distance would be too far to ever consider pursuing someone. It was late at night, and Mason was clicking on various profiles, which led to a random email to her, and she responded. Rather than sending multiple emails back and forth, after the third email exchange, they exchanged messenger names to chat further. Below are condensed parts of their chats over the messenger, which turned into three separate chats over roughly two weeks. After a long second chat and an unbelievable amount of talk and game, he convinced her to make the more than six-hour drive to his place. As you can see, he did this by making it seem as a simple drive and understating the significance of such a drive. By making it less of a big deal, it was not a big deal to her.

Conversation excerpts ranging from before they met to the conversation leading to them meeting

Mason: Im surprised youre still up!

> *Feedback—Quick introductory comment insinuating he thought she would be in bed at that time of night. The little poke of fun is sure to warrant a response.*

Rebecca: Well, hello to you too!
Rebecca: What do you mean surprised?
Mason: At your age, I would assume you'd be in bed by 9;)

> *Feedback—Innocent poke about her age and her being older, nice!*

Rebecca: haha very funny
Mason: so what are you up to?
Rebecca: just got done putting _____ to bed
Mason: so youre finally able to have a little "me" time eh?

> *Feedback—Hitting a hot button as any parent always yearns for "me" time.*

Rebecca: exactly, though doesn't happen nearly enough

> *Feedback—Stating she feels she doesn't have enough time for herself. This is a common feeling.*

Mason: true, though it is important to enjoy life too, lifes too short...

> *Feedback—Everyone agrees with this comment and this is meant to reaffirm that she needs to have some fun and time for herself. This is reiterating how she already said she feels.*

Mason: eventually youre going to have to take a day off to go get a massage at a spa, or have a girls night to a weekend getaway!

> *Feedback—Appealing to what she needs and doing it in a nice way by giving suggestions she's sure to like.*

Rebecca: that sounds soooo nice!

> *Feedback—Agreement from her. Her guard is slowly coming down = progress.*

159

Mason: don't talk abou tit, be about it!
Mason: *about *it, hahaha
Rebecca: lol
Mason: so today I got 2 weirdos who messaged me on pof...one was 55 & another was married!

> *Feedback—Great conversation starter and something everyone experiences who is dating online: weird people. This opens the gates for rapport and shared experiences. It also sets up rapport with you both agreeing there's more bad than good online, ugly than pretty, annoying than fascinating; well played.*

Rebecca: there was a man who was at least 400 pounds trying to hit on me by telling me he would love to take me and my son down to his condo in Florida for a weekend trip
Mason: sounds like a free trip...so when ya going?

> *Feedback—Joking.*

Rebecca: yea right!
Mason: you're not going!?
Rebecca: absolutely not
Mason: not a fan of florida?

> *Feedback—Sense of humor shining through!*

Rebecca: you're funny

> *Feedback—She's eating it up.*

Rebecca: first off the guy is over 400 lbs and more importantly I don't even know him!
Mason: oh the cry for attention by desperate men on the internet!
Mason: its nice to see you are looking for someone you are attracted too;)

> *Feedback—Acknowledging that you're picky too, and the wink is icing on the cake.*

Rebecca: of course
Mason: fyi Im not going to fly you to florida...
> *Feedback—Light humor, establishing differences between him and other guys.*
Rebecca: haha, you could only be so lucky
Mason: I doubt you could keep up...

> *Feedback—Fun poke about her being older though not meant to offend her.*

Rebecca: hey, its 11:30 now and I am just fine..
Rebecca: I am definitely not past my time, in fact I feel like im just hitting my stride

> *Feedback—She's taking the conversation elsewhere.*

Mason: nice, they say women don't hit their sexual peak til 35-40...
Mason: it seems like older women know their body better and what they like

Feedback—Very universal comment—with age and experience everyone becomes more comfortable in all aspects of work, life, and play.

Rebecca: big difference in me now vs me at 25
Mason: im 22 though

Feedback—Creating a challenge for her.

Rebecca: listen honey, I have years of experience
Rebecca: you should be the one worrying about keeping up
Mason: is that so...whats your favorite position

Feedback—Quick transition and gauging if she's comfortable to talk about this.

Rebecca: I like being on top

Feedback—Oh,, yes, she is.

Mason: oh, so you like being in control...makes sense

Feedback—Stating the obvious creates further agreement. Women can control more on top.

Mason: communication is huge, you have to know what the other person likes to make it a good experience for both parties

Feedback—No brainer, very agreeable. All women love this because it makes the man seem more engaged with her and satisfying her, too.

Rebecca: absolutely, my ex didn't care if I was able to enjoy it

Feedback—Expressing past frustrations gives insight on what to avoid and what she wants.

Mason: that's terrible...it all comes down to communication

Feedback—Generic, yet very relatable comment, perfection!

Rebecca: man, I cant believe I am talking to you about this
Feedback—Out of character for her though she is engaged enough to keep going.
Mason: its not a big deal, I cant believe I am either..but its been awhile so I guess it may has been a little while for you too...

Feedback—Lessening the "wow factor" of this discussion, while letting her know he's clean since he hasn't been sexually active for awhile; both make her feel more comfortable.

Mason: you said you don't have your son this weekend right?

Feedback—Using information given earlier to sell her on making the trip. Well done.

Rebecca: nope
Mason: you should make a trip this way...
Rebecca: whats your address?
Mason: can I trust giving it to you!?!

Feedback—Poking in an innocent, fun way to lighten the mood; it's important to shift from the previous conversation. The reality is he couldn't screw her now, and he doesn't want to end it awkwardly, so best to keep the mood light.

Mason: (address removed for privacy)
Rebecca: your like 6 hours and 21 minutes away
Mason: not spontaneous, eh?

Feedback—Little jab as she mentioned she doesn't have time for herself and reflecting on how she has lost her sense of adventure with responsibility and age. She has this on her mind now and will justify to herself making the trip.

Rebecca: oh I am..but that's a hike
Mason: excuses, excuses
Rebecca: ill see what I can do
Mason: lets plan on Saturday night

Feedback—Date is set. Conversation has not ended, though there's no reason to continue on. Go out on top and end the conversation.

Rebecca: alright, I will let you know
Mason: well get some rest Mrs. Robinson, I have to get a little too, busy day tomorrow
Rebecca: sweet dreams
Mason: you too, night
Rebecca: night
Mason: confidence is attractive

Feedback—Good response to get back on the same page and give indirect compliment.

Rebecca: so I'm told 😊
Mason: if u were to hang out with me....u would be calm...u would be relaxed and would forget about the everyday stresses of life...u would be excited for a movie by the fireplace...wine..dinner

Feedback—Change of subject matter to get her mind off being offended. Creation of a mental picture and hitting hot buttons such as having no stress and being relaxed, along with fireplace and wine creates a very desirable setting.

Rebecca: sure...I like wine too.

Feedback—She's in tune with the idea.

Rebecca: you cooking?

Feedback—She's showing she can joke a little too, great progress and paramount for success.

Rebecca: I'm just trying to understand the meaning of what you're saying, it takes a lil while when you start chatting with someone..

162

Feedback—Showing she's still trying to understand him and get his humor down.

Rebecca: 'and tone is everything...emails, etc, really suck

Feedback—True. It's hard to gauge tone online. We use this to our advantage in this book.

Mason: youre thinking too much

Feedback—Generic genius comment as everyone does and will admit to thinking too much; this will help someone let down her guard in acknowledgement.

Mason: settle down...every time I have looked for that it NEVER happens...so I try to go in open minded and if something develops I am NOT opposed, also I prefer not to use the term settle as it equates to settling, which I don't want to do :o)

Feedback—Generic comment, perfect!

Mason: with you.....i like the idea of us being in different areas to where it would be open and free if we were to hang out and not run into people each other would know

Feedback—Creating a desirable feature to getting together in secrecy and a getaway from home.

Rebecca: How long have you been online seeking someone for potential?
Mason: ive been on pof for a little while now and have not been impressed, actually creeped out

Feedback—Very relatable and nice humor to follow.

Mason: i have not hung out with a woman of your age and am somewhat attracted to it..
Mason: like the idea of if we were to hang out there would be no talk and it would be totally comfortable being from different areas and not knowing any of the same people

Feedback—Hitting her hot button as she obviously didn't like being the talk of the town when she was divorced (stated earlier in the conversation). The details make the difference.

Mason: u do think too much..i like your appearance, confidence and maturity
Mason: think of it as a vacation from reality...a weekend getaway

Feedback—Creating a desirable set up.

Rebecca: weekend getaway sounds like "friends with benefits"....but can't say haven't considered

Feedback—She's open to it.

Mason: see i dont know anything on you and have nothing but good to say....so getting away from that could be good for you...

Feedback—Telling her he isn't going to judge her. All women are afraid of judgment.

Mason: friends with benefits...havent crossed that bridge...but havent negated that either....

Rebecca: no, cuz I am wanting a meaningful partner to spend time with ...one who wants that just as much....the guys on here have so many mixed signals, I WON'T PUT UP WITH IT...

> *Feedback—Speaking with her heart in wanting a meaningful partner, though acting on desires when considering his proposition.*

Mason: realistically im 22 and you are 41, we are hours apart

> *Feedback—Straight shooter. Clarifying the reality of the situation and how unlikely it is that anything would develop due to the age difference.*

Rebecca: yes, and sounds like you want laid

> *Feedback—He has made himself clear.*

Mason: im upfront and a straight shooter...no need for lies and people getting hurt

> *Feedback—A response that any woman is sure to appreciate since no one likes to be lied to or misled, and every woman has experienced this. Additionally, by being honest she's sure to be on the same page and realistic in her expectations.*

Rebecca: no need for bullshit doesn't mean you forget about getting to know someone, for real, to see if meeting again is worth your time..I had a guy bolt when he learned I figured him out that he was not going to wait for sex, so he left...via text. can you believe THAT shit

> *Feedback—Showing she's a good girl and letting it be known that she has standards.*

Mason: however telling some stranger the truth at the beginning is going to scare most guys

Rebecca: what do you mean with that?

> *Feedback—She wants to know more about the ins and outs of dating since she's been out so long. Great opportunity to be nice and helpful to someone who deserves the help.*

Mason: dont want to scare someone off, esp if first date....okay to let them know where you stand and want out of life -leave out past relationships, exes, negativity

Rebecca: are you sharing with me the reasons I am probably scaring them off? I have been told the tenacity and assertiveness coupled with intelligence is what is doing it..I am too serious about this whole thing as its important..which is why I have thought that POF is not a place for me.

> *Feedback—She acknowledges friends have told her various things about what she's doing wrong, and she's reaching out for help.*

Mason: agree, POF is a joke, which is why im going to delete my acct

Rebecca: so, give me your opinion, what am I doing that is ineffective?

> *Feedback—Reaching for help.*

164

Mason: 1) being on pof, 2) online dating is a good concept...but what it is guys and girls picking ppl they would hang out with to make "bad" decisions or good depending on your perspective

Feedback—Confirming her reservations and thoughts of what she has experienced so far.

Mason: i gotta get going here shortly....but u need to protect yourself from the bad guys w/o scaring off the possible matches for u too

Feedback—He senses no meeting will take place immediately, so creates an escape route.

Mason: ok. I appreciate your standards..we may just get along.
Mason: First thing Rebecca is to BE HAPPY

Feedback—Generic, though brilliant response.

Rebecca: Well thank you. I AM happy, and will remain that way if I am single for the next 40 years....As asked by thousands....why I am still single...it's because I KNOW WHAT I'M WORTH. Thanks Mason...Have a good workout.

Feedback—Made her feel great.

Mason: EXACTLY
Mason: youve been through a lot. we all have. its what makes us who we are.
Mason: dont short sell yourself though too...nothing is EVER perfect

Feedback—Wise words from a wise man.

Rebecca: And you only know the last two months worth. that's okay. POF is a real joke, which is why I am going to give up on it too

Feedback—Great! Sooner she deletes account, less competition for you.

Rebecca: so what made you contact me anyway?

Feedback—She's still wanting and yearning for his approval so she feels she's good enough for him.

Mason: disagree, we ALL want to live happily ever after and find someone right for us

Feedback—Generic comment, nicely used.

Mason: i found u attractive, typically not attracted to older women and was intrigued...
Rebecca: oh, sorry, not that I forgot, but wondered if anything else came to mind after chatting with me....... enough said.

Feedback—She wants comments regarding something more than just looks, and he missed the boat on this.

Rebecca: you're still here aren't you?

Feedback—She's hooked and is really clicking in the conversation and the tone with him.

Mason: so what time are you heading this way?

Feedback—Assumptive close.

Mason: something tells me we might not get along...
Mason: u see im always right...and im afraid you wouldn't see it that way:P

Feedback—Witty response that almost anyone will smirk over. Very nice work.

Rebecca: I may give you a run for the money....I tend to be right mostly.....
Mason: haha, i like ur style

Feedback—Direct compliment as the two of them are in sync and hitting it off!

Rebecca: Are you cooking or picking a movie, as you said in that conversation was long time ago

Feedback—Confirmation she knows what they planned from prior communications.

Mason: you are out of control
Rebecca: who MMMMMMEEEEEEEEEEEEEEEEEEEEEE

Feedback—She's excited, all capital letters.

Mason: u have to meet ur atty anyway and still need a shower

Feedback—Pulling back the invitation to see if she's legit for tonight.

Rebecca: yes, I give him until 7 and I'm busy I'll tell him

Feedback—She's in for tonight!

Rebecca: you're cool, even at your age

Feedback—She's learning.

Mason: haha real smooth GIRL
Rebecca: of course I was too at that age
Mason: 123-456-7890 dont abuse it Rebecca

Feedback—Nice jab.

Rebecca: or, that could still be that you're alone............ooh that wasn't nice...sorry
Rebecca: cuz you repeated "getting off" thought you were in the gutter again
Rebecca: sorry
Mason: apology not accepted

Feedback—Hysterical.

Mason: text me if u feel the need...not to be confused with desire...texting can get costly:D

Feedback—Humor shining through.

- CASE STUDY -

TONYA
37 YEARS OLD

SCHOOL TEACHER
LIVED ON THE OPPOSITE SIDE OF TOWN

Tonya was a 34-year-old Catholic school teacher. She had two kids and had been divorced for a little less than a year from her high school sweetheart. She volunteered at the school often and babysat during the summers. Tonya had just joined Match, and this was the first site she had joined.

The following conversation shows how to initiate a conversation after exchanging information from the dating site directly. In the conversation, you can identify how to interact with humor and keep progressing toward hanging out. With each conversation you participate in, you should have a plan and a goal.

The goal of Mason's conversation with Tonya was to make contact, catch her attention, establish mutual interest, and get her number. He could sense that, because she had kids who lived with her, getting her to meet the first night was not realistic. Getting her phone number was important since he had kept an eye on his messenger contact list because she rarely got online. After getting the number, he established rapport and comfort to have her come over to his place.

Mason: So you do get on here!

> *Feedback—Quick way to initiate conversation as he has been on at various times, and she has not.*

Tonya: yea, not often though!
Mason: I respect that, someone who has a life
Tonya: yep, how are you?
Mason: im great, just got home from the gym

> *Feedback—Letting her know he has a life and doesn't just sit online, while giving her imagery of him being in shape.*

Tonya: I need to go to the gym
Mason: its crazy how much better of a mood I am in if I get some exercise, not only feel better physically but mentally

> *Feedback—Very relatable comment for anyone who works out.*

Tonya: when I run it feels like I get a break from life
Mason: that's a good way to put it
Mason: I have a 6:30 meeting to get to, so can only be on here for a few, but wanted to at least say hi

> *Feedback—Putting a limit on his time, showing he has a life and his time is in demand by others. Plus, this is useful as an excuse to get out of the conversation if it isn't going anywhere.*

Tonya: thanks
Mason: no problem, cute picture

> *Feedback—A compliment geared toward a picture of her with Mickey Mouse that she had on her profile.*

Tonya: picture?
Mason: yea the one on your profile, when you must have been at Disney

Feedback—Remember, the details make the difference.

Tonya: oh, I forgot I had that there..its an older pic, I just didn't have anything new I liked

Mason: so youre saying you look nothing like the picture now? Uh oh...youre not one of those people who look nothing like your pictures...please don't tell me your 500 lbs and have a moustache!

Feedback—Joking though serious since she stated it was an older picture, and he wanted to clarify the picture is not that old and that it isn't that different from her today.

Tonya: no no no, just a couple year old pic
Mason: ok, whew
Tonya: haha, I had you worried
Mason: ive heard stories!

Feedback—Letting her know he has reservations, as she most likely does too.

Tonya: youre not 500 lbs are you?

Feedback—She's joking, too.

Mason: yes.

Feedback—Funny.

Tonya: lol, youre not shallow are you;)
Mason: Of course!

Feedback—Showing a little sarcasm.

Mason: youre not shallow?
Tonya: haha, no

Feedback—She's trying to save face.

Mason: so you would like me if I were 500 lbs?

Feedback—He's calling her bluff.

Tonya: no, lol
Mason: hahaha, I like that you have standards and know somewhat what you like :P
Tonya: that I do
Mason: well hey im going to get off here..whats your cell, ill text you sometime

Feedback—Establishing his time is valuable and in demand, though he's interested in her and does not want to chance waiting for the next time she "might" sign online.

Mason: that is, if you know what texting is...at 34 yrs old I know you are on the borderline of knowing whats in and whats not :P

Feedback—Quick jab to keep her on her toes which makes asking for her number less serious by adding humor.

Tonya: (phone number removed for privacy)

Mason: cool, (phone number removed for privacy)
Mason: now don't abuse it!

> *Feedback—Fun poke.*

Tonya: you don't either!
Mason: no promises;)

> *Feedback—Funnier poke.*

Mason: see ya

- CASE STUDY -

RACHEL
35 YEARS OLD
DENTAL ASSISTANT
DROVE FROM AN HOUR AWAY

Mason met Rachel on Plenty of Fish. She was newer to the site, and he contacted her the same day she signed up. They exchanged emails over two consecutive days before catching her on Messenger. This was the first conversation Mason had with Rachel on Messenger, and he convinced her about why she should come over. Part of his approach was understanding that missing out is very powerful, and no one likes to miss out.

Mason overcame any questions and doubt Rachel had by reassuring her how nice it would be and by establishing how she was missing out if she didn't come. People are more driven by what they could miss than what they could have. At the end of the conversation, he even gave her his phone number. He did this to make her feel more comfortable. When she called him, all he had to do was be nice and normal, and he eliminated all her fears; she was more comfortable in making the trip to see him. All the while on the phone, he continually reassured her about what they were going to do and how she's making the right decision while building the excitement up to get her more excited.

Mason: hello!
Rachel: Hi
Mason: youre up late!

> *Feedback—Simple and friendly icebreaker.*

Rachel: yea, cant sleep
Mason: me either..its crazy the time I want to get some sleep I cant
Rachel: I just had a busy day and tough for me to unwind, im nowhere near tired
Mason: looks like you have the energy of a 21 year old..who would have thought;)

> *Feedback—Little jab about her age without crossing the line and offending her or turning her off completely.*

Rachel: I do at times...
Mason: nice

169

Rachel: so why are you still up??

Feedback—Multiple question marks shows she's engaged in the conversation and excited.

Mason: well, I was thinking about watching meet the parents, though cant drum up myself to go watch a movie by myself, kinda pathetic..

Feedback—Meet the Parents is a classic movie that many have watched. This led to her viually picturing scenes from the movie. The comment about watching it by himself is easily relatable and leaves the door open for her to invite herself.

Rachel: that's not pathetic

Mason: lol, well the fireplace is on, its really nice and toasty in here, smells great, though having all that and watching a movie solo is too much for me...that's where I draw a line!

Feedback—Creating visual imagery of what it's like there so that she can picture it and engage her senses to create her possible reality if she were to go over.

Rachel: I understand, it is a great movie!

Mason: agreed!

Mason: it is hilarious! Possibly one of the funniest movies!

Rachel: im going to have to watch it, ive heard a lot of great things about it and haven't seen it since it was at the movie theatres..

Mason: well if I knew you weren't crazy I would invite you over for a movie...but if I invited you, youd know where I live and that could be bad news if you were...

Feedback—Quick poke with invitation for her to come over though covered with humor to make the offer not too direct/serious.

Rachel: very true

Mason: so youre admitting to it:P

Feedback—Joke confirming she's not denying she's "bad news."

Rachel: of course not

Mason: well I appreciate the sincerity I can sense, haha

Rachel: haha

Mason: in all seriousness if you are in fact wide awake and are up for it, come over in comfy clothes and we'll watch meet the parents and keep the fire going..i think I have some popcorn too

Feedback—Creating a no-pressure, direct invitation for her to come over while painting a picture for her describing a relaxed atmosphere that's very unassuming. Telling her to wear comfy clothes eliminates any excuse she could create about not wanting to have to get ready and thoughts of having to dress up and paint her face.

Rachel: where do you live again?

Mason: Deerfield

Mason: you?

Rachel: Simeon

Mason: so you're not that far! If you are going to be up, might as well

Feedback—Making distance seem less because she's driving, and he's working hard to sell her on making the trip since it isn't that bad.

Rachel: it says youre like 50 minutes away
Mason: 50? No way, if youre just passed (Exit 56) then maybe 25 tops!

Feedback—Discounting potential excuse to not come by making trip seem shorter for her.

Rachel: are you sure?
Mason: yes, I drive by there all the time and have family there
Mason: if you go 10 below the speed limit in traffic it could take 50 minutes

Feedback—Poking fun at her driving and referencing that times on websites are for people who drive at a very conservative speed.

Mason: then again seeing how its 2:02 am right now, I seriously doubt youre going to run into traffic :P

Feedback—Further poking.

Rachel: idk..
Mason: just put on some shorts, a sweater and plan on a little cuddling if youre lucky!

Feedback—Pushing without pressuring her.

Rachel: that does sound good
Mason: the fireplace smells amazing too

Feedback—Appealing to her senses and how she'd feel; the fireplace makes you think of warmth, plus there's the image of the flames and the smell of the wood burning. When she thinks of this, she literally puts herself in the frame of being there, which is his goal. If she pictures herself there, half the battle is already over; she's more comfortable because it doesn't seem foreign to her mind.

Rachel: alright, whats your number? I at least want to call you...

Feedback—She wants reassurance everything is going to be okay and looks for any reason not to make the trip. Her brain is telling her no, though her desire is telling her yes.

Mason: (123) 456 7890, I trust you wont stalk!

Feedback—Quick joke to lighten the mood before she's going to call him.

Rachel: haha, ill call you in a few
Mason: alright, talk to ya in a few

JACKIE
28 YEARS OLD
NURSE LOCAL WOMAN
EXPERIENCED IN ONLINE DATING

It was late on a Friday night when they were chatting. She had been on various sites before, so she understood how most guys operated. Understanding this, Mason knew he had to be different and better to keep her attention since she has most likely encountered a lot of guys contacting her.

Mason established comfort and likeability Friday and Saturday; the timing was never perfect, though things ended up working out nicely. He put feelers out (noted in the conversations with feedback) and could tell quickly she wasn't having it. He also understood this wasn't her first online experience, so he had to avoid being too pushy and let the conversation play out based on both of their comfort levels.

CONVERSATION #1

Friday

Mason: hey you
Jackie: hey
Mason: what are you doing in on a Friday night?
Jackie: just got in early, met with a couple friends for dinner and drinks
Mason: sounds exciting
Jackie: so hows match working for you?
Mason: it's kinda weird to be honest

Feedback—Relatable topic to establish rapport and show his personality.

Jackie: yea, youll have that
Mason: I cant believe the things some of these older women say and some of the pictures, im speechless!

Feedback—Continuation of establishing rapport and showing humor.

Jackie: sounds like you've found some lookers:D
Mason: not good lookers, but definitely lookers
Mason: the hardest images to rid is the 65 year old wearing little to nothing, asking me if I liked what I saw, hahahaha

Feedback—Showing his sense of humor and giving her something to find humor in, too.

Jackie: oh my
Mason: yea...hard to forget those two inparticular..lol
Mason: what about you? Any new messages or pictures worth talking about?

Feedback—Trying to get her to open up to establish rapport more quickly and let her guard down.

Jackie: hmm..let me think

Mason: sounds dangerous;)

Feedback—Quick comment to keep her on her toes. Insinuating that her thinking sounds to be a dangerous thing!

Jackie: it can be!

Jackie: I haven't had anything recently, other than the typical we should hang out...I would treat you so good, blah blah blah

Feedback—She is telling him what she has experienced thus far and what has not worked.

Mason: I forgot you have experience in this online dating world

Jackie: that I do...these guys are so easy to read and see exactly what they are after, whether its to get laid (98% of the time) or to actually date and find someone

Feedback—Tired of people who present no challenge or originality.

Mason: interesting

Jackie: It really just cracks me up to see these guys think their game is so tight when it is beyond pathetic

Mason: ill be honest...I just want sex

Feedback—Humor and sarcasm

Jackie: lol

Mason: no seriously, I like sex

Feedback—Humor and sarcasm again

Jackie: haha, me too

Feedback—She likes the humor.

Mason: well im glad we at least have something in common..i cant say I know how you feel as I have only received 2 messages from guys and my polite response was, read the profile ONLY interested in women

Feedback—Showing the two of them are similar, while lightening the sex discussion with funny facts about two guys messaging him, even though he's straight.

Jackie: are you serious??

Mason: yea, one actually sent a rather vulgar message...I blocked him 😊

Feedback—She would appreciate this because women must get familiar with the blocking system on any site; there are so many people who can't take a hint or "no" for an answer.

Mason: that block button has quickly become my best friend, haha

Jackie: that's hysterical, I use it all the time!

Feedback—Point in case.

Mason: well, its getting late and I have wanted to watch Mission Impossible 8,465 since it was released on Netflex

Jackie: Mission Impossible 8,465 – haha. They definitely keep making them...

Mason: I would invite you over to watch it, though Im still new to this whole thing and you are a seasoned vet...don't know if it's a good idea..unless you prove through a thorough background check report that you are "normal"

> *Feedback—Extending invitation though not in a serious manner, only serious if she accepts.*

Jackie: I am nothing close to normal, just amazing :P have fun with your movie, we will have to chat again soon!

> *Feedback—Essentially saying no without being blunt. This ending is encouraging since she flirted with the smiley face with tongue sticking out and mentioning talking again soon. He's laid the groundwork laid— to be continued.*

Mason: sounds like a plan
 Jackie: seeya!
Mason: later

CONVERSATION #2

Saturday

Mason: You can't use the same excuse of drinks with the girls tonight and being tired miss!

> *Feedback—Initiating the conversation as he just caught her online and helping her recall he was the one she had a conversation with the day before. Mentioning being out with the girls shows he listened to her the previous night.*

Jackie: who you calling miss
Mason: this girl who is like an internet pirauna preying on younger men;)

> *Feedback—Hilarious!*

Jackie: hahahha
Mason: ohhh misses jonesssss!
Jackie: youre a comedian tonight
Mason: im a man on many talents, one of which is an amazing sense of humor:D

> *Feedback—Showing his personality with a witty response.*

Jackie: so what are you doing in?
Mason: friends are lame, im one of the single ones and everyone else is doing couples night

> *Feedback—Everyone can relate to this and has been there at some point.*

Jackie: been there done that
Mason: yea, half of them don't even want to be in relationships, its comical
Jackie: doesn't sound good
Mason: some are better than the others
Jackie: I don't get it, why be in a relationship if youre not happy

Feedback—Not intended to be a real question.

Jackie: 1) comfort 2) avoiding change 3) insecure

Feedback—Capitalizing on a great opportunity by answering with generic, acceptable answers. Most women would appreciate and see eye-to-eye with his comments.

Jackie: damn, look at you mr shrink!
Mason: I prefer dr. shrink
Jackie: lol
Mason: so every time I watch wedding crashers I come across something I must have missed the 500 other times I have watched it!

Jackie: that movie is better each time
Mason: yea, "Hey mom, can you get me some meatloaf? Mom the meatloaf!"
Jackie: chazz rhinehold
Mason: im livin the dream the man!

Feedback—Quoting the movie, lighthearted humor.

Jackie: "Grief is natures most powerful aphrodisiac"

Feedback—She knows it too = connection!

Mason: "I always knew I was never going to be a professional bull rider, but that's not why I did it"

Feedback—More.

Jackie: "Please don't take a turn to negative town"

Feedback—And more.

Mason: "So how's my protégé? Jeremy, believe it or not, is getting married! What? What an idiot! What a loser! Good! Good! More for you and me."

Feedback—Further connecting.

Jackie: I love that movie, I would so watch it right now, lol

Feedback—She's telling him she wants to watch it and to invite her over.

Mason: hell, I just watched it last night and I would watch it again!
Jackie: that's why its one of the bests
Mason: don't let this get to your head, but I like your sense of humor

Feedback—Compliment though powered by a little jab to keep her on her toes and make her smile.

Jackie: I was just thinking the same thing
Mason: It's because we both like seeing our own sense of humor in someone else, haha
Jackie: that's exactly what it is
Mason: so what part of town do you live on again
Jackie: I'm about ten minutes outside of downtown
Mason: got ya, which way
Jackie: what about you

Mason: Im a little outside of town as well, _____?
Jackie: youre not that far
Mason: are you serious?
Jackie: no.....yes, haha :P
Mason: hell I am literally a couple miles down
Mason: different city names, yet 3 miles apart...what are the odds
Jackie: crazy, right
Mason: alright, so its 10:15 now, the movie is is roughly an hour and a half...if you get here by 1030, we would be done by 12;)

Feedback—Eliminating the need for her to think by giving her the details; it makes sense for her to simply show up and hang out.

Jackie: you think just because we both have nothing going on on a Saturday night, that im just going to come over to your house?

Feedback—Trying to be snarky since she's not sold yet.

Mason: no, I think that since we both want to watch wedding crashers, my place is really toasty with the fireplace on and I have the dvd in the dvd player, so I already am steps ahead of you...and you and I are both talking online again and wedding crashers could be playing while were talking and reciting lines back and forth

Feedback—Nice use of "you and I" because it's assumptive. By saying that, it grouped both of them together as being on the same page and on the same team through a mutual understanding. Selling her in detail with instances as to how much she has enjoyed talking to him thus far and giving visual imagery to create a sense of comfort to show he's not a stranger.

Jackie: what if I like to watch my movies in peace and quiet

Feedback—She just jabbed him now.

Mason: that's not going to be possible tonight

Feedback—Two can play this game.

Jackie: lol I always talk during movies anyway!
Mason: I have a feeling we will be reciting lines and repeating what we hear through half of the movie, haha

Feedback—Smooth and most accurate after discussion with her where both recited lines back and forth.

Jackie: I could sooo see that happening
Mason: alright see you here in about 15, (address removed for privacy)

Feedback—Closing deal with assumptive close as she now needs to just head his way.

Jackie: see ya in a few

In Closing

Whether a woman is a few years older or quite a bit older, innocent little comments regarding their being too old to keep up combined with innocent pokes can create intrigue on their end. The intrigue garners responses because they don't typically encounter this type of banter since most men would never dare try it. This is what makes your approach that much more effective, so be thankful for these other guys. Making innocent comments and pokes about their age, stereotypes about where they're from, jokes about their background, pictures they've posted, responses they may have made in a chat, or things they do for fun or in general are all angles.

It's also common for a woman to respond in a way that she feels insulted and takes it personally. You must convey you're joking in good fun and aren't being malicious. As you can tell from the various conversations previously detailed, for every comment made you can typically predict the response that will follow. It's vital to understand the personality type of the person you're corresponding with. When you understand this, you can understand how they'll reply. This is Sales 101. Combine the understanding of the personality type with your ability to predict future responses, and dating will become simple for you. You can then plan, so you'll always be one step ahead.

CHAPTER 31:

THE IMPORTANCE OF AVOIDING THE "FRIEND" LABEL

"A guy's worst nightmare, when interested in a girl, is being called her friend."

—James Donaldson

A friend is the man who may have a crush on the woman but has never made his interest known to her. When and if the friend does come forward to express their "feelings," it's too late or too awkward at that time. Making the transition from friend to potential mate is a very tough transition to accomplish. The best, far more effective route is the route that can end in friendship but starts as two people having an interest in dating, hanging out, and potentially more.

Being friends first and then making your feelings known will 99 percent of the time create discomfort for her. This, then, forever ruins the friendship because it creates awkwardness.

There are however, instances where friends with benefits can work. Though, rarely do these people begin as friends, hang out, have sex, and then go back to being friends. The reason for this is that at least one of the parties has feelings involved, and most of the time jealousy will be present. In the movie *No Strings Attached*, starring Natalie Portman and Ashton Kutcher, the couple had an understanding that their relationship was strictly sexual. Both parties agreed to the arrangement because both were busy and not looking for a relationship. However, feelings developed as they spend increasingly more time with one another, and neither party likes seeing the other with other people, even though they aren't in a relationship. The moral of this story is to limit the time you spend with someone if you're looking to keep it strictly sexual. If you go out to a movie, eat together, or even hang around with the person doing nothing, you're entering relationship territory with the expectation to "make it official" soon thereafter.

Friends with benefits rarely end on a positive note. Eventually, one or both people develop feelings, and it ends poorly. However, the opportunity to be friends with benefits is greater when you're not friends to start.

Now, I'm not telling you to make the move the second you meet a woman to avoid the "friend" label or to be overly direct with your conversation; both can be turn-offs.

What I am telling you is to be selective about the sites you're on. One of the benefits of being on an app or dating site is that when you're talking to someone online, the facts are out in the open. You both are on a "dating" site, not a making "friends" site. With that already established, you must make a move to differentiate yourself from the "friend" category.

Guys don't want to hang out with women as "just friends" unless they feel no attraction to the woman or value the friendship more than their hormones. **Note**: Very seldom will a man choose a friendship over his animal extinct. Most men simply don't know how to. Guys have penises, and penises don't decipher between friends and possibilities unless attraction is missing.

SECTION V:

RECONGNIZING AND USING THE MODES OF COMMUNICATION

CHAPTER 32:

READING BETWEEN THE LINES OF EMAIL

"For a successful technology, reality must take precedence over public relations, for nature cannot be fooled."

—Richard P. Feynman

I recommend creating a new email address strictly for online dating and apps you join. Create an email address that does *not* include your name. For instance, if Joe.Johnson@gmail.com sends an email, there's no secret about who wrote it. Additionally, all information sent in that email now directly connects to Joe Johnson (could be you).

With search engines such as Google and social networking sites such as Facebook, one can access a person's background, family history, friends, pictures, place of employment, address, and more, simply by having a part of your name to use in a search. For these reasons, it's important to protect your identity because all these women are, in fact, strangers.

You should strive to have a sense of anonymity. I strongly suggest making a separation between your personal life and your online dating life.

Also avoid giving any pertinent information in relation to your job, nickname, location, or places you frequent in your conversations. These are easy and often overlooked details that could put you in an undesirable situation.

Instead, use a creative email address for security. For example: PoolShark@gmail.com is more anonymous. You should also delete any email history in case a friend, ex-girlfriend, or someone else accesses your email and uses the information against you. This isn't about hiding anything, it's about your personal information being just that—your personal information.

Correspondence via email used to be the most common way to interact. Now, everyone uses messaging services and texts. However, some still do use email, primarily the ones who aren't allowed to access their phones at work during the day. This chapter is for your interaction with them since using email has become a lost art.

Just as you may want to get her number to get her attention away from all the competition on app or site messaging service, email does the same. Plus, email can be not as personal for a woman to give up. By establishing direct contact with her email address away from the sites where her inbox is probably full of messages, you increase the odds of meeting and getting her to want to meet you.

The following are a couple of case studies with detailed analysis on the good and bad features of each of these two emails. Review the comments since they give reasoning why the highlighted parts are a positive or negative in terms of delivery. Note the email addresses used for these case studies are not the actual email addresses (for privacy purposes), though they are similar enough to give you insight into the reasoning and explanations through the detailed feedback below.

- CASE STUDY -

To: ILoveMyYorkies@gmail.com
From: SmithM33@msn.com
Subject: Can't wait to talk to you again :D

Have a great day! I am really looking forward to talking to you again, I woke up this morning thinking about you and you seem like a great girl. I will be on my email throughout the day, if you're bored and want to email back, I will get online tonight around 9 to chat some more!

Max

DETAILED ANALYSIS

"SmithM33@msn.com"

Feedback—I recommend never having your actual name or initials in your email address; it reveals too much personal information. Additionally, this chat is traceable directly to you with your name revealed and any significance with the number 33, which was his football number.

"Can't wait to talk to you again :D"

Feedback—Cute, though way too anxious. You want her to send this to you.

"Have a great day"

Feedback—Not bad, innocent, and nice without coming across as desperate.

"I am really looking forward to talking to you again"

Feedback—Not necessary to put yourself out there that much. You want her to think you're still a challenge, not already falling for her.

"I woke up this morning thinking about you and you seem like a great girl."

Feedback—Too much information. This will turn her off, and saying she seems like a great girl is not accurate; you don't know her, and she will most likely see through this.

"I will be on my email throughout the day, if you're bored and want to email back"

> *Feedback—Telling her you essentially have nothing to do, and you'll be waiting for her. This lessens your value and attractiveness by being so readily available.*

"I will get online tonight around 9 to chat some more!"

> *Feedback—If you didn't have the previous sentence, you could have simply tried to line up a future chat time or exchange information. However, having this with the previous sentence is too much and seems way overanxious.*

- CASE STUDY -

> To: M_RN_317@aol.com
> From: RoofDoctor@gmail.com
> Subject: Interested?
>
> So what did you think of the chat last night? Did you have fun? I sure did, you were really easy to talk to and not only do you look beautiful, you seem to be smart too. I like that ;) I have a pretty busy day today, driving from where I live by Northwest College to the jobs I have today should make for a tiring day. I guess it could be worst, right? Luckily, our work phone is (123) 456-ROOF, as it keeps us busy. So do you enjoy your job as a nurse? Which hospital do you work at? I could only imagine how sexy you look in your little nurse outfit..text me at (123) 456-7890 and we can message back and forth throughout the day.
>
> Talk to you soon sweetie,
> Justin

DETAILED ANALYSIS

"RoofDoctor@gmail.com"

> *Feedback—Not a discreet enough email address. This email is very specific and associates you with working on roofs.*

"Interested?"

> *Feedback—Putting the ball in her court and is seeking her approval to decide if anything will follow.*

"So, what did you think of the chat last night?"

> *Feedback—Again, seeking her approval. Showing a lack of confidence.*

"not only do you look beautiful, you seem to be smart too"

Feedback—Instantly aligning your email with ones she receives from every other guy (with no true game) telling her how great she is through compliments.

"Luckily, our work phone is (123) 456 – ROOF, as it keeps us busy."

Feedback—Not necessary or smart; you're giving her too much information to know everything about you. By simply searching that number online she can identify the company you work for, its location, and so much more.

"So do you enjoy your job as a nurse?"

Feedback—This doesn't fit in the tone of the email and would be better to have during a chat, on the phone or in person.

"Which hospital do you work at?"

Feedback—Can make her feel you're asking too much personal information, which can lead her to feel uncomfortable and classify you as creepy since she doesn't know you yet.

"I could only imagine how sexy you look in your little nurse outfit."

Feedback—Not appropriate, could result in an instant turn-off and a cut off any communication moving forward.

"text me at (123) 456-7890 and we can message back and forth throughout the day."

Feedback—Last act of desperation. Coming across as way too available and demonstrating little to no value.

"Talk to you soon sweetie"

Feedback—Giving her an intimate nickname when you're getting to know her is a little odd and most women will be uncomfortable with you doing so.

CHAPTER 33:
UNDERSTANDING INSTANT MESSENGERS ONLINE AND ON APPS

"Show off your own style and uniqueness to stand out. That's the advice I'd give to people getting started online now."

-Conor Maynard

Text messages are to a phone call what direct/instant messages are to an email. They're less personal, quicker, and more convenient. There's an element of excitement with messengers. Anticipation builds while waiting to receive a response, with some showing at the bottom of the screen when the other party is typing back to you. Women like to be pursued, which holds true for app and dating site messengers, as well.

The appearance of messengers varies from app to app and site to site, though below is a quick example of a more detailed version of a chat box, which you may see out there. Others will be far simpler without a photo and detailed information. You must use any information you can to gain an advantage and the more information provided, the more you have to work with.

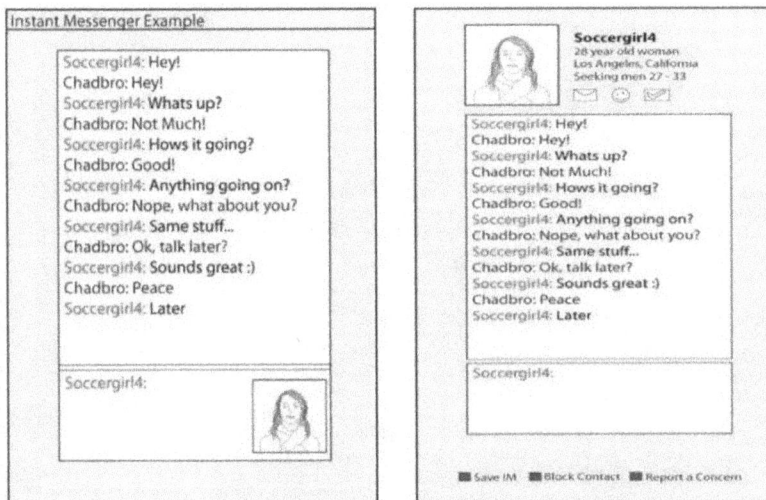

Instant Messenger Example

Soccergirl4: Hey!
Chadbro: Hey!
Soccergirl4: Whats up?
Chadbro: Not Much!
Soccergirl4: Hows it going?
Chadbro: Good!
Soccergirl4: Anything going on?
Chadbro: Nope, what about you?
Soccergirl4: Same stuff...
Chadbro: Ok, talk later?
Soccergirl4: Sounds great :)
Chadbro: Peace
Soccergirl4: Later

Soccergirl4:

Soccergirl4
28 year old woman
Los Angeles, California
Seeking men 27 - 33

Soccergirl4: Hey!
Chadbro: Hey!
Soccergirl4: Whats up?
Chadbro: Not Much!
Soccergirl4: Hows it going?
Chadbro: Good!
Soccergirl4: Anything going on?
Chadbro: Nope, what about you?
Soccergirl4: Same stuff...
Chadbro: Ok, talk later?
Soccergirl4: Sounds great :)
Chadbro: Peace
Soccergirl4: Later

Soccergirl4:

Save IM   Block Contact   Report a Concern

As displayed above, some messengers have more options than others. As you see at the top of the following examples, you can click on the envelope icon to send an email, the wink icon to send a wink, or the check icon to mark them as a favorite. There are also buttons that allow one to save the instant messenger conversation, to block the person, and to report a concern to the site's administrator (if you're chatting within the app of the site's messenger). Being able to block people is a very valuable feature because you'll want to block those who are creeping you out.

It's equally important to know you can save your conversation (all fonts and photos sent). Be sure to keep this in mind because you're, in a sense, being monitored, and this is an example of how something you say can be used against you if it's bad, so be smart. Delete any chats before exiting the conversation box; there's no reason you should save these or have the settings set to save these conversations.

CHAPTER 34:

HOW TO CHAT

"Just be you, but better."

- Molly Napolitano

The secret to learning how to chat is learning how to break the ice to eliminate the initial nerves or awkwardness and ultimately create small talk about common items. If this is your first time or you have very little confidence, Practice on women who are from distant cities or women you have no interest in. The reason for this is that you have absolutely nothing to lose and everything to gain with real-time interaction.

This is your opportunity to learn how women respond to comments you make, stories you tell, and more. Whether it is or isn't your first time on a site or app, the reality is that you talk to random people every day. You can use this interaction to benefit other parts of your life, as well, business, friendships, etc.

You may comment on how nice of a day it is, how close a game it was last night, how expensive gas is, how ready you are for a vacation, or how tired you are of the current weather. Inevitably, one statement leads to a conversation, and that can carry on into many other conversations, a name, number, or date.

Chatting is no different. Just imagine the person on the other end of the computer as someone you already have enough information on (based on her profile) to establish common interests and develop a good rapport with. From what I've seen, most women will feel a connection and forget all about everything they included in their profile, which gave you a cheat sheet on what their likes and interests are.

Also, be sure not to be too available. I know this sounds crazy, but it works because your perceived value increases if you're not too readily available or if you're the one who needs to get offline because you have plans.

In *The Rules: Time-tested Secrets for Capturing the Heart of Mr. Right* by Ellen Fein
and Sherrie Schneider, the authors hit the nail on the head. The book advises you to always end the phone call first to seem "busy." [27] You want to appear busy so that any woman you may be talking to will think you're sought after by others, which, in turn, increases your desirability and value.

Once you're comfortable with chatting, you should have a goal with each conversation. Below is an outline of questions to ask yourself; it will help you stay on track if you're trying to get to know a woman, learn more about her, or hang out.

SEVEN INTERNAL QUESTIONS TO STAY FOCUSED

1. What is my goal in this chat? To get a number? Meet up? Planting a seed for next time?
2. What is the other person expecting out of this chat?
3. What are the potential results from this chat?
4. How will I handle the various responses she could give?
5. What is my exit strategy if I'm not interested?
6. Where will I suggest meeting if we agree to meet at a public place?
7. What's my game plan to get out of a dead-end conversation?

All effective communicators use this process.

Some train themselves to use this process intentionally, while others do it naturally since they're more experienced. Remember, each experience is one you learn something from. It's essential that you organize your various conversations to review. You should review these for the following reasons a) to see how the interaction progressed after stepping away from the chat to analyze the overall interaction b) to identify anything you could have done better c) to see her responses and determine whether you had any missed openings for you to know in the future and d) to improve your overall communication skills for more effective chatting. The benefit you have in texting or messaging is you have time to think; on the phone it is much quicker. Use this to your advantage.

Whether it's using a messenger, text messages, or another service, you may be messaging more than one woman at a time, so you must keep track of each conversation. You also must keep the progress moving forward with each woman. Luckily for you, most messengers, including text messaging, allow you to scroll up to see the previous messages. This is a nice bailout for you, though paying attention is vital since scrolling back up delays the interaction and doesn't bode well for any progress or connection. In Chapter 35, you'll learn the secret to making progress in a chat.

CHAPTER 35:

THE SECRET TO MAKING PROGRESS IN A CHAT

"A good plan, violently executed now, is better than a perfect plan next week."

—US General George S. Patton

Let's begin by understanding there isn't just one secret method to having a successful chat. There are several secrets to experiencing good results with women. I've noticed in the various interviews and case studies conducted that many of the successful "chatters" have taken very similar paths. After analyzing these paths, I created a list of the seven most powerful steps that have created their predictable results. These steps are comfort, humor, interests, attraction, timing, synchronization, and potential regret. This chapter details these steps with tips for further understanding so you can successfully implement.

1.) **Comfort**: Establish comfort by being less aggressive and more laid back. Being too aggressive will turn most women off immediately. You need to differentiate yourself from others. Remember, a random woman won't want to meet you unless she feels somewhat comfortable with you when talking, texting, or chatting. With the advances in technology, women meet to a lot of strange people. She's going to be screening and dealing with a lot of players and weirdos. This is your time to show you're not that guy. You must create a sense of normalcy. Creating a feeling of normalcy will help her let her guard down to feel comfortable with you. You should be a "breath of fresh air" from most guys she meets online.

Tip *Find out what she enjoys and let her talk. Ask open-ended questions regarding interests on her profile. She will, in turn, feel comfortable talking to you because she's talking about what she likes. If she's comfortable with you, the percentages of meeting increase drastically.*

2.) **Humor**: Marilyn Monroe once said, "If you can make a girl laugh, you can make her do anything." What else is there to say? Get her to laugh. To identify her personality and humor type, start by dissecting her profile. Figure out her likes and dislikes and pay close attention to her responses when talking to her. Also, pay attention to what she finds funny and any random comments she may make. Women tell us what they like, we just have to listen.

For example, she may have said, "My boss's breath smells horrible, and he's such a close talker." This is your opening to connect and voice a similar experience you had with the subject at hand. You can even add how bad breath is a pet peeve of yours, so you chew gum or mints after each meal, and you always have some in your pocket, if not for you, but for others. Once you can identify her sense of humor, you'll understand whether she's very proper with a reserved sense of humor, a dry sense of humor, or a provocative sense of humor. From there, you can connect with her style. In doing so, she'll find herself much more attracted to you, comfortable, and interested. The reason for this is that she'll see so many of her own characteristics in you. We like people who are like us.

3.) **Interests**: People tend to gravitate to those who are like them. It's how most of us are programmed. For example, my best friend and I hit it off because we have very similar senses of humor and share many interests, including favorite vacation spots and sport teams. We both liked that we saw ourselves in the other person. So, if a woman feels the two of you have many common characteristics and interests, she'll feel drawn to you. Because you now have this knowledge, it's important to identify the woman's interests. The easiest way to find out this information is by viewing everything listed on her profile and your typed conversations. One overlooked but great resource is any photos she posted; they may show her interests (pictures at a sporting event, hobbies she has, etc.). Additionally, just ask her questions and listen. Her answers will typically give you a very clear picture about what her interests are and what she enjoys in life.

Tip *Because you can do preliminary research on a woman by viewing her profile, you should always be a step ahead. This is an obvious, yet underused advantage most guys have. This is comparable to a cheat sheet before the big test. You can use this information by reflecting on an experience or mentioning a story regarding a subject you know would pique her interest. An example of this is, "I'm so tired, I just got back from going on a 10-mile bike ride." If she lists cycling as an interest in her profile or has a picture of herself on a bike, you're obviously appealing to her immediately. Your goal is to use the information she provides you to connect further.*

4.) **Attraction**: Attraction involves much more than physical looks. It can also stem from comfort, humor, and interests. If you're on the same page with a woman by creating comfort, connecting through common interests, and interacting on a level where she sees you have a good sense of humor, you're good as gold. This will give you an advantage over other guys, including those who may be better looking. These are often undervalued aspects of attraction, though I assure you they're equally, if not more, valuable than looks alone.

Tip *Practice makes perfect. When joining a site and initiating conversations with different women, message women you have no interest in. The reason for this is to familiarize yourself with the site, its features, and figure out what works and what doesn't. By messaging a woman you don't have any interest in allows you to focus on your approach and interaction and prevents emotion or nerves from distracting you. As you practice more, you'll become better, and your confidence will create momentum. That momentum will lead to becoming more attractive to women. Make it a top priority to identify her type of humor and interests. From* there, connect with her, and through trial and error decide which techniques work best for you. The more experiences you have, the more natural you'll become.

5.) **Timing**: Timing is everything. If the woman has had a horrible day, she may not talk to you and may not want to talk to anyone. You will have to judge the timing based on how the conversation progresses, her availability, the amount of time between responses, and the number of distractions she may or may not have (work, kids, roommates, responsibilities, etc.). Be sure to look for comments she might make such as, "I am so bored," "I wish I could go (insert place)," and "I am the only single one of all my friends." I consider these comments to be reaching out for help. She wants an invitation for you to occupy her time and excite her.

Tip *Be patient and let the woman dictate her timing. We both know you'll change your schedule around if she's ready and willing to hang out. If the timing is right, less is more. The only way things will not progress is if you act out or turn her off in some way. Essentially, you should do your best not to mess up the most powerful thing on your side—timing.*

6.) **Synchronization**: Synchronizing is being on the same page. In online dating sites and through messages, it's the closest thing to mirroring in person. Determine the mood of the woman you're communicating with. If she's upset, be upset, too. If she's upset about a speeding ticket, feed her fire by mentioning a speeding ticket you had in your past and tell her why it still ticks you off with a little humor. This will lighten her upset mood and provide a needed distraction, while also connecting with her. Once it's obvious you're in-sync, simply move the conversation to whatever you choose. If you're not in-sync, it will seem as though you aren't on the same page, and you don't understand where she's coming from.

Tip *To successfully synchronize with another person, you must focus on understanding exactly what they're feeling and thinking. The only way to do that is to put yourself in their shoes and to listen and understand. You must pay close attention to details in the conversation as well as to body language to successfully synchronize. (Body language applies if you're with her in person or if you're on a video chat.). Self-discipline is vital for your success and thorough understanding. Once you have practiced this, it will become second nature to you in any situation. You must discipline yourself to successfully synchronize.*

7.) **Potential Regret**: Last, the feeling she could be missing out on something, referred to as potential regret, is often more powerful than the actual benefit. Regardless of the decision a woman makes, the other option immediately looks better to her before she makes the choice because of the feeling of commitment. There's a reason cell phone companies advertise having no contracts (commitment), that dealers offer the option to lease a car instead of purchasing one (commitment), and why companies offer a money-back guarantee (protection from making the wrong choice). It's common that the closer someone gets to their wedding day, the more likely they are to get cold feet and express doubt about being with one person the rest of their life. Hence the reason men and women tend to act out on their last chance before the "forever commitment of marriage" known as their bachelor and bachelorette parties. It's human nature for someone to overthink and second-guess any major decision.

Doubt amplifies when a person has time to think. The longer someone has had time to think about the concept of commitment; the more their reality will feel compromised. The only way you can combat this is to avoid making her feel any sense of commitment. For instance, if you want to hang out with her, never ask her directly. Rather, joke with her about hanging out as it lessens any feeling of commitment. If she's interested, you were being serious and want her to come over. If she's not interested, then you were, of course, just joking.

If she's on the fence, you can always drop in the word because. For example, "I'm thinking of staying in tonight to watch a movie because the weather is miserable." Using because is important. As Warren Buffet's partner, the great Charles Munger, has said, "If you always tell people why, they'll understand it better, they'll consider it more important, and they'll be more likely to comply." If you don't insert because into your vocabulary, you'll come across as a dictator.

You must be careful not to pour it on too heavily, though. If you do, expect buyer's remorse or her losing interest altogether. If you want her to be a repeat customer, avoid this. Remember, if the salesman pushes too hard, they often push the customer away. The same is true with meeting women online. Describe a setting that hits all her senses to help her paint a picture in her mind and imagine what it would be like being there with you.

Tell her what movie you'd watch, how the surround sound makes you feel as if you're in the theater, the temperature of the room with the fireplace, the smell of popcorn, the taste of wine, and the toasty feeling you have with the down blanket covering you to keep warm on this cold winter night.

The last sentence of the previous paragraph hits on all five senses: seeing, hearing, smelling, tasting, and touching. This is a textbook example of how you can create a mental picture to help the woman envision how it would feel to be there. Once she's already pictured herself there in her mind, more than half the battle of getting her physically there is won.

Tip *The more descriptive you are about how great whatever it is the two of you will do is, the more effective it is. The clearer the mental picture is, the greater she'll desire it. The reason for this is mentally she's already pictured herself there and created a pleasurable time. This works to your advantage because she's even more intrigued to experience the real thing.*

Bear in mind that by engaging the senses, you become more interesting to listen to, and if people are attentive and interested, they're much more likely to get your point. [28] That info came from a book analyzing how some of the most successful lawyers use techniques to influence the courtroom to do what they want.

As Tim Ferriss, the author of The 4-Hour Workweek said, "It is easier to pick up the one perfect 10 at the bar than the five 8's." [29] Don't be afraid to go after someone you may not normally pursue. The worst-case scenario is that it will be live practice and you'll learn; the best-case scenario is that you'll succeed. You never know until you go for it. One thing is for certain, you have no chance if you don't take one.

CHAPTER 36:

THE BEAUTY OF TEXT MESSAGING

"It has become appallingly obvious that our technology has exceeded our humanity."

—Albert Einstein

First and most important, imperative for you to understand you should never, ever send nude or compromising photos of yourself through any mode of communication. If you do, you should expect trouble, blackmail, and humiliation. Frankly, absolutely nothing positive can come from sending any nude or compromising photos to anyone, period.

Despite the beliefs that certain apps delete these photos once sent, there are always ways around it. For instance, a screenshot is a quick and easy way to save anything sent.

The following is a thorough analysis of what messaging is and how it works. I've simplified this information into an easy-to understand format that will make it easy for a novice to understand the ins and outs, but also for the most tech-savvy to learn more tips and insights. My goal is for you to use text messaging to your advantage.

Text messaging has become the main type of communication for individuals and businesses alike. Bulk text messages to cell phones have replaced telemarketing. Rather than calling to see if someone wants to hang out or to finalize plans, people send text messages, instead. Texts have even replaced emailing back and forth. Talking on the phone 20 times a day is a thing of the past. People now text message; it's much easier and more efficient.

Text messaging is efficient because it enables you to multi-task while still having a conversation. Text messages are also a great way to communicate with different women at the same time. One of the main benefits to text messaging is that it gives you the time to digest the text and respond to each message without feeling caught off-guard by a question or comment. As we both know, while talking on the phone, a woman can question whether you were paying attention to the specific details of a conversation or question, wondering whether you heard what she just said. If you weren't paying attention, it will be difficult to respond correctly.

However, with text messages you can view prior texts, which eliminates the issue of not paying attention. It makes it difficult for a woman to ask, "What did I just say?" or "Are you listening to me?" and that should bring a smile to your face since the conversation is in writing, and we both know you always pay 100 percent attention to what she's talking about.

Another nice thing about text messages is that thelabels are names you've given people in your phonebook. This helps organize the conversations you may be having with more than one woman at once. It's acceptable when texting not to use proper punctuation or complete sentences, as long as it appears understandable.

TOP EIGHT REASONS PEOPLE TEXT MESSAGE

1. **Convenience**: You can text message in an environment where it may be too loud to talk on the phone or where you can't talk on the phone, such as a work environment.
2. **Multi-Tasking**: You can send texts to multiple people at a time without having to focus 100 percent on one conversation.
3. **Options**: You can choose not to reply to a text message, or you can respond at your leisure. You don't have to worry about being stuck on the phone when you don't have the time or when you frankly don't want to be on the phone.
4. **Connection**: Talking on the phone is much more personal. Texting is not as personal; you're communicating via messages and not actually hearing someone's voice on the other end.
5. **Fun**: People tend to enjoy texting, and it makes them feel popular.
6. **Speed**: Communicating in real time allows for instant responses and saves you time.
7. **Avoidance**: You can avoid being stuck talking to someone for an extended period. We all cringe when certain people call us. They either talk too much or have nothing else to do than talk on the phone.
8. **Time**: In a world where everyone is so busy, getting answers and being able to communicate as effectively as possible is more important than ever.

TOP FOUR THINGS TO AVOID WHEN TEXT MESSAGING

1. **Capital Letters**: Capital letters are the equivalent of yelling, going overboard, and being dramatic. Use all lowercase letters or use a capital letter to begin a sentence when communicating via text.
2. **Pictures**: Be careful with pictures, especially nude or racy ones; someone can use them against you, and they can spread rapidly. These can easily spread to others without your knowledge since there's no way to track your message to see whether someone forwarded it or sent it to others.
3. **Racy Jokes**: These may seem funny to you, but if things fall through, someone can use them against you as blackmail, and they can trace them to your number. Topics to avoid include race, handicaps, politics, and religion.
4. **Sexual Thoughts**: These could be in good fun, but they'll be in writing, someone can potentially use them against you. Do not send anything you wouldn't want your boss or mother to see.

TOP SEVEN ABBREVIATIONS DEFINED

1. **lol**—laugh out loud (something is funny)
2. **hmu**—hit me up
3. **ex**—for example
4. **idk**—I don't know
5. **wtf**—what the fuck
6. **nmu**—not much u
7. **haha**—laughing

How soon should I respond?

As Ellen Fein and Sherrie Schneider say in their book *All the Rules: Time-tested Secrets for Capturing the Heart of Mr. Right*, "Don't think playing games is bad. Sometimes game playing is good." That quote came directly from a book written for women on how to get a man. [30]

Even if you're a punctual person (answering and responding quickly) who dislikes mind games, you must play the "game."

It's vital for you to understand that the more accessible you are, the less desirable you are. We know the things that are difficult to get are typically better than those that are easy to get. [31] If a woman takes five minutes to respond to a text, you take six. You can direct the conversation without their noticing. You don't respond to her immediately unless she has responded immediately to you. This is leading and is necessary to get equal respect established.

Some people consider these games, and yes, they are, in fact, mind games. Your goal is to win these "games," and directing a conversation by leading is at times necessary for her to value your presence. If she doesn't answer when you call, be too busy to answer when she calls. Think about it—the women you don't like continually call you after you ignore them or turn them away, right? If you answer immediately on the first call or even so much as the first ring, it spells out desperation. You're not desperate, you're in control, and you must believe that.

- CASE STUDY -

WITTY TEXTS WITH HIGH SUCCESS RATES!

<u>You</u>: I know I know....
<u>Her</u>: you know what?
<u>You</u>: you can't stop thinking about me;)

Rationale: This is an excuse to contact her. If she weren't thinking about you then, she most certainly is now. This also is sure to bring a smirk to her face since she has most likely never received a text like this before. The wink is like a smile, semi-serious, yet totally kidding.

<u>You</u>: ps when we meet later, I prefer chocolate
<u>Her</u>: chocolate??
<u>You</u>: chocolate over flowers as flowers typically don't last as long;)

Her: haha, right..

Rationale: You're creating an easy-going atmosphere for later. You're also laying the groundwork so she'll feel you're worth hanging out with because you can keep her on her toes, and you have a good personality. Predictability and failure to keep a woman on her toes are where most guys fail. The chances of her bringing flowers or chocolate are slim to none. However, if she does, that's great. The goal is not to get either, but rather to show you're different from other guys she's met and are much more intriguing.

You: is there any way you could wear the same outfit you have in your profile picture, so I recognize you if you look nothing like your picture :P
Her: I look just like my picture.
You: well, you wearing those ridiculous polka dot earrings would make it a little easier to pick you out...
Her: you're funny
You: im glad you noticed!

Rationale: You're poking fun at her, while confirming you're still on without directly asking if she's still going to meet you later. If you were to ask directly whether she's still on for later and hasn't forgotten, you might come across as desperate or uncertain if she's into you. Handling her this way makes you come across as the complete opposite and confident. Poking fun with the earring comment showed your wit, and she knows she's going to have to be on her A game.

CHAPTER 37:

THE ART OF THE PHONE CALL

"Attraction can be enhanced, both in person and through technology."

—Michael Anthony

Today, the first thing that enters your mind when you think of your phone may be the features it has such as searching the internet, apps, email access, GPS, camera, and more. One of the most forgotten aspects of the phone is the original purpose of making calls. The phone call is a lost art.

While it should be your last resort for communication because it's the least efficient and requires the most attention, it can be extremely effective. In this chapter, you'll learn there's an art to mastering the phone call. I personally am not a fan of talking on the phone. I use my phone for more than 5,000 minutes some months and look forward to the day I can get rid of it, but I understand a phone is necessary for certain things. I use other technologies to make the time I talk on the phone as efficient as possible, and you should do the same.

It's important to screen all your phone calls to avoid being unprepared. You can do this by saving her number in your phone as soon as you receive it so you know it's her when she calls. If you receive a "private" call, never answer.

Though talking on the phone requires more attention to detail and attentiveness, it's also one of the greatest opportunities since most women want to talk on the phone before hanging out.

When answering your phone, put a smile on your face, and she'll sense it through the phone. This may seem tacky, but Fortune 500 companies have their employees trained using this technique. Use your smart phone or tape recorder to record your voice with a frown and record it with a smile on your face and notice the difference.

When you're talking on the phone with a woman, ignore any text messages your phone may be receiving because she'll hear you pushing buttons on the other end. This will turn her off and ruin all the work you've previously done. Plus, it's rude.

The phone conversation should be very easy-going and light. The goal is to have a smooth yet fun talk. You want her to enjoy talking to you. Talk to her about the good parts of your life and your day, not the bad. Talking about the bad will simply portray you as a negative person. Being in a good mood and having good energy is contagious, and she will eat it up. Ask her questions, and she'll engage further since nearly all women love to talk about themselves. Also, listen with the intent to understand. As Stephen Covey points out in the ultra-successful book *The 7 Habits of Highly Effective People,* far too many people listen with the intent to reply, not understand. [32]

If you listen with the intent to understand, you can understand their perspective and will continue to elevate your knowledge of women to unforeseen levels.

- CASE STUDY -

There was a study I saw in which one man spoke with 10 different women for five minutes each about themselves. Once the study was complete, the researchers surveyed the women, and nine of the 10 found him to be charming while only one did not. You may ask, what made him charming? His instructions were to nod, ask questions about the woman he was with, and smile while listening attentively. He followed those instructions for nine of the 10 women. With the other woman, his instruction was to talk about himself and make it his goal for her to get to know him better. From these results, you can conclude that people enjoy talking about themselves and find others who listen to be charming.

I know what you're thinking, "Well that's great, but I don't want to be stuck on the phone for an hour listening." I don't blame you, and neither would I! That is exactly why you must be or appear to be busy to keep the conversation length to a minimum. For instance, if she calls you at 4:54 p.m., inform her you have a 5:15 p.m. conference call and that you took her call because you wanted to talk to her; this way, you're letting her know you only have so many minutes to talk. This will twist the reality from you not wanting to talk on the phone to her believing you made the time to take her call while still having your own life.

If the conversation is going well, it's equally important to end it before it becomes repetitive and yields awkward silence. For example, if you two are really hitting it off, be sure to appear busy and tell her you will talk to her later. This prevents you from committing to calling her and keeps her yearning for more of your attention.

FROM PHONE CALL TO FACETIME

"Videotaping anything does not sound like a good idea."

—Jordan Banck

With video chat, Snapchat, Skype and FaceTime and many others so easily accessible on your phone, many move quickly from a phone call or skip the phone call altogether. Don't use these services if you're not 100 percent certain you can behave well in the conversation because more bad than good can come from your being on video.

However, if a woman is willing to get on FaceTime, Skype or any other video app, this can be a positive for you. It allows you to see what she truly looks like, not the selected photos she wants to have everyone see, which are sure to be most favorable to her.

Be cautious about using any of these outlets and getting caught up in the moment, if you're attracted to her. Do not make inappropriate comments, compliments or ask her to do anything such as stand up or show you her body.

Men tend to think they have nothing to lose when they're hiding behind a phone or tablet. You do. Make your actions PG-rated; there's no need to cross the line to get a woman to want you; it typically does the opposite. My rule of thumb is to ask yourself if this is something you would be comfortable with your mother seeing.

SECTION VI:

COMMUNICATING EFFECTIVELY

CHAPTER 38:

THE DECISION-MAKING PROCESS EXPLAINED

*"If economists were any good at business, they would be rich men
instead of advisers to rich men."*

—Kirk Kerkorian

The quote above rings true for this book. The case studies I use are not advisers; they're living proof of men who have gotten women to want them.

As you understand more of how others think and how you think, you'll gain valuable insight into how decisions and thoughts are made. As you study these processes, relate them to your personal experiences. When you spot similarities, pay attention to ways you might adjust to learn better and improve your influence of others.

The following is an example of the decision-making process someone would go through in deciding to hang out with someone they met online.

DECISION-MAKING PROCESS [33]

Situation Presented—You must make a decision in the given scenario.

Benefits vs. Drawbacks Evaluated—You must weigh the benefits against the drawbacks to make a decision.

Timing—The timing must be right. This can include your location, current plans, and responsibilities.

Adrenaline/Excitement—As adrenaline/excitement builds, the benefit increases for the person to act in the moment.

Justification—Before coming to a decision, you must build a case for her subconscious mind to take these actions.

Availability/Ease—If the timing is right and the convenience makes it easier, it proceeds on to the next phase.

No Roadblocks—Without anyone to intervene, the path to deciding is on the path to completion.

Commitment to Decision—The benefit amplifies and the good feelings take over, enhancing commitment.

Action—With a decision made, any potential actions are complete.

Reflection—This is when it's time for potential regret for a poor decision or happiness from a good decision.

Next, let's look at the process of turning thoughts into action. The significance of the thoughts turned to action process is to gain insight into how humans decide when to act. This is a general outline for almost any action someone takes that may surprise you or that seems out of character for them. The following section detailing this process provides insight into each stage before reaching the point where they decide to act.

THE PROCESS OF THOUGHTS TURNED TO ACTION [34]

Hesitation—At this stage, they're not sure. They're too reserved and unsure to make a decision; doubt is present.

Frustration—Frustration builds since there are items they're not happy with.

Impatience—The lack of action to ease their frustrations amplifies the impatient feelings they have.

Desire—They have hope and expectations that there's something better for them than the current situation they're in.

Action—After enough frustration and impatience builds up, the light at the end of the tunnel appears in the form of desire, and they act.

VALUABLE INSIGHT

Whenever you want to change someone's beliefs, don't state your case but rather get them to question their own beliefs. Once someone questions anything, enough doubts will follow, and change is inevitable.

CHAPTER 39:
UNDERSTANDING WHAT TO SAY

"Sometimes less is more."

—Jan Denise

Now, you're going to learn what to say and, more important, what not to say. This chapter is short, sweet, and to the point.

- Be as politically correct as possible to avoid negative feedback and energy from the beginning. This will create a good synergy, which rapport needs.
- You want to identify her personality type and avoid awkward silences by making general comments that connect with her, about your day and the people surrounding you.
- When making comments, don't say anything offensive; ensure all your comments are innocent in nature and in good fun. Remember, she'll like you more, and there's fun in learning about others, if you let her talk about herself.
- The goal is to make it impossible not to be liked since you're not offensive to anyone, pleasant to be around, and genuinely funny.

Sometimes less really is more. People don't want to know everything about you or your opinions on everything. What will benefit you is having the woman like you, and one of the easiest ways for a woman to like a man is for the man to listen. It's simple, yet so few of us men have the restraint to shut up and listen to someone talk besides ourselves.

Don't ask questions they obviously don't have the answers to, and if you do ask a question they can't answer, don't pry further into it; this will immediately turn them off. Few people seem to recognize that others tend to feel bothered and frustrated by questions they can't answer. This can lead to awkward pauses and halt any previously made progress.

However, the exact opposite is true for questions they do understand and can answer. Asking questions regarding an area they know about will ensure passionate, genuine responses. These passionate and genuine responses will create rapport and advance the conversation because they feel valued. In return, they'll view you positively. People like to feel valued and important.

As Stephen Covey says in his book The 7 Habits of Highly Effective People, it's crucial to understand before prescribing. Translated, this means before you can determine what you're going to do (prescribe), you must identify (understand) the person you're talking to, their personality types, hot buttons, and mindset at the moment to decide how best to approach it.

DIFFERENT APPROACHES TO ASKING A WOMAN OUT

1.) *Are you free...*

Example: Are you free for dinner Tuesday or Wednesday?

*Not a question requiring much thought or commitment. Most would answer quickly with a yes or no, since it's natural to be honest if they are, in fact, free.

2.) *Would you...*

Example: Would you like to go out on a Tuesday or Wednesday?

*Too vague, makes them think too much instead of a simple yes or no answer. It's too much a commitment about going on a date. "Would you" requires more thought, while "are you" is interpreted more as an opinion, so a quick answer will typically follow, without much consideration or thought.

CHAPTER 40:

COMMUNICATING TO REACH YOUR GOAL

"Making an assumption is the mark of a lazy communicator. It's one of the most dangerous things you can do in dealing with others."

—Tony Robbins

As Tony Robbins wrote in his book Unlimited Power, the way to communicate exactly how you feel without compromising your integrity and without having to disagree with someone is through the agreement frame. While it's common for most of us to state our thoughts, the reality is the masses won't receive our opinion and thoughts communicated in a direct manner. However, if you implement the agreement frames below, you can voice your opinion without coming off in a combative manner if someone doesn't see eye to eye with you. In doing so, it will increase the odds that others will agree with you and understand your viewpoint.

These three phrases are directly from Unlimited Power:

"I appreciate and..."
"I respect and..."
"I agree and..." [35]

In addition, The Institute of Human Understanding has found the following four techniques are equally as effective in communicating with others. When intertwined with the three phrases above, you'll have a complete vocabulary to be both very influential and well received by all types of people you may encounter, regardless of differentiating beliefs.

1. **Rather than using *but*, use *and*.**

For example, when someone says they agree with you followed by *but*, it rescinds the agreement because *but* triggers a hot button in our minds during the conversation.
For example, compare the following two sentences:
"I agree with you, but it's priced too high." rather than "I agree with you, and just imagine what your sales would be if the price was less than $50."

The latter is much more direct and detailed. The *and* eliminates the reaction to the word *but* and is much more effective in getting the other party to see your viewpoint without feeling there's a disagreement.

2. **Repeat what they said and then insert your response**.

Repeating what someone says conveys to them you were listening. Because they feel you're respecting them, they'll give you their attention. Simply repeat what they said and insert your response directly after that; their attention will be yours to make a response.

3. **Universal response to any statements made by others: "Yes, and..."**

Whenever someone gives a thought, opinion, or statement, before responding in any way, simply add a *yes* before your response. The yes conveys agreement with their previous statement, and they will instantly become more receptive to what is following the *yes*.

4. **Insert *because* after your response.**

Once someone hears *because*, it almost instantly adds credibility. From a young age, we all asked the question "Why?" Parents, teachers, bosses or supervisors, and other people of authority encounter and answer this question all the time, and most of the time, they begin their response with *because*. Think of the times you may have witnessed someone respond with "Because I said so," which is one of the least direct answers and lacks true reasoning. However, many people accept it because of the presence of the word *because*. From a very young age, we learned to hold any statement beginning with *because* to a much higher level of credibility. [36]

THREE PARAMOUNT NEURO-LINGUISTIC PROGRAMMING™ STRATEGIES

Tempo of Speaking

Matching your speaking tempo with the person you're speaking to conveys to their subconscious mind a sense of congruency and that they're on the same page as you.

Pitch Level

Matching your pitch level as well as your speaking tempo enhances the level of congruency and works both on the subconscious and conscious mind as the rapport becomes more intertwined and more easily and consciously identifiable.

Breathing Pattern (match = in sync)

When people have similar or identical breathing patterns, it directly affects the nervous system, and each feels in sync with the other. To correctly do this, you must take notice of their mouth, nose, and chest to see how often they inhale and exhale; you must also pay attention to the duration of time between their breaths to match them correctly.

Linguist Dr. John Grinder and physicist Richard Brandler founded Neuro-Linguistic Programming, also called NLP. Many believe they were years ahead of their time and showed insight into representations and reactions through the brain and the psychological effects it has, providing the reasoning behind it.

Neuro-Linguistic Programming (NLP) studies the structure of subjective experience and what it can calculate from that and is predicated on the belief that all behavior has structure.

If you'd like, you can do further research into Neuro-Linguistic Programming.NLP beliefs regarding communication relate directly to Albert Mehrabian's beliefs that we relate to people in three ways: verbally (with words), vocally (tone of voice), and visually (body language). [37] Albert Mehrabian, PhD, is professor emeritus of psychology at UCLA and author of the book *Silent Messages*.

IN CLOSING

If you familiarize yourself with and use these concepts, the immediate results will amaze you. We already do many of these things naturally. Implementing these techniques will quickly develop your understanding of women and men alike as you experience the effectiveness of these strategies.

Within a short period of time, these behaviors will feel natural to you. Once they become natural, they will require little to no thought to implement them. The best part about becoming a natural with these valuable techniques is that when you don't experience any type of resistance in the conversation, there's no conflict or isolation separating your goal to possibly hang out, date, or something more. This also puts the odds in your favor to win over almost any person in any situation. Your goal is to be liked and offer value to others. This is a true win/win for you and anyone you meet.

CHAPTER 41:
HOW TO HAVE COVERT INFLUENCE

"You know, Debbie, has anyone ever told you you could be a model?"

"Really?"

"Yeah. It's too bad you're not sexy."

"Really? - Bull! I can be sexy."

"Uh-huh. All right. Show me sexy."

(She does)

"Very nice."

—Zack Phillippe's character Sebastian from the movie, *Cruel Intentions*

The first step to having any influence is to understand the way the person hears and understands, not how you want to say it. This requires thought and discipline.

The key to being influential is to influence without those you're influencing knowing it. Once someone feels someone is intentionally influencing them, they'll feel manipulated. Their guard will immediately go up, and they'll feel that person is pushing their beliefs.

You must integrate certain words and language patterns into your vocabulary. You must also use them consciously on a regular basis, which will ingrain these words and language patterns into your daily communication.

We all have been in a discussion or argument when we knew we were clearly in the right and were beyond frustrated with the other party for not seeing our viewpoint. Some would think of this as arguing with an idiot. I call this everyday life.

While the right way or the right answer may have been obvious to *us*, the most effective way to get people to see our view is by changing how we communicate *our* message. It's important to understand you cannot and will not get someone to change their position or beliefs by telling them to change and forcing your beliefs on them. Presenting statistical data and examples are typically useless, too. However, getting someone to *question* their beliefs is the absolute, most effective way to get them to change their beliefs.

Once they begin to question their beliefs, there's doubt, and a shift in their mind takes place. Often, this leads them to consider different viewpoints, and they become more open to outside perspectives.

Another covert tactic is to ask questions that can lead them to the answer you want without giving what you're doing away. If they feel you're manipulating them, it directly insults their intelligence. However, if you can get them to "see the light" on their own, they're much more likely to understand the other position and be open to changing their once-concrete stance.

In his autobiography, Ben Franklin described his strategy for communicating his opinions while keeping rapport by saying, "I continued this method some few years, but gradually left it, retaining only the habit of expressing myself in terms of modest diffidence; never using, when I advanced anything that may possibly be disputed, the words *certainly, undoubtedly,* or any others that give the air of positiveness to an opinion; but rather say, I conceive or apprehend a thing to be so and so; it appears to me, or *I should think it so or so,* for such and such reasons; or *I imagine it to be so; or it is so,* if *I am not mistaken.* This habit, I believe, has been of great advantage to me when I have had occasion to inculcate my opinions and persuade men into measures that I have been from time to time engaged in promoting..."

I have hand-selected words that the book *Covert Persuasion* lists as being crucial to implement into your vocabulary, while staying on course with your message:

YOU

PROVEN

NOW

HOW

EASY

FAST

IMAGINE

WHY

FREE

BECAUSE [38]

SEVEN IMPACTFUL CLOSING OPENERS

1. I have to go, but you seem like a cool person...
2. I should go, though I'd like to continue this sometime...
3. I'm bad for you...
4. We probably wouldn't get along...
5. I don't know how much fun we'd have since you....
6. You seem like...
7. I'm more of a...

You can use these when closing/ending a conversation online and in person. By using these as closers, you're leaving the door open for them to disagree, which is what you want. If they disagree with you, they're playing into your strategy. For example, "I don't know how much fun we'd have since you seem more reserved, and I'm more adventurous and active." Immediately, many women will disagree and attempt to prove how she's adventurous and active, as well. This leads to you opening the door for her to come over or hang out.

In contrast, when you're using this as an opener, you're standing out with a far different approach from other men and when using the time constraint such as "I should go, though I'd like to continue this sometime..." you're letting it be known you're busy, yet interested. This gives the appearance that you're more valuable, as is your time.

Language techniques are another great asset to have and use. Language techniques are the identification of techniques and patterns to make your communication more effective. I incorporated some of my personal favorites with ones from the book Covert Persuasion, which highlights them as "Using Hypnotic Language Patterns." These language techniques are highly productive when implemented in the right way at the right time.

I WOULDN'T TELL YOU TO...
HOW DO YOU GO ABOUT DECIDING...
YOU MIGHT WANT TO...
WHAT IS IT THAT WOULD HELP YOU KNOW...
YOU DON'T HAVE TO...
IMAGINE WHAT WOULD HAPPEN IF...
DON'T YOU FEEL...
WHAT WOULD IT BE LIKE IF YOU...
ARE YOU INTERESTED IN...
IF YOU WERE TO COME OVER...
WHY IS IT THAT SOME PEOPLE... [39]

Another personal favorite is "I don't want you to do anything unless you feel it's the right thing to do...." The last part is very powerful since it's a direct command about the right thing to do. You can implement these however you see fit to get your point across. For instance, rather than saying, "You shouldn't go out to the movies tonight!" you can simply say, "I wouldn't tell you to hang out with me over going to a boring movie." By using effective communication techniques, you plant an influential seed in the sentence by inserting the direct command, "hang out with me over going to a boring movie." Direct commands are effective in getting your way as they speak directly to the subconscious mind.

Another example is rather than asking whether she would like to come over, you can say, "If you were to come over, we could watch a movie by the fireplace." By using these language techniques, you get your point across without being offensive or pushy. It's also much easier for them to respond since there's no commitment; it is solely based on "whether or not." The presupposition is very powerful. A presupposition is an assumption without confirmation, assuming something not actually verbalized. The term presupposition is from the Foundation of Hypnotic Language Patterns.

Two examples of presupposition are:

1. "When you change into comfy clothes, you'll feel much more relaxed." This sentence is telling their subconscious mind how they should feel once they change. You do this with the wording of "when" since it's assuming they're going

to change clothing. It's easy to see how this could help if you're trying to get a woman to relax when she seems distracted, stressed, or upset due to any work or personal life situation.

2. "Hey, after we go out to eat, let's get ice cream. Okay?" "Okay" follows the direct message of getting ice cream, acknowledging they'll eat ice cream as well as go out to eat.

Often, the presupposition is picked up subconsciously without any second thought or questioning. A presupposition supposes beforehand. When you use this, you'll be amazed at the effectiveness of presuppositions and how often they're used in daily communication.

SECTION VII:

IMPLEMENTING YOUR KNOWLEDGE INTO REAL-LIFE INTERACTION

CHAPTER 42:
DECIDING WHERE TO MEET FIRST

"All men can see these tactics whereby I conquer, but what none can see is the strategy out of which victory is evolved."

—Sun Tzu, The Art of War

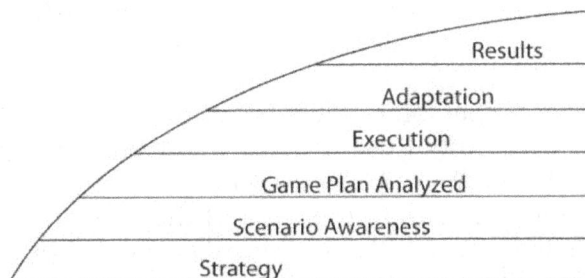

Results

Adaptation

Execution

Game Plan Analyzed

Scenario Awareness

Strategy

The best way for you to get predictable results is to have a strategy in place.

Are you going to meet her at a public place, a bar, a restaurant, the local mall, or are you going to hang out at your place? Without a clear strategy in place, the odds of success are against you. With a defined strategy, the odds of success are on your side. The reason for this is because you must have a clear goal in mind that you can work toward, otherwise you can't determine if the progress is on track.

I recommend meeting at a location relatively close to your place, so you're more comfortable.

The location should be a public one that's well-known or visible to make her feel comfortable, preferably low-key. Focus on her and limit potential distractions. Another reason for a low-key location is to avoid potentially running into someone she may know. Nothing is worse than running into someone you don't want to see, especially when out on a date. Our goal in this strategy is to decrease the odds of this happening. We want to control as much as we can, so both of you can have the most enjoyable time as possible getting to know one another.

When you're setting up the date, never ask an open-ended question about where to meet or at what time. You should ask her a question with two options (that you have already decided are good for you) built into the question. An example of this is asking, "Will 7:00 or 7:30 work better for you tonight?" This is an "assumption close" that she's going to meet you, and you're just ironing out the time. By simply giving her a couple of options, she's more likely to choose which time works for her based on her availability alone.

Furthermore, you can continue leading the conversation with details such as location and additional plans. Asking in a manner that doesn't appear to be too direct and forceful is vital to prevent her from having or feeling any sort of commitment.

If you do run into someone you know that you may have dated or hung out with, be friendly toward them and comfortable so that it doesn't create an awkward situation. Act in the same way if she runs into someone she knows unless she's rude to you. You must also understand that if she's interested in you, she'll make time for you. If she isn't, she will find excuses. If she completely blows you off by giving that person all the attention, this is disrespectful, and you should either call her out or simply end the date. If you call her out, be sure to do it in a direct, yet noncombative manner and, again, use the word "because." If you show her how she acted, she might then understand the awkward position she put you in and apologize.

Harvard psychologist Dr. Ellen Langer conducted an experiment in which she used a college setting where students were waiting in line to use the copier. She had her subject use three different techniques to cut a long line to use a copy machine.

- She sent in a person to go to the front of the line who asked, "Excuse me, I have five pages. May I use the Xerox machine?" This yielded a 60 percent success rate.
- Next, she sent a person to the front of the line who asked, "Excuse me, I have five pages. May I use the Xerox machine **because** I'm in a rush?" This yielded a 94 percent success rate.
- Last, she sent a person to the front of the line who asked, "Excuse me, I have five pages. May I use the Xerox machine **because** I have to make some copies?" This yielded a 93 percent success rate. [40]

Crazy, isn't it? The word *because* increased the success rate when combined with asking for compliance with a defined reason. **Note**: The success rate was high even though many others could have been in a rush, too. Just by asking and using "because" yielded exceptional results.

The same is true for talking to a woman and deciding where to meet. Rather than stating,

"Let's meet for a drink," give a better reason. How much better does, "Let's meet at the Martini Mixer on Main Street for a drink because they have a great band with a cool atmosphere and because it's great for people-watching!" sounds better than "Let's grab a drink?" Make sense?

In my studies and throughout all the interviews conducted, one thing remains the most important for men and women alike: control. You lose it; you most likely won't get it back. The goal is to understand and agree to the amount of control you need or want. Remember, you only possess control when the other person grants it. Leaders cannot lead without the followers to follow them. You must show them you deserve it.

CHAPTER 43:

HOW TO CREATE A COMFORTABLE AND RELAXED ATMOSPHERE

"Advertising is the genie which is transforming America into a place of comfort, luxury and ease for millions."

—William Allen White

Most people are anxious and nervous when they venture into unfamiliar territory because they simply do not know what to expect. As humans, we're notorious for over-thinking everything. When we over-think, it's natural for our minds to gravitate toward the worst-case scenarios. When we allow our minds to do this, the time we spend thinking about it is often more stressful and worse than whatever it is we're thinking about. Have you ever been stressed out or worried about something, only to find out that once whatever it was you were worried about had passed, there was nothing to have been stressed or worried about at all? Join the club, we all have!

The point of this is to understand that it's normal for almost everyone to be nervous about meeting someone for the first time. You're about to learn how to calm the nerves of others and create a sense of comfort for them, as well as yourself. One of the most effective ways to calm the nerves of someone is to understand how they process information. If they're very fast talkers, they'll process information quickly. If they're slow talkers, chances are they're slow in processing information, so they think each sentence through much slower.

Identifying how someone processes information plays a major role in effectively communicating your message. If you're talking fast to a slow processor, you won't be effective. If you're speaking very slowly to a fast processor, they'll lose patience and attention. You must match their speech patterns as well as thought patterns to be effective.

One of the most efficient ways to lessen the nervousness of a situation is to "break the ice." The easiest way to do this is to create rapport.

Rapport—(n) relation, connection, especially harmonious or sympathetic relation[41]

The best way to establish rapport when meeting a woman for the first time is to express your nervousness. Mention that you're new to this and that you were worried because you've heard online horror stories, so you're glad she seems normal and smile or wink. You're saying everything that has gone through her mind prior to meeting you. This will lighten the mood and be relatable. She will smile and respond, stating she was worried about the same things, and that she even told friends about it in case something happened to her. With both parties thinking the same way and both having expressed their feelings, it not only lightens the pressure that had built up before meeting in person, it also creates a sense of normalcy and comfort. From there, joke back and forth about trusting she's not a weirdo, joke, joke, laugh, laugh. She'll love it, and you'll be off to a phenomenal start.

CHAPTER 44:
UNDERSTANDING HOW TO CONTROL YOUR NERVOUSNESS

"Since your brain is always thinking, you might as well have it think thoughts that are useful and positive for you rather than destructive and negative."

—Michael Anthony

About nervousness: When you're nervous, you unconsciously contract your muscles. But when your stomach and chest muscles are tight, you don't breathe in enough air to properly support your voice, and you get the same tightness and constriction mentioned earlier about improper breathing, with the same results: a tight, constricted and therefore high-pitched voice. In addition, when you're nervous, you tighten the throat muscles, which further constrict your voice. [42]

The easiest way to control your nervousness is by doing the following:

- Take five breaths during which you inhale only through your nose for a three-second count and exhale only through your mouth for six seconds.
- Use perspective on the situation by thinking about something more serious. This acts as a necessary distraction to change your reality. Things aren't as big a deal or as bad as many would like to believe they are. Perspective is necessary.
- Close your eyes and think of three obstacles you've overcome and smile while thinking of each. This reminds you that you have overcome past obstacles, increases your confidence, and the smile changes your mood.

TOP FIVE ATMOSPHERE TIPS

1. Do not text at all while in her company. This will come across as rude and may give her a player vibe.
2. Do not take or make any phone calls while in her company. This will also come across as rude and may give her a bad vibe.
3. Do not talk about an ex—ever. This will come across as if you aren't over her. If she asks, change the subject and let it be known your exes don't deserve the opportunity to distract from the time you're hanging out together.

4. Do make eye contact. This will come across as if you're genuinely interested in what she's talking about.
5. Do smile. This will come across that you're a fun person to be around.

The Top Five Atmosphere Tips combined with the information provided throughout Section II provides a solid foundation for your future growth toward having success with women online and in person. Remember, it's equally important not to turn her off as it is to turn her on.

CHAPTER 45:

DON'T SPEND ANY MONEY ON A WOMAN!

"It has been said that Casanova's first experience was with two girls, sisters at that. He didn't choose between the two of them because he didn't know he was supposed to."

—Brady Collins

THE DATING PIGGY BANK

This piggy bank illustration may be elementary, but it's true that the less you spend on women, the more money you have to do whatever else you want.

Chances are, you've courted a woman by buying her a drink, dinner, tickets to a movie, etc. None of these are free. They cost you your hard-earned money.

The hope for most men is a trade-off in the form of time, attention, or possibly more. Few women will openly acknowledge this because it makes them seem bad or shallow, though it's reality. The main problem with this is that she is in complete control and you're like a lapdog begging for attention. This is not a fair or promising way to get off on the right foot.

Think of a date you may have gone on, where you spent money on dinner and a movie only for her to blow you off or never hang out again. Does it seem fair to you that you spent your hard-earned money, while she simply showed up and reaped the benefits without any investment on her end?

This whole setup puts the man at a disadvantage and gives the woman an upper hand. In fact, this has even been advice given to women. In the book The Rules: Time-tested Secrets for Capturing the Heart of Mr. Right, it says, "It's nice of you (female) to care about his finances, but remember that he is deriving great pleasure from taking you out. Why deprive him of the joy of feeling chivalrous? The best way you can repay him is by being appreciative. Say thank you and please." [43]

REALLY?? I don't know about you, but I wouldn't feel deprived if I didn't spend my money. I'll even propose a trade. I'd be more than willing to allow any woman to take me out and spend all her hard-earned money on me, and I'll be sure to say thank you and please.

The problem is not you. The problem is what society has come to expect.

The respect a woman expects a man to give, men should get, also. If you stand out from the others and get women to want you, spending money on them won't be important. They will enjoy your company, which is substance in the dating world.

- CASE STUDY -

TODD'S EXPENSIVE AND TIME-CONSUMING WAYS TO IMPRESS A WOMAN

Todd met a woman online and was very interested in her, so he decided he wanted to really impress her. He researched the top sushi and Italian restaurants in town. He decided on the Italian restaurant because it overlooked the water and was far more impressive. With the city views, white tablecloths, and candles on each table, came a big bill.

- Upon pulling into the restaurant, he used the valet to park his car: $25.
- Before ordering their meal, they ordered an appetizer and best bottle of wine: $330.
- Dinner came a la carte, though was fantastic: $110
- She drooled over the chocolate lava tower dessert: $14
- Tax: 8%
- Tip: 20%

Total $620.78

Oh wait, there's more! He had plans to take her to a comedy show after. After seeing the bill, he saw he went overboard and was concerned about how it got so out of hand. However, the comedy show tickets were non- refundable.

- Tickets for the comedy show: $80

Grand Total $700.78

At the end of the night, she thanked him for a great time as he dropped her off at her house. She mentioned they should do it again sometime soon. This, of course, made him feel good but also had him concerned since he realized he set her expectations for this type of night out. He frankly couldn't afford it. She was clearly enjoying the experience, but I voiced concerns. If she was paying she wouldn't have loved a $14 dessert, much less have ordered the way she had. In fact, she most likely wouldn't have recommended this sort of restaurant.

A connection is the goal. Attempting to impress them doesn't create a connection, it distracts. Simplifying is better, always.

Steve Jobs said it best, "Simplicity is the ultimate sophistication." [44] This is coming from a man who created the most innovative products of the century (if not ever), transforming six different industries, music (iPod/iTunes), film (Pixar), computer (PC), mobile phone (iPhone) and retail shopping (Apple stores).

Now if Steve Jobs, the Thomas Edison of our generation, thought the best way to achieve great results was through simplifying, I'm certain the simplicity in this book will yield success for you in an area as sophisticated as women.

The first thing you can do to simplify your contacts with women is to let loose. There's no pressure for you to pay, line up things to do, or to wow her, other than the pressure you put on yourself. When men act as though they must impress a woman or prove their value to her, it makes them appear insecure. It also distracts from being yourself to see if you two connect.

It's as though some men feel obligated to pay to be in the woman's presence; they don't feel they have enough to offer.

Paying for a woman and continually trying to impress her sets unrealistic expectations. Think about it. Do you want to have to entertain the woman every time you meet by having to one-up what you previously did? The answer is, of course, no.

Deciding where you may meet is important to understand the setting for your connection. Despite waiters and waitresses alike wanting to put the bill on one tab, you can politely ask them to split the tab if she gets up to use the restroom or you can do so discreetly by going to the bathroom. **Note**: You don't want her to catch you doing this; some women may see this unfavorably, despite being fair.

Sure, this may surprise the woman, but she couldn't dare act offended since she'd come across as snobby and awkward if she did. The fact is she's only paying for what she rightfully ordered. That is 100 percent fair.

It's amazing how different a woman may order if she knows she's paying for it. Some women try to take advantage of a man's generosity by ordering items she normally wouldn't. This is not right.

Dating can be expensive. Start saving your money and connecting with women from a different position, the position of respect. You have absolutely nothing to lose and everything to gain. Many women become even more intrigued and perceive this as a challenge, which is attractive to them. You cannot be better than the rest if you act the same as the rest. This is your time, be different.

CHAPTER 46:
THE INS AND OUTS OF ALCOHOL

*"I watch men go after women all the time. I can tell you with
absolute certainty when a guy buys a girl a drink she's in charge.
The successful men I've witnessed are those who don't purchase
drinks and have more of the woman's attention. I see this with all
ages and encounters. I see new customers daily on vacation, and it's
a recurring scene in Vegas."*

—Kasen Gregg, Las Vegas bartender

In the world today, almost all women accept alcohol in some way, shape, or form. You could go out for a beer, have a nice glass of wine, or load up on shots. Each of these represents something different to us. The person drinking a beer could be trying to stay low-key and have a good time. The person having a glass of wine could be looking for something a little classier. The person loading up on shots may be a big partier.

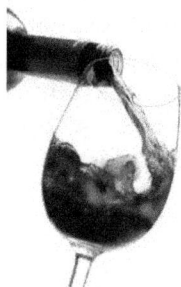

WINE

HOW CLASSY PEOPLE GET WASTED.

Wine is one of the most innocent drinks to have with a woman. It naturally loosens her up to make her feel more comfortable. Despite your goal of her being comfortable, I would shy away from pushing or offering alcohol. If she insists or requests a glass of wine, then go with it cautiously. Despite wine helping to let her guard down, it can also get her intoxicated. Wine can have a higher percentage of alcohol, so you must be responsible. Despite the temptation to hang out further or let her drive after drinking, you must make sure you also protect yourself. Consent is important, as is safety. Alcohol can impact both ethically and legally.

If you were to personally have a drink, limit yourself to one. It shows you can be social, yet responsible. Typically, more bad than good can come from a man drinking a lot of alcohol. Limiting yourself to one displays self-control, which is attractive to women. It also makes a woman feel better about you since it confirms you're different from the guys she's dated in the past and has no fond memories regarding alcohol. These memories of guys drinking too much can range from poor treatment, to embarrassment and annoyance.

In addition, you never want to drink too much on your first date (or ever) as you may act out, talk too much, and ultimately turn her away from you. This is not the type of first impression you want to make. First impressions never go away. Most importantly though, having too much to drink lessens your judgment and can lead to bad behavior. You limit yourself to one drink, you remain in control.

If you were to have drinks with her, there's etiquette to follow, as well. Avoid being the guy continually offering (pushing) drink after drink on her. She'll view this as a red flag and understand what you're doing. I cannot tell you how many times I've seen this in a college setting. The most popular drinks and shots are the fruity flavors with hard liquor. Even young, naïve college girls understand nothing is free and you're not just being nice. Pushing drinks on any woman is too obvious and will make you look desperate by trying to get her drunk to take advantage of her.

Alcohol has never caused someone to do something they didn't want to do. This is a built-in excuse our society has accepted, though I believe to be highly inaccurate. The reality is that alcohol builds in an excuse for most women to justify their actions, such as "I don't remember." or "I was drunk." Simply put, you cannot allow yourself to be in this type of position. Nor should you allow a woman in your presence get to this level of intoxication.

There's a quote, "A drunk man's words are a sober man's thoughts." The same rings true for actions. A drunk woman's actions are a sober woman's thoughts, hence the expression "liquid courage." Despite this being true, you still must be responsible and respectful.

If a woman brings wine to your place or opens a bottle when at her place, she's planning on a night of fun. Go with the flow, while being responsible and respectful. She's in control at this point.

- CASE STUDY -

While visiting friends in San Diego, a friend of a friend named Joe met a woman online. The first night they just hung out. They hit it off, and he established enough comfort for her to meet him at his place the next night for a movie. While Joe was telling us he was meeting her again, I mentioned to his roommate Brandon that if Joe got some wine, it would be a done deal. Shortly thereafter the doorbell rang, she brought a bottle of wine.

Despite her clearly understanding she was going to a man's house with a bottle of wine, I cautioned my friend to tell him to still be smart. As it turns out, they had a great time together, but the wine bottle was nearly full the next day. She liked him without the wine but was clearly nervous so brought the wine, just in case.

CHAPTER 47:
SEX—THE PERCEPTION AND THE REALITY

"Life is all perspective. From the glass is half empty to this girl isn't into me. The reality is the glass is half full, and there are 50 other girls in the room while you've only talked to one, and she's the one that may not be into you. There are 49 others."

—Unknown

The perception is a woman controls sex. The reality is two people who are dating must both agree to have sex; men give women the control without knowingly doing so.

Sex is a powerful thing. It can lead to acting out or complete obedience. Ultimately, each person decides how they view sex and how it fits into their lives. Their group of friends, popular culture, religion, and upbringing can shape these views. With beliefs come contradictions, and with attraction comes action.

Humans are like animals in their instincts. If they feel attracted or want something, their first instinct is to act. Women gain the upper hand because they harness their attraction through self-discipline.

Men, on the other hand, are quick to stare at a woman who's showing off skin, pay any compliment they think will increase their odds and oblige any command or request a woman makes—dinner, gifts, time, and more as they become so consumed with the idea of having sex.

When men behave like this, they relinquish any control and value proposition they have. Regardless of how attracted you may be to someone, you must show your value as detailed in this book. By simply using the techniques outlined, they should lead to naturally having women want you.

The typical approach men use regarding sex immediately lowers their value more times than not, which leads to failure. They don't show themselves as being any different, nor do they display anything they bring to the table. They're just an easy option a woman can take if she chooses to. If you're just another option, you'll never truly be an option for her.

Women would much rather hang out with someone they perceive to have higher value. The issue is men get so sidetracked they throw out everything they may have to offer.

Women know it takes two to tango. Would you give up all your leverage if you had it? Of course not.

Women don't either. Up until now they were just better than you at the game and outplayed you at every turn. That was **BTB**, *Before This Book*. Now that you have these tips and tools in your arsenal, you can change your reality. Gone are the days of getting sidetracked. Here are the days of presenting value, acting differently, and being treated differently—having women want you.

Below is an excerpt from the article, "*Has Dating Become More Egalitarian: A 35 Year Review Using Sex Roles.*"

> *"During the 'lusting stage' (of dating) the woman can take complete control of the budding relationship by not giving him sex...The carrot of sex will keep him around long enough to become attached."*
> *[45]*

You're an equal partner. Show them you're part of the equation and demonstrate some self-control. Most women tend to like guys who make them work for it (challenge).

Now think about that statement: "Most women tend to like guys who make them work for it." Sounds about right, doesn't it? It's human nature for people to want to be liked, which is why most feel surprised when they learn someone dislikes them. Once someone hears that someone else doesn't like them, they want to understand why and often go to great lengths to earn that person's friendship through actions, humor, or small talk to establish some type of rapport.

Relating this to online dating, if you tend to gravitate more toward a woman who makes you work for it, then why are you not making her work for it, too? You now see what we as humans are more drawn to—a challenge.

We place a higher value on something that's typically more difficult to get because if it were easy to get, everyone would have it and the value placed on it would decrease. It starts with you placing a higher value on yourself, and others will start to view you as offering a higher value, and your transformation will begin.

Creating a role reversal by being the one in charge is a very effective way to differentiate yourself. For instance, men think of the woman as the one who may pull back and make a remark about moving too fast and not being "like that." Imagine if, in the middle of a hot and heavy encounter, you pull back and remark, "We should slow down" because you don't know her that well yet. Can you imagine her shock and her speechlessness? It would leave her questioning what just happened. It would also make her desire you more because of the anticipation on future meetings.

It's also very important that you change your vocabulary because this will change the way you think and process information. You must change your perception that she's the only one who has anything to give, and you have nothing to offer. Remember, 50/50.

This will also level the playing field. Since you both are equal in value, make all decisions together, not based on one person holding the power, whether it's choosing what to eat for dinner, where to meet, or anything on a physical level.

The brain is continually thinking and predicting "what's next" to be prepared. Being aware of this and controlling how you think and where your mind drifts is of paramount importance.

Changing your vocabulary is also important to your subconscious mind; it's always listening. John A. Bargh, a professor of psychology at Yale, wrote, "Well, we're finding that we have these subconscious behavioral guidance systems that are continually furnishing suggestions through the day about what to do next, and the brain is considering and often acting on those, all before conscious awareness." [46] Choosing your vocabulary carefully will strongly affect how you perceive women, experience encounters, and respond.

*Remember, the most valuable currency for women is attention. The more you give, the less valuable it becomes to them.

- CASE STUDY -

My friend Jared always gravitated toward the low-hanging fruit. He didn't like a challenge and would go after the girls who expressed any interest in him, regardless of their looks, personality, or various other traits. When he first tried online dating, I mentioned to him there's no reason for him to not raise his expectations and standards. To make him feel more confident, I gave him some of the strategies. While discussing in detail the strategies, I could tell he was intrigued. He was attentively listening, asking questions and all at once, it seemed to click for him.

A few days later, he called me, and the first words I heard after answering the phone were, "I think talking to women online may be as exciting as meeting them!" He told me how many options there were online and the potential he saw.

He decided to go for quality women, not quantity like the old Jared. Spending less time and money than if he were to go on a normal date, he invested his time in searching, talking, and meeting women online. He got much better results.

The women he would never dare approach in person, he could easily approach online since he didn't fear the rejection or humiliation of someone turning him down in public.

I cautioned him to enjoy his time online but remember what worked. His key to success was that he never rushed any of the progress he was making.

Note: To establish that you're in control, you need to make it clear to her (without telling her) that she needs you for sex. Surefire ways to do this are:

- Stop in the middle of kissing and give her some excuse, such as, "I feel we're going too fast." This will baffle her.
- Touch her, but do not attempt to remove any of her clothes. She will grow impatient and make her want you even more.
- Do not let her do anything to you other than kiss. You're in charge.

By doing this, you make it clear she needs you to participate as much as you need her. She'll most likely be confused and surprised at the same time since these actions are the last thing any woman expects. These actions create tension and excitement, making her want you even more. Once you decide the time is right, prepare for an unbelievable time because the buildup of sexual tension she experienced will be very rewarding for you.

CHAPTER 48:
HOW TO INTERPRET AND RESPOND TO MIXED SIGNALS

"Janice, I apologize to you if I don't seem real eager to jump into a forced awkward intimate situation that people like to call dating. I don't like the feeling. You're sitting there, you're wondering do I have food on my face, am I eating, am I talking too much, are they talking enough, am I interested, I'm not really interested, should I play like I'm interested but I'm not that interested but I think she might be interested but do I want to be interested but now she's not interested? So, all of the sudden I'm getting, I'm starting to get interested... And when am I supposed to kiss her? Do I have to wait for the door 'cause then it's awkward, it's like, well, goodnight. Do you do like that ass-out hug? Where you like, you hug each other like this and your ass sticks out 'cause you're trying not to get too close or do you just go right in and kiss them on the lips or don't kiss them at all? It's very difficult trying to read the situation. And all the while you're just really wondering are we gonna get hopped up enough to make some bad decisions?
Perhaps play a little game called "just the tip."
Just for a second, just to see how it feels."

—Vince Vaughn's character Jeremy from Wedding Crashers

As Vince Vaughn's character Jeremy clearly points out, dating and trying to figure out when is right and whether someone is into you can be a challenge and overwhelming. Thoughts run through your mind such as: "When should I move in for the kiss?" "Would it be awkward if I put my arm around her?" "What if I held her hand?" "Is she looking at me in the eyes because she wants me to make a move?" "Do I have something she's staring at on my face?"

Interpreting and responding to mixed signals lead us to over-think every detail. It's perfectly normal to over-think when attempting to identify and respond to a woman because there's so much to take into consideration. I like to reflect on a quote by NLP master practitioner and trainer Steve Boyley regarding reverse engineering, "What has to be true for this to be true?" The following are signals, moves, and reactions to assist you in understanding how to act.

Kiss: When she kisses back, that's a green light. When she doesn't return the kiss or just keeps her face still, you should back off. If she kisses you on the cheek, she is either not interested in you, or she wants you to invest more time with her before she's willing to reciprocate.

Hold Hands: Holding hands registers on an emotional level for a woman. If you're looking for a true connection, go for it. If not, this is too far. Holding a woman's hand will lead her to believe you're interested in her and want to establish a connection. This connection is emotional for women, but it's physical for a guy. Most guys view holding hands as not a big deal. Don't hold hands if you're not looking to date a woman exclusively; it's far too emotional for the woman.

Eye Contact: When you make eye contact and a woman gives some type of flirty facial expression, you're in business. Eye contact is one of the hardest things to hide; most people can feel when someone is looking at them, and it's easy to see. If a woman makes direct eye contact with you more than just a couple of times, that's a sign she's interested and likes what she sees. A simple smile to acknowledge her looking at you lightens the mood and the potential embarrassment she may have of your catching her staring at you. Smiling back is the best way to initiate a conversation after you and she make eye contact. If a woman smiles back after making eye contact, this is a green light to initiate a conversation with her. The following is an illustration based on research findings of the founders of NLP, Richard Bandler and Dr. John Grinder.

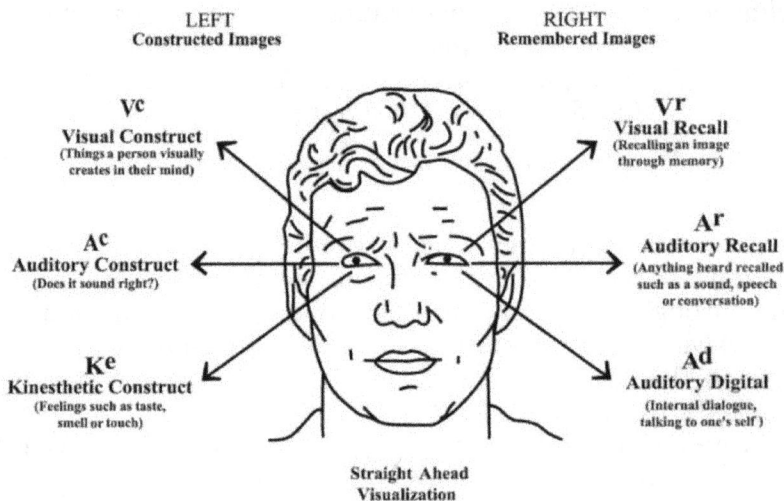

LEFT
Constructed Images

RIGHT
Remembered Images

Vc
Visual Construct
(Things a person visually creates in their mind)

Vr
Visual Recall
(Recalling an image through memory)

Ac
Auditory Construct
(Does it sound right?)

Ar
Auditory Recall
(Anything heard recalled such as a sound, speech or conversation)

Ke
Kinesthetic Construct
(Feelings such as taste, smell or touch)

Ad
Auditory Digital
(Internal dialogue, talking to one's self)

Straight Ahead
Visualization

Eye positions as looking at another person

Smile: A smile can be "nice," to express interest or to blow someone off. A genuine smile is rather easy to identify because it's hard for a person to hide their facial expressions with a fake smile. It's important to view how she smiles and interacts with others to avoid total embarrassment. She could very well just be a flirt. If she's smiling at everyone else too, proceed with caution. Also, identify the interest she gives you through her actions and mannerisms. Compare those actions and mannerisms with those she gives to others to gauge whether the attention you're getting from her is legit.

Body Language: You can conclude a girl is interested in you if she faces you without her arms or legs crossed. (The exception is if her toes point toward you while crossing her legs since she's still directing her body toward you.) If she crosses her arms, looks at everything but you, is easily distracted, rarely makes eye contact with you in a conversation, or has her shoulders turned away from you, then you should cut your losses; these are all signs she isn't interested in you. If she's interested, she will make it known 95 percent of the time through her body language. The same holds true if she isn't.

Hesitation: The hesitation a woman may give when she pulls back regarding anything physical is an immediate response to her not being comfortable. Physical hesitations include her pulling back in the middle of a kiss, her not holding your hand when you attempt to hold hers, and her moving away when you put an arm around her. The reasons for the hesitation and reactions are that she's either not feeling you or has started second-guessing what she's doing in the moment, and her mind is telling her this isn't right. When her subconscious mind tells her, "This isn't right," she becomes hesitant to proceed or interact. It's possible she may be a little self-conscious and may feel awkward due to poor self-esteem. The most likely reason is that she's not comfortable enough with you. Luckily for you, her comfort with you is something you can control (within reason). When this happens, it's very important to never force her. If the timing isn't right for whatever reason, and you can't create the right comfort zone, move on.

Comments: In any interaction, both parties are going to make comments in a conversation. Rather than just hearing what a woman says, pay attention and listen to her words and how she's saying them. Her comments will tell you how she thinks and what she wants. One of the easiest ways to understand the root of a comment is by asking yourself this general question:

"WHAT HAS TO BE TRUE FOR THIS TO BE TRUE?"

This open question can yield many in-depth and insightful answers that will be very useful for you. The key to asking yourself this question is to determine what's not being said.

Example: "I'm not looking for anything serious."

What has to be true for this to be true?
She's obviously looking to have fun; she doesn't want a relationship from the start. She has most likely had men express interest in her for something more serious, and she avoids it for one reason or another. There are reasons behind her not wanting anything serious now. It could be her current career path, a bad recent relationship, her lack of time, her lack of desire, or the timing isn't right. Identifying how she feels creates a clear picture for you, and you can decide if there's an arrangement in which both parties can be happy.

Example: "It was so boring hanging out with this guy I met last week."

What has to be true for this to be true?
She doesn't want to be bored. She's telling you she wasn't happy about being bored. She's looking for excitement. This tells you that if you're boring, she won't hang out with you. She's telling you exactly what she wants, and that's excitement and something different.

Example: "I can't tell you the last time I could go out, relax, and have a good laugh."

What has to be true for this to be true?
She must not get out much. She has been busy, and she's cherishing the opportunity to relax. Her life is most likely too serious if she's grateful for a good laugh, especially if she can't recall the last time this has happened. She's also acknowledging the fun she's having with you at that moment.

IN CLOSING

Mixed signals are a part of life. People shy away from making decisions and committing often. We see this with people trying to make decisions as minor as what to eat for lunch or deciding on clothes to wear. We see the lack of commitment being attractive enough that large companies, including cell phone carriers and cable companies, offer no contracts. Since this is common, you must expect it and adapt. Those who adapt succeed.

CHAPTER 49:
WHEN IS THE "RIGHT TIME" TO MAKE THE MOVE?

Jerry, "Look at George; he's on his ninth date with Betsy. He still hasn't gotten anywhere with her. Every time he tries to make a move, something screws up. Like on their last date, they were on the couch, but she was on his wrong side."

Elaine, "Wrong side?"

Jerry, "Yeah, she was on his right side. He can't make a move with his left hand. Can't go left... What about women? Do they go left or right?"

Elaine, "Nah, we just play defense."

—Dialogue from an episode of Seinfeld

We've all been in the position where we think, "When is the right time to make the move?"

Most women think it's just an easy move for a guy to make. They never think about the number of details a guy must cover and the thoughts running through his mind before making his move. For example, the following thoughts enter a guy's mind before making his move:

- Which side should I be on, the right or left?
- Should I get a piece of gum or a mint in preparation, or is that too obvious?
- Is it too assumptive to ask her if she'd like a mint or piece of gum?
- Am I better off to make the move on the couch or standing?
- Should I make sure we're eye level before making the move?
- Should I offer her a massage or recommend her giving me a massage to lighten the mood?

The guys who have the most experience with women typically have a strategy they've used as their "go-to" move. My advice is to create your own. This "go-to" move is necessary for you not to create awkwardness. This will also help you to not think about all the details that can get overwhelming.

Obviously, the more comfortable you are with a move the better you'll be at it, which helps your confidence moving forward. It will become natural to you, so you just do it rather than think about doing it. From there, success will follow, and you'll gain momentum.

The best time to make the move is when you're making eye contact and receiving positive affirmations. Positive affirmations include the following:

- She's smiling directly at you for no reason.
- She's continually making eye contact with you.
- Her body posture toward you is open and facing you.
- She's touching you in some way, your hand, hair, arm, or body.
- She has complimented you in some way (smell, clothes, looks, etc.).
- She's stroking her hair; this is a nervous tendency.

The absolute key for success with making the move is comfort. If she's comfortable with you, the timing is right. If for any reason she isn't comfortable, the timing will never be right.

Making the move is an important start, though progress you cannot make unless both parties participate. Remember, half the jokes or comments women make are serious thoughts expressed. The reason they're hesitant to just say them in a serious normal conversation is they don't know what the reaction will be. Keep an ear out for these jokes and comments; they're opportunities for the two of you to connect further. For women, connection = comfort.

One of the best ways to encourage participation is through give and take. Give and take plays an important role before making the move, successfully making the move, and after making the move. This begins with the conversation, take turns so it isn't a one-sided conversation. If she reveals something important to her, you should reciprocate.

After you make this move, you must continue with the give and take. If you expect kissing, touching or the removal of clothes, you must participate, too. If a woman looks over and sees you fully clothed while she's completely naked, she'll feel exposed and vulnerable. This could lead to her reacting by putting her clothes back on (the exact opposite of what you want). Through give and take, this situation will never arise.

From my discussions with case studies, they've said they take the initiative by taking off their shirt first and placing the woman's hand on his abs or chest (giving first before taking). The goal is to get her to feel comfortable seeing him with his shirt off and letting her touch him with the expectation that he can do the same in return. If she does not "give back" after "taking," she's not comfortable enough for one reason or another. You never want to force the action if she's not on the same page.

There are cases in which guys read the signals wrong. If you were ever to experience that, just back off and try to lessen the awkwardness by recommending something else to do or cracking an innocent joke to lighten the mood. If she's still interested, she'll contact you again.

It's important to remember there's no time limit. So, don't rush it, take your time, and enjoy it. The buildup can be equally as valuable in terms of excitement and anticipation for the woman as the act itself. What you'll notice in give and take is that it's the best way for both parties to be satisfied.

Often, the anticipation alone has the woman making the first move.

SECTION VIII:

THE HONOR CODE AND YOUR COURSE OF ACTION

CHAPTER 50:

RESPECT THE HONOR CODE

*"Without feelings of respect, what is there to distinguish
men from beasts?"*

—Confucius

If a woman is married, she's off limits. There are no excuses—a married woman or a woman in a relationship is off limits. The "I'm not happy," "It's on the rocks," or "He cheated on me" descriptions do not make it right, and karma is a bitch, so don't do it.

Additionally, be safe. There are many sexually transmitted diseases out there. Being responsible by using protection and getting tested regularly is expected for all parties. The excuse that it feels better without a condom is no excuse at all. STDs are a real problem today, and if you're going to have sex with a woman, you owe it to her to be safe and clean. You should expect the same. This is very clear—cut and dried. There are no exceptions, period.

You owe it to yourself and to others to abide by these principles. If you choose not to, you're not only disrespecting yourself, you're disrespecting others and risking a potentially harmful outcome. No one wins if someone catches an STD, has an unwanted child, or attracts a more serious, deadly disease. Be responsible and don't be selfish.

This chapter is one of the shorter ones because it's as simple as "doing the right thing." You'll know if it's the right thing to do. There's no gray area, so don't attempt to create one. It's black and white. If you question whether something is okay or right, you already know it isn't. The only reason a question arises in your mind is that your conscience is bringing it to your attention because it's obviously not right.

Success without fulfillment is ultimate failure.

CHAPTER 51:

SUCCESS—YOUR COURSE OF ACTION

"The main difference between the successful and unsuccessful is the lack of action."

—Brian Tracy

We have covered a lot of great information. How you decide to use this information is up to you. This book gives you the information you need and has taught you skills and strategies to help you complete your desired transformation. You must make the commitment to act and change. If you don't, you've made the subconscious decision to continue in your current situation.

YOU HEAR, YOU FORGET.
YOU SEE, YOU REMEMBER.
YOU DO, YOU UNDERSTAND. [47]

Let's review the main things you've learned:

- How to become the type of person you envision
- Identifying, classifying, and understanding women
- Establishing rapport with any type of woman in any situation
- How to dress to look better and get women to want you
- Becoming a desired man and how to have the "it" factor
- How to be charming
- Creating a profile to maximize results online and on apps
- Leveraging your time through technology
- How women think and seeing through a woman's eyes
- How to be the "right guy" for any woman at any time
- Influencing any situation through covert persuasion and language patterns
- Identifying when the timing is right to make the move
- Creating desire and anticipation for a woman

I want to personally challenge you to join a site immediately and implement everything you now know. Applying the skills and strategies you learned in this book will generate immediate results.

As the founder of IHU, The Institute of Human Understanding, I commend you for making the commitment to change your life. Welcome to your new life. Remember this moment. It will be a life-changing experience, and your life-changing experience will soon become the envy of others. Anyone can say they want to improve their understanding and results, but you did. Now take this information and live the life you deserve.

Until next time,
Michael Anthony

ABOUT THE AUTHOR

Michael Anthony is the founder of The Institute of Human Understanding. The Institute of Human Understanding believes that human decision-making is predictable, once the person's classification is identified and understood. Mr. Anthony is nationally known for his research and understanding of human interaction and reaction. The Institute of Human Understanding has conducted more than 10 years of research for this book.

The research includes understanding the psychology behind the different personality types, how to effectively communicate verbally and non-verbally, and interpreting body language. It also includes how to create a presence (the "it" factor), establish rapport, and analyze the details of real-life case studies.

Additionally, Mr. Anthony has traveled extensively throughout the United States and abroad.

He has worked with people from more than 30 countries, including the United States, Canada, Sweden, India, Australia, Saudi Arabia, Egypt, Jordan, Germany, the Netherlands, Costa Rica, Italy, Spain, France, South Africa, Russia, England, Pakistan, Mexico, Israel, Syria, Malaysia, Lebanon, Turkey, North Korea, Slovakia, Finland, Thailand, Brazil, Japan, Puerto Rico, China, and Singapore.

He is a certified Neuro-Linguistic Programmer after having completed intense training in the field of Neuro-Linguistic Programming. Neuro-Linguistic Programming details from a linguists' and physicists' perspective on how people think and make decisions. Mr. Anthony is also a certified Master Practitioner of Neuro-Linguistic Programming after completing further training and certification on the Master Practitioner level for effectiveness and practice in the field.

Mr. Anthony's vast experience includes psychology, human interaction, language patterns, sales techniques, training efficiency, communication strategies and dating interaction. The author has tweaked this book continually over the years as new advances were made. The final product is the result of years of research, development, and most importantly, human understanding.

The Institute
of
Human Understanding

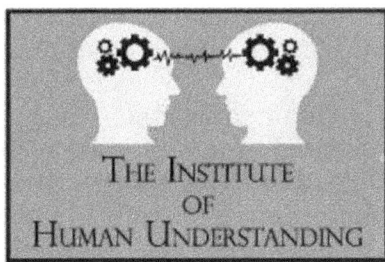

Principles for Success

- Strive to be happy, not content.
- Do not ever settle; the things you accept can become the things you regret.
- Timing is everything.
- Don't acknowledge or participate in timetables for the sake of timing alone.
- Be aware of how you think so you avoid falling into past failures.
- The implementation of little tests (without the woman knowing you're testing her) is essential.
- Knowledge without implementation is worse than implementation without knowledge.

REFERENCES

[1]*Trading Up: Why Consumers Want New Luxury Goods—and How Companies Create Them* pp.41-42
Michael J. Silverstein and Neil Fiske
Portfolio of Penguin
New York, New York 2005

[2]*How to Marry a Multi-millionaire: The Ultimate Guide to High Net Worth Dating* p. 19
Ted Morgan and Serena Worth
Specialist Press International
New York, New York 2005

[3]*The 7 Habits of Highly Effective People* p. 37
Stephen R. Covey
Free Press
New York New York 2004

[4]Site http://www.FitzVillaFuerte.com
Link: http://www.FitzVillaFuerte.com/The-Importance-of-Writing-Down-Your-Goals-On-Paper.html

[5]*Influence* p. 148
Robert B. Cialdini
Pearson Education 5th Edition
Boston, Massachusetts 2009

[6]*Winning!: Using Lawyers' Courtroom Techniques to Get Your Way in Everyday Situations* p. 158 Noelle C. Nelson, PhD
Prentice-Hall
Paramus, New Jersey 1997

[7]*Winning!: Using Lawyers' Courtroom Techniques to Get Your Way in Everyday Situations* p. 158 Noelle C. Nelson, PhD
Prentice-Hall
Paramus, New Jersey 1997

[8]Dustin Goot
Site: www.happenmag.com
Link:
http://www.happenmag.com/y/article.aspx?articleid=8716&TrackingID=526103
&BannerID=682739

[9]*First Impressions: What You Don't Know About How Others See You*
Anne Damarais, PhD and Valerie White, PhD
Random House
New York, NY 2005

[10]*Kinesics and Context: Essays on Body Motion Communication*
Ray L. Birdwhistell
University of Pennsylvania Press
Philadelphia, PA 1970

[11]Site: www.TonyaReiman.com
Link:
http://www.TonyaReiman.com/Articles/Building_Rapport_Through_Body_Language

[12]*Unlimited Power* p. 210
Tony Robbins
Simon and Schuster
New York, New York 1986

[13]*Think and Grow Rich* p. 87
Napoleon Hill
Highroads Media, Inc.
Los Angeles, California 1960

[14]*Winning!: Using Lawyers' Courtroom Techniques to Get Your Way in Everyday Situations* p. 9 Noelle C. Nelson, PhD
Prentice-Hall
Paramus, New Jersey 1997

[15]*How to Win Friends and Influence People*
Dale Carnegie
Pocket Books, Simon & Schuster
New York, New York 1936

[16]*How to Marry a Multi-millionaire: The Ultimate Guide to High Net Worth Dating* p. 20
Ted Morgan and Serena Worth
Specialist Press International
New York, New York 2005

[17]*The Power of Charm: How to Win Anyone Over in Any Situation* p. 22
Brian Tracy and Ron Arden
Amacom
New York, New York 2006

[18]*The Power of Charm: How to Win Anyone Over in Any Situation* pp. 38-62
Brian Tracy and Ron Arden
Amacom
New York, New York 2006

[19]*Silent Messages: Implicit Communication of Emotions and Attitudes*
Albert Mehrabian Wadsworth
Belmont, CA: 1981

[20]*Kinesics and Context: Essays on Body Motion Communication*
Ray L. Birdwhistell
University of Pennsylvania Press
Philadelphia, PA 1970

[21]*Winning!: Using Lawyers' Courtroom Techniques to Get Your Way in Everyday Situations* p. 42
Noelle C. Nelson, PhD
Prentice-Hall
Paramus, New Jersey 1997

[22]Site: www.Wikipedia.org
Link: http://en.Wikipedia.org/Wiki/Improvisation

[23]*All the Rules: Time-tested Secrets for Capturing the Heart of Mr. Right* p.15
Ellen Fein and Sherrie Schneider
Warner Books
New York, New York 1995

[24]Site: www.DivorceRate.org
Link: http://www.DivorceRate.org

[25]Site: www.Marriage101.org
Link: http://www.Marriage101.org/Divorce-Rates-In-America/

[26]Site: www.BoldOpinion.com
Link: http://www.BoldOpinion.com/Sexual.htm

[27]*All the Rules: Time-tested Secrets for Capturing the Heart of Mr. Right* p.45
Ellen Fein and Sherrie Schneider
Warner Books
New York, New York 1995

[28]*Winning!: Using Lawyers' Courtroom Techniques to Get Your Way in Everyday Situations* p. 139
Noelle C. Nelson, PhD
Prentice Hall
Paramus, New Jersey
1997

[29]*The 4-Hour Workweek* p. 50
Timothy Ferriss
Crown
New York, New York 2007

[30]*All the Rules: Time-tested Secrets for Capturing the Heart of Mr. Right* p.49
Ellen Fein and Sherrie Schneider
Warner Books
New York, New York 1995

[31]Scarcity Effect on Value: Mediated by Assumed Expensiveness pp.10, 257-274
Michael Lynn
Journal of Economic Psychology 1989

[32]*The 7 Habits of Highly Effective People* p.239
Stephen R. Covey
Free Press
New York New York 2004

[33]*The Institute of Human Understanding*
www.TheInstituteOfHumanUnderstanding.com

[34]*The Institute of Human Understanding*
www.TheInstituteOfHumanUnderstanding.com

[35]*Unlimited Power* p. 245
Tony Robbins
Simon and Schuster
New York, New York 1986

[36]*The Institute of Human Understanding*
www.TheInstituteOfHumanUnderstanding.com

[37]*Silent Messages: Implicit Communication of Emotions and Attitudes.*
Albert Mehrabian
Wadsworth
Belmont, CA: 1981

[38]*Covert Persuasion: Psychological Tactics and Tricks to Win the Game* p. 211
Kevin Hogan and James Speakman
John Wiley & Sons
Hoboken, New Jersey 2006

[39]*Covert Persuasion: Psychological Tactics and Tricks to Win the Game* pp. 81, 213
Kevin Hogan and James Speakman
John Wiley & Sons
Hoboken, New Jersey 2006

[40]The Mindless of Ostensibly Thoughtful Action: The role of "placebic" information in interpersonal interaction. pp. 36, 635-642
Ellen Langer, Blank, A. and Chanowitz, B.
Journal of Personality and Social Psychology 1978

[41]Site: www.Dictionary.com
Link: http://www.Dictionary.Reference.com/Browse/Rapport

[42]*Winning!: Using Lawyers' Courtroom Techniques to Get Your Way in Everyday Situations* p. 119
Noelle C. Nelson, PhD
Prentice-Hall
Paramus, New Jersey 1997

[43]*All the Rules: Time-tested Secrets for Capturing the Heart of Mr. Right* pp.38-39
Ellen Fein and Sherrie Schneider
Warner Books
New York, New York 1995

[44]*Steve Jobs* p. 127
Water Isaacson
Simon and Schuster
New York, New York 2011

[45]Has Dating Become More Egalitarian: A 35 Year Review Using Sex Roles p. 1
Asia Anna Easton and Susanne Rose
School of Integrated Science and Humanity at Florida International University, Miami, FL 33199, USA
Springer Science + Business Media, LLC 2011

[46]"Who's Minding the Mind?"
Benedict Carey
The New York Times
New York, New York 2007

[47]*Leading with the Heart: Coach K's Successful Strategies for Basketball, Business, and Life* p. 88
Mike Krzyzewski and Donald T. Phillips
Warner Books
New York, New York 2000

www.ingramcontent.com/pod-product-compliance
Lightning Source LLC
Chambersburg PA
CBHW080047280326
41934CB00014B/3243